Six For The Tolpuddle Martyrs

Six For The Tolpuddle Martyrs

The Epic Struggle for Justice and Freedom

Alan Gallop

PEN & SWORD
HISTORY

First published in Great Britain in 2017 by
Pen & Sword History
an imprint of
Pen & Sword Books Ltd
47 Church Street
Barnsley
South Yorkshire
S70 2AS

Copyright © Alan Gallop 2017

ISBN 978 1 52671 250 9

A CIP catalogue record for this book is available from the British Library

Typeset in Ehrhardt by
Mac Style Ltd, Bridlington, East Yorkshire
Printed and bound in the Malta by Gutenberg Press Ltd.

Pen & Sword Books Ltd incorporates the imprints of Pen & Sword Archaeology, Atlas, Aviation, Battleground, Discovery, Family History, History, Maritime, Military, Naval, Politics, Railways, Select, Transport, True Crime, Fiction, Frontline Books, Leo Cooper, Praetorian Press, Seaforth Publishing and Wharncliffe.

For a complete list of Pen & Sword titles please contact
PEN & SWORD BOOKS LIMITED
47 Church Street, Barnsley, South Yorkshire, S70 2AS, England
E-mail: enquiries@pen-and-sword.co.uk
Website: www.pen-and-sword.co.uk

Contents

Foreword

Why 'Six For The Tolpuddle Martyrs?'

Many people reading this book might be asking what the title 'Six for the Tolpuddle Martyrs' means and where it came from. When I was a young boy in the Cubs – the junior version of the Boy Scouts – we used to sing a quasi-religious song called 'Green Grow the Rushes, O', an English folk song which appeared during the first half of the 19th century, the same period as this book is set. The song is sung in twelve different stanzas, starting at number one and rising to number 12. It is designed to be sung by either a pair of voices or two choirs – one asking questions and the second giving answers. It begins:

First voices: *I'll sing you one song, green grow the rushes, O.*
Second voices: *What is your one song?*
First voices: *One is one and all alone and ever more shall be so.*

The 'one is one' refers to God and other verses refer to 'Four for the Gospel makers' (Matthew, Mark, Luke and John), 'Ten for the ten commandments,' 'Twelve for the twelve Apostles' and verses in between making sometimes obscure references to Christian and/or astronomical meanings.

It was a very popular song which we enjoying singing around a camp fire or in our tin tabernacle Scout hut six decades ago, even though most verses were meaningless to us and everyone else singing the same song in school choirs, scout camps, sing-along groups or along with recordings played on the BBC Saturday morning radio show 'Children's Choice' presented by Derek 'Uncle Mack' McCulloch.

There is, however, another version of the song; one more political than the original and expressing (often tongue-in-cheek) certain Marxist-Leninist views but still sung to the tune of *Green Grow the Rushes, O.*

It begins:

First voices: *I'll sing you one song, Red fly the banners, O*
Second voices: *What is your one song?*
First voices: *One is workers' unity and evermore shall be so!*

And so it goes on up to: *'Twelve for the hours on the Kremlin clock, Thirteen for the holes in Trotsky's head* and *Fourteen for the IQ of the average Trot.'*

When the song reaches number six, following *'Five for the years of a five year plan'* comes the line *'Six for the Tolpuddle Martyrs'*, which is highly appropriate as there were six agricultural labours deported to Australia and Tasmania in 1834 for swearing an unlawful oath as they initiated members into their new agricultural trade union. Four of them were staunch Methodists, a fifth later converted to Methodism and a sixth avoided being a member of any religious denomination. I'm not sure if the men themselves would approve of the song if they were able to come back and hear it today.

There are different versions of the song and new verses are probably being written as you read these lines. Verse six, however, always remains the same: *'Six for the Tolpuddle Martyrs* – and long may it remain, O.

Alan Gallop

Acknowledgements

It would not be possible to write a book such as this without help from a variety of people and organisations that assisted me over a two year period and shared their time, knowledge and patience. I particularly wish to thank the following for their interest and assistance:

The Allport Library and Museum of Fine Arts, 91 Murray Street Hobart, Tasmania 7000.
Andrew McCarthy, Chairman, Tolpuddle Old Chapel Trust.
British Library's Newspaper Library.
Convict Records of Australia – *http://www.convictrecords.com.au.*
David Joliffe – Museum of Australian Democracy (Australian Prime Minister's Centre Co-ordinator), Canberra.
Dean Sully – UCL Institute of Archaeology.
Dorchester Circuit of the Southampton District of the Methodist Church.
Dr Catriona Mills, Senior Researcher and Indexer, AustLit, School of Communication and Arts, University of Queensland, Brisbane, Queensland.
Gale News Vault (Cengage Learning).
Jan Pickering – former manager of the Tolpuddle's Martyr's Museum and Festival.
Jim Nunn.
Methodist Heritage: *http://www.methodistheritage.org.uk.*
Mrs. Janet Johnson, who with her husband owns Martyr's Cottage, Tolpuddle and allowed me to visit the upper room which the village's agricultural labourers used for their union meetings.
National Archives, Kew.
People's History Museum, Spinningfields, Manchester.
Peter S. Forsaith – Oxford Centre for Methodism and Church History, Oxford Brookes University, Oxford.
Ruben van den Broek at Tigris Old Prints, Udenhout, Noord Brabant, Netherlands.
Staff at the Dorset History Centre, home of many Tolpuddle-related archives.
Trades Union Congress.
Henry Wilson, Chris Robinson, Matt Jones and Mat Blurton at Pen & Sword Books.

> *'Give me the liberty to think,*
> *to speak, and to argue freely according to*
> *conscience, above all other liberties.'*
> *John Milton*

This book is dedicated to the memory of my father, John Gallop, a shop steward for the Amalgamated Engineering Union (AEU) at Petters Limited, Staines who first introduced me to the Tolpuddle Martyrs. It is also dedicated my late cousin, Michael Convery, who was an active and passionate trade union supporter at several factories in Middlesex.

The Arrest

Monday 24 February, 1834 (daybreak)

Come all ye bold fellows that follow the plough,
Either hedging or ditching or milking the cow;
The time has arrived and the Union flag waves:
We won't be kept down like a lot of white slaves.
So be ready boys, be ready,
For the union be steady,
The white slaves of England will soon gain the day.
19th century broadside ballad – date unknown

Petty Police Constable James Brine was far from happy. He had left his small cottage in the Dorset farming village of Tolpiddle the previous afternoon to walk seven miles to Dorchester to collect a special warrant for the arrest of six farm labourers. Now he had to leave his nice warm bunk in Dorchester Police Barracks at 4:00am to trudge back to his village through the cold and frosty winter morning to make the arrests.

Brine was Tolpiddle's single Petty Parish Constable, a job which paid him one guinea a year for a 12-month term plus other expenses including one shilling for escorting prisoners to court or to jail. This meant that today was to be a good day as he was escorting six prisoners, which would earn him four shillings. One prisoner was worth one shilling, two prisoners one shilling and sixpence and three prisoners two shillings. Six prisoners, therefore, earned him four shillings which was supposed to be borne by the prisoners themselves providing they had the money to pay. If they did not, the constable's fee would be paid by the local Justice of the Peace – in this

A Petty Police Constable in full uniform, including a top hat, blue tunic, a pair of light coloured trousers and carrying a stick, only to be used when trying to quell a disturbance. (*Author's collection*)

case, James Frampton, Lord of the Manor of Morton, Justice of the Peace, High Sheriff of Dorset, a local landowner and magistrate.

Petty Constable Brine's parish was a quiet patch and he only made two or three arrests each month, mostly drunkards who had downed too much cider and had staggered down Tolpiddle's single street knocking on doors and windows and making a nuisance of themselves. Otherwise he dealt with minor misdemeanours including serving summonses for poaching, evicting unlicensed peddlers and fortune tellers from the village and discovering vagrants illegally sleeping in barns, outhouses or in farm wagons. He also had to keep an eye open for runaway husbands, collect rates and taxes, deal with thieves stealing dogs, hares, pigeons, doves and beasts and pursue anyone 'wantonly and cruelly beating, ill-treating, abusing or torturing horses, cattle or domestic animals'. Brine was also charged with apprehending military deserters, anyone 'profanely cursing or swearing' in

A fanciful – and highly inaccurate – interpretation of how George Loveless was arrested at daybreak on 24 February from *The Annals of Crime & Newgate Calendar* (Number 37, 17 May, 1834). Instead of wearing working clothes, including a smock, Loveless (second from left) is seen here in clothing worthy of a middle class landowner. In the picture, Mrs. Loveless and her daughter are seen wearing fine clothes instead of cast-offs and the family home includes a grandfather clock, upholstered chair and leaded window – none of which would have appeared in a poor labourer's cottage. (*Author's collection*)

his presence and evicting 'idle and disorderly persons, rogues, vagabonds and incorrigible rogues' from the parish. But very few of these types ever came to Tolpuddle to commit such terrible crimes.

On this day the Petty Constable had been ordered to rise early and give himself plenty of time to arrest the unfortunate labourers before they left their homes to begin their day's work in Tolpiddle's barns and fields. Brine was instructed to read the contents of the special arrest warrant to the men and then escort them to Dorchester to appear before the magistrate. He wasn't looking forward to making the arrests. He knew all the men and their families personally. They were his neighbours, peaceful folk and not trouble makers and he knew his task would be distasteful and likely to bring embarrassment upon himself.

It was still dark when he left the barracks. He was tired, irritable and hungry, having departed before eating his usual morning brew of porridge oats. He walked into Tolpiddle's misty road towards the first dwelling on his list, the home of ploughman George Loveless, his brother James and their families. As he approached the small rural home known as Sheppey Cottage, the door opened and out came two men. One of them quietly closed the door behind them so as not to wake the family still sleeping inside.

Brine walked over and asked the men if they might be George and James Loveless. They looked at him strangely, as if to say 'why are you asking who we are? You know darn well who we are. We live in the same village.' But neither man said what was on their minds and simply answered that they were, indeed, George and James Loveless. 'Then I have a warrant for you from the magistrates,' said the constable. 'What are its contents, sir?' asked George Loveless after a pause. 'Take it yourself, you can read it as well as I can,' said Brine handing over a rolled up document to the older brother who read it carefully. It stated that he, his brother and four other Tolpiddle men – all members of the recently formed Friendly Society of Agricultural Labourers – were to be charged with having participated in the administration of an illegal oath. It was signed by the magistrate James Frampton, a man well known to both Loveless brothers.

After reading the warrant, Loveless rolled it up again and handed it back to the Petty Constable who asked him: 'Are you willing to go to the magistrates with me?' At this point George and James Loveless could have made a run for it down the street leaving Constable Brine far behind. They were strong and fit men, used to working with heavy horses and farm equipment and could have outrun almost any other man in Tolpiddle. But running away would have made them marked men with no respect for the law. It would have brought trouble upon their families. So instead of running away, George Loveless told Brine: 'I will go with you to any place wherever you wish me.'

Brine then took the Loveless brothers around the village, knocking on the doors of other men whose name also appeared on his list. Together the three men walked

One of the six arrested farm labourers bids farewell to his wife and baby before being marched with the rest of the men to Dorchester by Petty Constable Brine. (*Artist unknown*)

further through the quiet street, past the small Wesleyan Chapel where both Loveless brothers were lay preachers and towards a house on the north side of the main street – home of the Standfield family.

The Petty Constable banged on the door. There was no reply. He banged again and from inside a voice could be heard saying that he was coming to open up. The door was opened by a young man who was fully dressed in work clothes and still rubbing sleep from his eyes. 'Is your name Standfield – John Standfield?' The young man said of course it was. 'And is your father Thomas Standfield?' The young man said that was correct and was about to ask why he was requesting him to confirm names he already knew when the constable quickly cut in with: 'Then in that case I must tell you that I have a warrant from the magistrates and you must both come with me.' By this time a second, older man, had appeared in the doorway in time to hear most of what Constable Brine had said. They both spotted the Loveless brothers standing in the narrow street and without another word pulled on jackets and quietly slipped out pulling the door closed behind them.

The five men now continued towards the Crown Inn. The constable told his prisoners to stay together in the middle of the narrow street while he made two further calls. He first went to one of two cottages behind the inn known as Drew's Tenements and thumped on the door which was opened by James Hammett who lived there with his wife and younger brother John. According to local Tolpiddle legend, Hammett's young wife Harriet appeared from her bedroom in her nightclothes and began remonstrating with Petty Constable Brine. She screamed and wailed that her husband was to be taken from her and cried for help. Her pitiful cries were heard by neighbours who came to their windows and doors to see what the fuss was at such an early hour. Harriet was calmed by her husband's brother as James Hammett came out of his cottage to join the others. The look on his face showed he had expected such a call of this sort sooner or later and now the time had arrived.

The Petty Constable crossed back across the street and knocked at the home of the Brine family. The door was opened by a young boy who was asked by the constable if he was James Brine (no relation to the Petty Constable – the name 'Brine' was common in these parts). 'No, I'm his brother Charles. What do you want with him?' After hearing the constable Charles Brine called to his brother inside who appeared in the doorway looking scared and confused. But, seeing the Loveless brothers and other men waiting in the street, he calmed down and followed the constable.

Constable Brine told the men that they were now in his custody and he was going to march them to Dorchester without placing them in shackles or manacles – and they were to come quietly. He said they would first be making another call to a house on the edge of the town. And so the six farm labourers from Tolpiddle followed him silently down the road just as the wintery sun was starting to rise and half a dozen cocks began to crow.

They left expecting to return to their families later that day having lost a day's pay due to their sudden absence. The next time they would see their wives, parents, siblings, children and friends again would be after an humiliating 'trial' in Dorchester, a journey half way around the world locked into chains, brutal treatment on convict hulks, prison ships and in penal colonies; they were to cause a stir in parliament, embarrassing both the Prime Minister and the King, and walk into English history as early trades union heroes.

oOo

The men travelled almost in silence on the rough road to Dorchester, their only remarks being short mutterings made in low voices which could not be overheard by the constable. They walked in a westerly direction towards Burleston and Puddletown following the road that ran down Yellowham Hill and through Yellowham Wood before skirting around the village of Stinsford, one mile from Dorchester. The journey took them along stony roads passing through farming communities similar to Tolpiddle, where early risers stood back and gaped as Constable Brine and his prisoners – many of them known to local families – looked straight ahead and passed by in silence. The 'prisoners' might have felt nervous inside but knew they had nothing to fear because they had committed no crime.

With Dorchester now in their sights, they marched along the narrow road which cut through water meadows leading to the Grey's Bridge crossing over the River Frome where a notice had been set into the wall reminding anyone foolish enough that *Any person wilfully Injuring any part of this County Bridge will be guilty of Felony and upon conviction Liable to be Transported for Life By the Court.'*

The village of Tolpuddle is located seven miles from Dorchester. Little has changed in the village over 130 years after the six farm labourers were arrested and transported. The streets are still lined with attractive thatched cottages and landmarks associated with The Tolpuddle Martyrs. (*TUC*)

Tolpuddle's High Street runs past West Farm (left) where George Loveless and other members of the Tolpuddle Six worked in a variety of agricultural roles. (*Hills & Rowney*)

They trudged onwards into London Road towards the pointed spire of All Saint's Church, passed the stone archway of the Pale Ale Brewery and site of the Old Dorchester Prison before turning into High East Street and Durngate Street towards an imposing red brick-built house with high sash windows and a slate roof. Pointing to the building Constable Brine informed his charges that this was Woolaston House, home of Mr. Charles Woolaston, Chairman of the Quarter

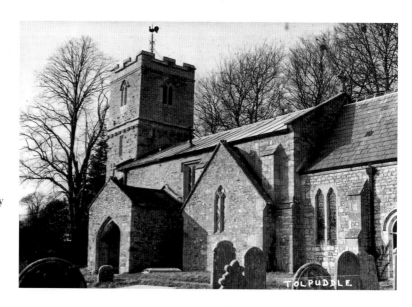

Tolpuddle's 12th century Church of St. John the Evangelist. (*Author's collection*)

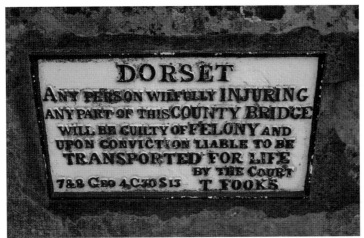

The warning on Grey's Bridge crossing the River Frome outside of Dorchester. (*Photograph: Alan Gallop*)

Sessions of the Country of Dorset. Petty Constable Brine pulled a cord hanging down inside the stone columned porch over the front door. A bell could be heard ringing somewhere deep inside the house. Shortly afterwards a servant girl opened the door and without saying a word admitted the Petty Constable and his charges and led them into a vestibule after first pointing out the doormat where they were all expected to wipe their boots – including the Constable. She also indicated that they needed to remove their hats.

And there they waited. None of the Tolpiddle men had ever been inside such a fine house as this before. The house was much warmer inside than it was outside and they looked up at the grand ceiling which covered a corridor leading towards a staircase at the end. They heard voices nearby and could smell breakfast cooking in a kitchen somewhere within the building. After their long hike into Dorchester they were ready for some refreshment but knew they would be offered nothing here.

After five minutes a door opened further along the corridor and two men came out, crossed the passageway without looking at the prisoners and entered a room opposite. Then a voice called out to Petty Constable Brine and he, too, entered the room after being told to shut the door behind him.

This was a chance for the Tolpiddle men to talk freely among themselves although George Loveless motioned them to speak quietly. Some of them thought they were going to get a good telling off – but for what? Others said it had something to do with the fact that most of them were Methodists and that some Dorchester people thought Methodists were dissenters – but in what way?

The door opened again and the Petty Constable appeared and motioned the men to come forward and enter. They slowly shuffled forward in single file, entered the room and gathered in line in front of a pair of smart leather winged armchairs in which the two men lounged comfortably. A fire crackled in the fireplace. Petty Constable Brine was the first to speak and he addressed the Tolpiddle men directly:

Woolaston House, Dorchester, home of Charlton Woolaston, Chairman of the Quarter Sessions of the County of Dorset and half brother of the Magistrate James Frampton. Today the house has been converted into offices for various agricultural and community-based organisations, including NFU Mutual, an insurance organisation founded by farmers for farmers in 1910. (*Photograph: Alan Gallop*)

Gentlemen, this is the Honourable Magistrate Mr. James Frampton, squire of Moreton Hall and who many of you will know. And this gentleman is Mr. Charlton Woolaston whose house you have the privilege of entering today and who is Chairman of the Quarter Sessions of the County of Dorset.

The constable went on to introduce each of the Tolpiddle men while Frampton and Woolaston – who they later learned were half-brothers – sat with their legs crossed, elbows resting on the sides of their chairs and hands carefully folded together. The officials looked intensely at the Tolpiddle men.

Although Frampton knew some of the prisoners, the Petty Constable still introduced them individually for Wollaston's benefit. While this took place, George Loveless noticed another figure in the room hiding in shadows away from the window. He could not make out his face, but he appeared to be wearing the same type of clothing as himself, meaning he must also be a man of the land, a farm labourer. But who was he, and why was he trying to hide himself?

Frampton did most of the talking. He asked them if they were aware that by asking those present to take a secret oath at a meeting of the Friendly Society of

Agricultural Labourers in an upper room at the Tolpiddle home of the Standfield family on December 8, 1833 they were breaking the law. George Loveless replied: 'We are not aware that we have violated any law; if so, we must be amenable, I suppose, to that law.'

Frampton then turned towards the figure lurking in the shadows and summoned him to step forward. 'You will be familiar with this fellow?' Frampton asked. Most of the Dorchester men knew who he was alright. His name was Edward Legg, a Tolpiddle labourer like themselves, who had asked to be admitted both to the December 8 meeting and the Friendly Society.

Legg stood there looking embarrassed, his eyes cast downwards. He was reminded that he was under oath and asked if he could identify the men in front of him as being present at the union meeting. He said they were all present and Frampton promptly closed the meeting, got to his feet along with Woolaston and the two men escorted Legg from the room.

Once they had left, Petty Constable Brine turned to the men and told them to follow him to the door. He didn't say where they were going, how far away it was or for how long, but they followed him out into the cold.

As they followed the Petty Constable up the hill he was asked what was going to happen next. He turned and said with some regret: 'I'm afraid you're going to jail.'

An engraving of Charlton Byam Woolaston, magistrate to Dorchester prison, painted by William Holl, Jr. (*National Portrait Gallery*)

Part I

'Captain Swing'

1815/30

Oh Captain Swing, he'll come in the night,
To set all your buildings and crops alight,
And smash your machines with all his might,
That dastardly Captain Swing!

The early years of the 19th century witnessed difficult times for farming communities and citizens living in Britain's towns and cities. In the Napoleonic wars of 1801-15 prayers were offered for Nelson's victory at Trafalgar and the nation lived in fear of an invasion by Bonaparte's armies. The cost of training and sending fighting men to defend their country from the French plunged Britain's farming communities into fourteen years of depression. Common lands had been divided up by the Enclosure Acts, a series of Acts of Parliament which enclosed open fields and common land in the country, creating legal rights to land that was previously considered common property. Hedges were planted widely to denote new boundaries and, almost overnight, the country began to resemble a patchwork quilt.

With the rise of the Industrial Revolution landowners sought better financial returns with more efficient farming techniques – including introducing new mechanised farm equipment which created lower wages and unemployment. Enclosures also allowed landowners to charge higher rent to the people working on their land. This was at least partially responsible for farm labourers deserting country villages to seek work in city factories. These were hard years for labourers who worked daily for sixteen hours or more on the land to feed their wives and children and survive on a diet of bread, potatoes and turnip tops if they were lucky. Turnips were easy to source, highly nutritious and small enough to slip into a labourer's smock pocket to bring home for the cooking pot.

o0o

Following the Napoleonic Wars disturbances erupted across southern England. Violent protests were made by farm labourers worried that their wages would be

Éch. 0 = 0⁄20 P.M.
Fig. 349. — *Batteuse Damey à manège direct placé sous la batteuse.*

The arrival of mechanised agricultural machinery, such as early threshing machines, meant that fewer men were needed to operate them and machines built to separate golden brown grain from straw and chaff could achieve a day's work equivalent to 12 hand thrashing labourers. (*Dictionnaire d'arts industriels*)

slashed following introduction of mechanised machinery. This meant that fewer men would be needed to operate them and it was estimated that the machines, built to separate golden brown grain from straw and chaff, could achieve a day's work equivalent to 10-12 individual hand-threshing labourers. As a protest, wheat ricks were burnt, mills smashed to pieces and angry demonstrations held in fields and town squares. For a while, mob rule was the order of the day.

By 1830 the rural wars fought by labourers and village artisans had become more serious with some southern counties bordering on insurrection. London was in panic and the Duke of Buckingham told the House of Commons that if disorders continued the government 'would be beyond the reach of almost any power to control them'.

In Kent masked arsonists attacked farmers' homes and destroyed wheat ricks. In an agricultural village near Canterbury, 400 labourers turned out to smash a wooden thrashing machine – later known as a threshing machine – into splinters. Before wrecking the device they had heard a magistrate express strong views against mechanisation. He stated that while mechanisation would 'take the drudgery out of farm labour' it would also replace farm workers who would no longer be needed. The labourers proceeded to wreck the machine – originally costing its owner £10 – whereupon the magistrate turned on them and sent them to jail. In revenge the mob burnt his hay ricks to the ground.

A Kentish farmer said: 'Ah, I should be well pleased if a plague were to break out among them, and then I should have their carcases as manure and right good stuff it would make for my hops.' This remark was probably made in jest but his hop field and stacks were soon ablaze.

Wrecking riots in southern England closely followed similar unrest which had occurred in and around Manchester between 1811 and 1817 when textile workers protested against mechanised labour-saving cotton looms replacing less-skilled and lowly paid labourers. The mill workers, known as Luddites, gathered under cover of darkness and broke into mills and factories and took their axes to the new machines. This was more than simply an act of violence; there was both method and reason in it. Textile workers, like farm labourers, were among the few jobs left for non-skilled men to exist above starvation level.

A landowner wrote to the *Kent Herald* on 30 September, 1830:

In my parish, where no machines have been introduced, there are twenty-three barns. I calculate that in these barns fifteen men, at least, find employment threshing corn until May. If we suppose that each man has a wife and three children, this employment will affect seventy-five persons. An industrious man who has a barn never requires poor relief; he can earn from 15s and 20s per week; he considers it almost as his little freehold, and that in effect it certainly is. It is easy to imagine what the sight of one of these hated engines might mean to such a parish; the fifteen men, their wives and families would find cold comfort, when they had become submerged in the morass of parish relief, in the reflection that the new machine extracted for their master's and the public's benefit ten per cent more corn than they could hammer out by their free arms.

The rise of mechanisation and machine wrecking by radicals continued unchecked throughout October 1830. By the end of the month most active rioters were in custody and magistrates predicated there would be more voluntary surrenders. But the disturbances spread over a wider area. There was a riot at Lyminge, at which the High Sheriff of Kent Sir Edward Knatchbull and the local Rector, Rev. Ralph Price (with a little help from their estate workers and stable lads), succeeded in arresting ringleaders and bound over another fifty men. In writing to the Home Office, Knatchbull stated that labourers claimed 'they would rather do anything than encounter such a winter as the last'. But the Rev. Price paid his penalty for his part in the affair. His wheat ricks were set alight and burning sprees spread steadily across Kent for another month.

Later that month *The Times* reported that Sir Edward Knatchbull had been invited to address a meeting of radicals who listened to what he had to say with rapt attention, but before dispersing one of them said publicly: 'We will destroy wheat stacks and threshing machines this year, next year we will have a turn with the parsons, and the third we will make war upon the statesmen.'

The following month 22 men were brought before Knatchbull at the Special Sessions for East Kent in Canterbury for rioting and machine wrecking. They pleaded guilty and were issued with sentences ranging from transportation for life (one prisoner) or seven years (five prisoners). Others were sentenced to between twelve months and a few days in confinement.

Later in November disturbances led 'by working men and women demanding a living wage' had engulfed 22 counties across southern England. Farm labourers pauperised by low wages and made redundant by the arrival of new farm machines were forced into taking parish relief. To receive this, labourers had to jump through a number of legal hoops to prove they had been born 'of legally settled parents, lived in the parish for three years, been hired by a legally settled inhabitant for a continuous period of 365 days and by the time you were married had proved your worth'. Labourers seeking relief were also required to have 'served a full apprenticeship to a legally settled man for a full 7 years'.

By 1832 over 400 agricultural machines – mostly used for threshing – had been smashed. Some 350 cases of arson and over 300 riots occurred between January 1830 and September 1832. The final cost of this destruction was estimated to be in the region of £120,000 (equivalent to around £136 million today).

1. The rioting and arson was even noticed by Princess Victoria who wrote in her journal in August 1832: 'I just now see an extraordinary building flaming with fire. The country continues black, engines flaming, coals, in abundance, everywhere, smoking and burning coal heaps ...'
2. And then mysterious letters began arriving at homes of farmers and landowners threatening that their houses, barns and wheat ricks would be raised to the ground if mechanised machines were brought onto their land. The letters were signed by 'Captain Swing', a wild, romantic and mythical figure who – it was said – rode through England by night stirring the peasantry into insurrection. The working population believed in 'Captain Swing', although not one person ever claimed to have actually seen him. Swing's name was designed to spread fear among landowners and act as a form of morbid humour that echoed the gallows fate awaiting rebels involved in machine wrecking and arson. 'Captain Swing' spread terror over agricultural England as self-organised gangs of labourers continued with the brazen destruction of machinery and wreaked revenge on classes exploiting their labour. There were other demonstrations over wages and tithes when workhouses and factories were set on fire and local parsons, 'gentry' landowners, and overseers of the poor were attacked.

Here are two typical threatening letters supposedly written by 'Captain Swing':

'Captain Swing' was a wild, romantic and mythical figure who, it is said, rode through southern England by night stirring peasantry into insurrection, including rick burning. (*British Museum*)

Sir – Your name is down amongst the Black hearts in the Black Book and this is to advise you and the like of you, who are Parson Justasses, to make your wills. Ye have been the Blackguard Enemies of the People on all occasions; Ye have not yet done as ye ought … Swing.

Sir – This is to acquaint you that if your thrashing machines are not destroyed by you directly we shall commence our labours. Signed on behalf of the whole, Swing

Following these 'Swing' riots, 252 people were sentenced to death (but only 19 were actually executed), 644 rioters imprisoned and 500 sentenced to transportation to Australia for terms of between seven years and life with little hope of ever returning – the largest group of prisoners ever transported from England for a common crime.

Rioters arrived in Dorset in the autumn 1830 just as post-summer seasonal jobs were starting. After the harvest had been gathered, one of the main seasonal jobs for the county's farm labourers was hand threshing. Some Dorset farmers had already introduced machines to undertake this work leaving their labourers without jobs or money to buy food, clothing and other goods to see them through the winter months. Poor harvests in recent years also resulted in hunger protests across the county.

Mary Frampton, sister of Dorchester magistrate and squire James Frampton, who kept a diary between 1779-1846, recorded that 'the first rising took place in this county on 22nd November' 1830 in Bere Regis, a village close to Tolpiddle. It was here that a large gathering of farm workers and families from surrounding villages – including Tolpiddle – assembled early outside the property of Liberal MP and landowner Henry Portman to demand better wages. Mary wrote:

The Farmer, the Rick Burner and his Family, one of many publications produced in 1830 promoting agricultural insurrection in Southern England. (*Author's Collection*)

> Mr. Portman immediately promised to raise the wages of his labourers, and by doing this without concert with other gentlemen, greatly increased their difficulties. My brother, Frampton, harangued the people at Bere Regis, and argued with them on the impropriety of their conduct, refusing to concede to their demands whilst asked with menaces. This spirited conduct caused him to be very unpopular, and threats were issued against him and his house.

Frampton, the Lord High Sheriff of Dorset and a Captain in the Dorset Yeomanry, had been tipped off that further 'intended risings of people at adjacent villages of Winfrith, Wool, and Lulworth were to take place on the 30th,' recorded Mary.

> Mr. Frampton was joined very early on that morning by a large body of (land owning) farmers from his immediate neighbourhood, as well as some from a distance, special constables amounting to upwards of 150 armed only with a short staff, the pattern for which had been sent by order of the government to equip what was called the Constabulary force. The numbers increased as they rode on towards Winfrith, where the clergyman was unpopular, and his premises supposed to be in danger. The mob, urged on from behind hedges by a number of women and children, advanced rather respectfully, and with hats in their hands, demanded an increase of wages, but would not listen to

the request that they would disperse. The Riot Act was read. They still urged forwards and came close up to Mr. Frampton's horse. He then collared one man, but he slipped from his captor by leaving his smock-frock in their hands. Another mob from Lulworth were said to be advancing, and as the first mob seemed to have dispersed, Mr. F. was going, almost alone, to speak to them, when he was cautioned to beware, as the others had retreated only to advance again with more effect in the rear. The whole body of the constabulary then advanced with Mr. Frampton, and, after an ineffectual parley, charged them, when three men were taken, and were conveyed by my brother and his son Henry, and part of the constabulary force, to Dorchester, and committed to gaol.

Although riots achieved nothing, Dorset's normally docile farm labourers remained unbowed before their employers who now recognised a new independence in the bearing and demeanour of their workers. All around there seemed to be a new awakening; unwillingness on the part of farm labourers to continue working for starvation wages and to voice their support for betterment for themselves and their families.

The life of an agricultural labourer in 1830s England was wretched and levels of wages paid throughout the year varied. They were at their highest during summer periods leading up to the grain harvest when farmers paid employees nearly twice as much as during the winter for the long hours they were expected to work. In the summer farm workers worked up to 16 hours at a time Monday-Saturday. Some farmers included up to three and a half pints of cider per labourer into their wages. For tee-total Methodists such as the Loveless brothers, forsaking cider earned them a few extra pennies each week in lieu of alcohol.

Labourers in the south west of England lived in hovels not fit to shelter cattle. William Cobbett (1763-1835) was an English pamphleteer, farmer and journalist. In his book *Rural Rides* he described a typical rural labourer's cottage in the south-west:

The labourers seem miserably poor. Their dwellings are little better than pig-beds, and their looks indicate that their food is not nearly as equal to that of a pig. Their wretched hovels are stuck upon little bits of ground on the road side, where the space has been wider than the road demanded. In many places they have not two rods to a hovel. It seems as if they had been swept off the fields by a hurricane, and had dropped and found shelter under the banks on the road side...In my whole life I never saw human wretchedness equal to this: no, not even amongst the free negroes in America, who, on an average, do not work one day out of four. And this is 'prosperity' is it? The land all along here is good. Fine fields and pastures all around; and yet the cultivators of those fields are so miserable!

INTERIOR OF A DORSETSHIRE LABOURER'S COTTAGE.

LABOURER'S COTTAGE, NEAR BLANDFORD.

Labourers in Dorset lived in wretched hovels not fit to shelter cattle and little better than pig holes. They often accommodated as many as twelve people in tiny rooms just ten feet square. (*Illustrated London News*)

Typical of housing conditions in Dorset is recorded in the case of a family of eleven who slept in a room ten feet square with an open thatched roof only seven feet high in the middle and with a single window measuring fifteen inches square and the floor covered in compacted earth. A Dorset clergyman who provided evidence before a Committee on farm worker's wages paid seven years before the 'Captain Swing' riots said that on a good week labouring families 'lived mainly on whey, made from the liquid part of fresh milk left over from the making of cheese and poured over beans. They also lived on tea, potatoes and turnips. Tea cost *6d* per pound, sugar *6d* per pound, soap *5d* per pound and candles *6½d* per pound.' He wrote that farming families 'learned to live without sugar and soap, but labourer's wives desperately tried to find enough money to bake a loaf or two of bread for their families once a week. But wheat used to make their bread was of the poorest quality and made from what was locally known as 'smutty wheat'. This was named after a disease known as 'smut' that covered crops with black, foul smelling spores and contaminated clean wheat. Farmers should have burn their diseased crops but greedy ones told labourers to harvest it to grind down into flour to sell at knock-down prices. Instead of the crust being a golden toasted colour, the bread was black, unwholesome and foul tasting.

To light their dingy homes, farming families either made their own moulded candles from tallow – a rendered form of beef or mutton fat, processed from suet – or purchased them from those who could afford beef or mutton. For those too poor to buy homemade tallow candles, the 'tallow dip' – a strip of burning cloth in a saucer of tallow grease – was a poor substitute.

For warmth, entire families foraged woods and country lanes for material to burn in their fireplaces. The easiest fuel to find and carry home was faggots – dry brushwood and sticks which could be bound into large bundles. Faggots gave out a good deal of heat, but burned quickly so a plentiful supply was always needed around the year for heating cooking pots and water. Anyone caught removing larger parts of a tree such as branches fallen in a storm and big enough to saw into logs did so at their peril. This was stealing and the punishment could be severe including periods in prison or – if sufficient wood for burning had been removed and the thief apprehended – transportation to the other side of the world. As a result, most raids on nearby forests, woods and lanes took place at night.

The standard of life for a Dorsetshire farm labourer and his family was, therefore, desperately low. Many were afraid of complaining for fear of being identified as trouble makers and thrown out of their jobs and homes. Some resorted to asking for Parish Relief while others went begging among their neighbours. A small number decided to do something about their situation. One of them was George Loveless, the village of Tolpiddle's master ploughman, part-time Methodist lay preacher, the seventh out of ten children and the man looked upon by many farm labourers as a leader prepared to stand up and fight for fair wages.

Chapter 1

Seven Shillings A Week

1830/34

Come all ye bold Britons, where'er you may be
I pray give attention, and listen to me,
There once was good times, but they're gone by complete.
For a poor man lives now on seven shillings a week

Most families in Tolpiddle could not read or write and knew little of what was going on outside of their community. Although they lived in a village populated by poor and illiterate farm labourers, at least five of the men known today as the Tolpuddle Martyrs could read and write. Four of them regularly studied the bible and three were Methodist lay preachers. It is not recorded if they were regular visitors to Tolpiddle's local ale house, The Crown Inn, but they probably drank locally brewed cider, especially when it came in the form of part payment for working long hot hours in the fields during late summer harvest time when the need to quench their thirst was never greater.

The 1842 *Tithe Map of Tolpiddle* was produced showing every parcel of land, road, lane, house, barn and stream alongside names of land owners and building occupiers. Most labourers living there were employed in land occupations producing barley, wheat, corn and root crops such as turnips, carrots, parsnips, potatoes and beetroot.

Like everyone else, the Tolpiddle men lived in primitive homes with their large families. Each of them knew that farm labourers were at the bottom of Britain's social hierarchy, along with coal miners and domestic servants. Their lives differed greatly from large landowners, such as Lord of the Manor, William Morton Pitt who offered for sale the freehold of three farms to tenants James and Susannah Northover who leased West Farm, East Farm and Middle Farm at Tolpiddle covering a total 1,190 acres. The farms included plenty of pasture, arable meadows, water meadows and coppice woodland along with farm houses, barns, a dairy, yards, stables and allotments. The lease also included 37 small tenements with cottages lived in by the Tolpiddle men and their families. The Northovers themselves lived in a substantial house known as Northover Manor, which, in addition to their own living quarters, had rooms for baking, brewing, making butter and cheese plus

A detailed 1842 map of West Farm, Tolpiddle where George Loveless worked as a Master Ploughman. (*Dorset History Centre*)

room for a small number of unmarried farm workers who lodged there for rent taken out of their wages.

All six men arrested by the Petty Police Constable in 1834 were good, simple and hardworking farm labourers. George Loveless, a self-educated, cultured and self-reliant man was age 37 at the time of his arrest. This master ploughman worked with his brother James at the Northovers' West and East Farms. George married Elizabeth (Betsy) Snook from Dorchester in 1824 and by 1834 they had three children, George (age 9), Robert (age 7) and Thomas (age 5). The family was originally supported by the ploughman's wage of nine shillings a week. By 1830 George Loveless had become respected in Tolpiddle and neighbouring villages as a community leader and Wesleyan preacher at chapels throughout the Dorchester region. He had learned to read and write at an early age and collected a small library of spiritual and secular material from which he would draw inspiration for his sermons. His writings and his part in the agricultural workers' movement from the 1830s indicate that he had also read the works of Welsh-born social reformer Robert Owen and became familiar with attempts to establish trades unions in London, Birmingham and elsewhere. Loveless claimed he played no part in the Swing disturbances that convulsed the southern counties in 1830, but over the next two years he represented Tolpiddle's agricultural labourers in discussions with farmers and land owners, who agreed to raise wages to 10 weekly shillings before denying they had ever made such a promise. As a direct result of this George Loveless made the first moves to form a trade union for Tolpiddle's land workers.

James Loveless was 11 years younger than his brother, George, and was 25 at the time of his arrest. James was married to Sarah and the couple had two children, Eli Wesley and Emily with a third on the way. Like his brother, he, too, was a Wesleyan preacher. Thomas and John Standfield worked on the same farms as the Loveless brothers. The oldest, Thomas, was age 44 in 1834 and married to the Loveless brothers' sister, Dinniah. By February 1834 the couple had five children (with another on the way) of whom John, age 21, was the oldest. Thomas and John were also Methodists and co-founders of The Friendly Society of Agricultural Labours and many of the society's meetings and investitures were held in the upstairs room of the Standfields' cottage.

James Brine was born in 1813 and was not yet 21 or married when he was arrested. He lived with his widowed mother, Catherine, and four younger brothers and sisters. Brine did not attend Methodist services and was only an occasional member of the local parish church congregation.

James Hammett, Tolpiddle's mystery man, was 22 when arrested; he lived with his wife Harriett, their one year old son, his brother John and his wife who was about to give birth to their first child. Of the six men arrested and transported, Hammett was the quiet one. He never spoke or wrote about his experiences as one of the Tolpiddle Six, apart from uttering a few words to an audience on the forty-first anniversary of his conviction.

o0o

George Loveless, aged 41.

James Loveless, aged 29.

John Standfield, aged 25.

James Brine, aged 25.

Thomas Standfield, aged 51.

Five of the six Tolpuddle men. (*Cleave's London Satirist* (*1838*))

In 1837 George Loveless recalled:

In 1831–2 there was a general movement of the working classes for an increase of wages, and the labouring men in the parish where I lived gathered together and met their employers to ask them for an advance of wages, and they came to a mutual agreement, the masters in Tolpiddle promising to give the men as much for their labour as other masters in the district.

The whole of the men then went to their work, and the time that was spent in this affair did not exceed two hours. No language of intimidation or threatening was used on the occasion. Shortly after we learnt that in almost every place around us the masters were giving their men money to the amount of ten shillings per week. We expected to be entitled to as much—but no—nine shillings must be our portion.

After some months we were reduced to eight shillings per week. This caused great dissatisfaction, and all the labouring men in the village, with the exception of two or three individuals, made application to a neighbouring magistrate, namely, William Morden Pitt, Esq., of Kingston House [a popular local MP who spent much of his fortune creating employment in Dorchester] and asked his advice. He told us that if the labourers would appoint two or three of their body, and come to the County Hall the following Saturday, he would apprize the chief magistrate, James Frampton, Esq. (whose name I shall not soon forget), and at the same time our employers should be sent for to settle the subject.

I was the one nominated to appear, and when there we were told that we must work for what our employers thought fit to give us, as there was no law to compel masters to give any fixed sum of money to their servants. In vain we remonstrated that an agreement was made, and that the minister of the parish (Rev. Dr. Thomas Warren, Vicar of Tolpiddle's Anglican church of St. John the Evangelist) was witness between the masters and the men; for this hireling parson, who at that time said, of his own accord, 'I am witness between you men and your masters, that if you will go quietly to your work, you shall receive for your labour as much as any men in the district; and if your masters should attempt to run from their word, I will undertake to see you righted, so help me God!'

So, soon as reference was made to him, he denied having any knowledge of any such thing. From this time we were reduced to seven shillings per week, and shortly after our employers told us they must lower us to six shillings per week. We consulted together what had better be done, knowing it was impossible to live honestly on such scanty means.

The labourers were alarmed by the rapid way their wages were falling and shocked at how 65-year old Dr. Warren had betrayed them and sided with the landowners. They likened him to Judas by denying he had made any promises 'to see you righted'. Under the cover of darkness, and in revenge, some of them threw stones and smashed the vicarage windows. They ran off into the night before anyone caught them or reported them to the constable.

In mid-1834 George Loveless sent word around the village that a meeting of farm labourers was to be held after work on Tolpiddle's village green beneath the spreading branches of a giant sycamore tree that had stood on the site for over 150 years. People had met under trees to discuss problems and celebrate festivals for centuries. But spaces under trees were public places and users needed to be careful about what they said in public for fear of negative remarks getting back to those whose names might be taken in vain.

Word about the meeting spread and about 50 men turned out to hear George Loveless tell the assembly that the time had come for Tolpiddle's farm workers to unite and present their employers with reasonable arguments to revert their wages to ten shillings a week in line with other Dorset farm workers in return for a six day working week in all weathers throughout the year. He told them he 'had read accounts of Trade Societies' and was considering contacting one of the new unions that existed for the benefit of industrial workers; he reminded the assembly that unions had been legal since 1824 and membership was not a crime. He closed the meeting telling the assembly that once he had found out how and where to contact the union and written them a letter outlining their situation he would call another meeting to expand his plan.

James Frampton would have heard about the village green meeting from one of several secret spies he had appointed around the district. The spies, made up of farm labourers, were told to examine any suggestions of unrest or insurrection

George Loveless (left with his hand in the air) sent word around the village that a meeting of farm labourers was to be held after work on Tolpiddle's village green, beneath the branches of a giant sycamore tree. Little did the 50 or so people who met together that day realise that a spy (crouching under the tree trunk) would report the meeting's activities back to squire James Frampton. (*W. H. D. Tilley, Wimborne*)

brewing in the neighbourhood. They were to note the names of as many people as possible attending meetings like the one on the village green. Frampton was determined that anyone found supporting trade union activity or making monetary demands on Tolpiddle's landowners and farmers would suffer the consequences.

Frampton's previous experience confronting what he considered to be a disrespectful mob of angry peasants had sent him into a rage and he intended to seek out the culprits and punish them. But there was no rush. He did not connect George and James Loveless with the insurrection but, as soon as he heard from village green informants that the elder of the two Loveless brothers planned to become involved with a trade union, the ploughman and his brother became his principal targets.

Edward Berkeley Portman, a magistrate and former Member of Parliament for Dorset from Bryanston, was one of the first members of the local gentry to look into trade union activities in and around Tolpiddle. He considered that trade unionism was an evil that had to be stamped out. Crushing the unions was his highest ambition and with great care and industry he began to piece evidence together which might bring an end to unions in his home county. He was eager to supply information which might spur Home Secretary Lord Melbourne into declaring the unions unlawful.

Today the sycamore tree under which the farm labourers first met is known as The Martyrs' Tree. (*TUC*)

Portman knew that Frampton was similarly committed and had written to Lord Digby, the Lord Lieutenant of Dorset on 30 January 1834 informing him that 'nightly meetings have been held by the agricultural labourers in the parishes of Tolpiddle and Bere Regis where societies – or as I believe they are called 'unions' – are formed and where they bind themselves by an oath to certain activity.'

And so began the task of attempting to destroy Tolpiddle's little union society and the key men elected to run it in a bid to smash the entire union movement and frighten members into withdrawing their support. Frampton informed Digby he had learned that members

… are conveyed blindfolded to the place and do not see the person who administers the oath, and I cannot as yet get any information as to the precise nature of the activity to which they are sworn but I am informed they are to strike work whenever ordered by their superiors and that this is to take place at a time when labour is most required by farmers; that they are to demand an increase of wages; that they are bound to some other points which I cannot exactly ascertain … Under these circumstances we have thought it our duty to write a letter to the Secretary of State and make him acquainted generally with what is going on.

As we can get no information on oath as yet, and only pick it up by degrees, and from the conversations of the labourers, who now often speak openly of such meetings being held, we have only mentioned very generally to Lord Melbourne what is going on, as we are not certain of the exact particulars.

Portman urged Frampton to forge ahead with his enquiries into the workings of local unions telling him he hoped he (Frampton) had a true case for conviction. In a postscript he asked Frampton: 'Do you mean to proceed at the next Assizes? Ponsonby has written to me to know this fact as he will in that event do his best to attend – it seems desirable to expedite the Blow and to allow it to come from the Judges if possible at once.' The Ponsonby referred to was the Right Hon. William Ponsonby, brother of Lord Melbourne and soon to be appointed Foreman of the Grand Jury at the trial of the Tolpiddle Six.

The Tolpiddle men were condemned before they were even arrested and Frampton, Portman and Ponsonby were determined by hook or by crook to smash the union.

In later correspondence to Home Secretary Lord Melbourne, dated 29 March 1834, Frampton claimed that George Loveless 'was very active in the riots of 1830'. He claimed that James Loveless was also active and Thomas Standfield was 'a very discontented man and if any disturbance is going on he is sure to be in it'. Standfield's son John was 'very saucy and ready for any disturbance', while

James Hammett was 'always a very idle man and ready for mischief'. Frampton stated that James Brine 'was about 17 years of age at the time of the riots, when he behaved well and tried to keep out of them, but since that time has become very idle and kept company with James Hammett'.

It is likely that some of the men had taken part in the unrest at Bere Regis and neighbouring villages but the Methodists among them would have prevented them from burning wheat ricks or helping smash threshing machines.

When asked by Lord Melbourne to provide further details about the labourers' involvement in the 1830 wages riots, Frampton wrote on 2 April, 1834:

> I have this morning seen a very respectable farmer of the Parish of Tolpiddle who occupies a farm about a mile from the village; and I have the honour to inform you that he states that, at the time of the riots in November, 1830, on hearing that all the Labourers of the Parish of Tolpiddle had assembled before it was daylight he went to them; and on his coming near, enquired

As Home Secretary, William Lamb, 2nd Viscount Melbourne, began looking into Tolpiddle's trade union activities in March 1834. (*From The History of White's by the Hon. Algernon Bourke*)

whether any of his labourers were there – on which George Loveless to whose voice he can swear, answered: 'Some of them are here and we have sent for the rest.' My informant together with the other farmers who were by that time present, told the labourers that altho' they would not promise them any particular sum, if they went to their work quietly they should have the same pay as was agreed to be given in other parishes. On which George Loveless said that the first man who started should have his head cracked. It was at this time light enough for the farmers to see who were there. James Loveless was also very active, appeared much dissatisfied and tried to persuade the men to go and join the mob which had assembled in Piddletown, a village about two miles off. At last, however, by persuasion and threatening to take down the names of every man who left the parish, the labourers did not go to Piddletown but returned to work.

Riots and rick burnings had ended by September 1832, and Captain Swing had faded into the background, but discontent about low wages continued in angry exchanges in fields, taverns and outside the doors of local churches. The Tolpiddle men, however, were not prepared for further dispute about decent wages and looked to George Loveless as their leader and the man who would deliver them from their bondage. Loveless remembers:

We consulted together what had better be done, knowing it was impossible to live honestly on such scanty means. I had seen at different times accounts of Trade Societies; I mentioned this, and it was resolved to form a friendly society among the labourers, having sufficiently learnt that it would be vain to seek redress either of employers, magistrates or parsons.

Chapter 2

The Travelling Preacher

1830/34

The Travelling Preachers, volunteer'd for the Lord,
Commence their attack from the press and his Word,
They boldly march forward, opposing their foe,
And come off victorious wherever they go.

George Loveless moved in a wide circle. As Wesleyan preachers, he and brother James were part of a team of more than 20 'travelling preachers' who walked to their country appointments every Sunday on the by-ways and bridle paths that criss-crossed the Weymouth Circuit. They were often called upon to lead up to three Sunday services which were eloquently and sincerely delivered by George and John and commanded admiration from their congregations.

The Weymouth circuit comprised 19 different chapels scattered across farming communities between Weymouth and Bere Regis. Services took place in chapels but, if these were unavailable, also in private homes or barns and sometimes in the open

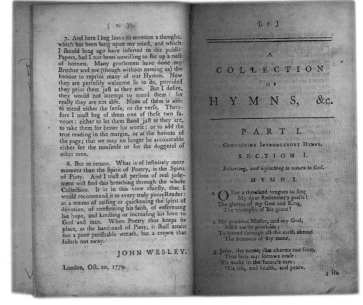

A page from John Wesley's Collection of Hymns 'exhorting and beseeching a return to God'. (*Open Library*)

air. The Loveless home in Tolpiddle was between three and a half miles and nine and a half miles distance from other chapels in parts of the circuit. The preacher's 'Plan' for November and December 1829 and January–March 1830 saw George Loveless conduct 21 different services in Tolpiddle, Winterbourne Houghton, Bere Regis, Tinkleton, Dewlish, Clenson and Bereheath. On 31 January 1830 he walked nearly four miles to preach at Bere Regis at 10:30am before walking another two miles to a second service in Bere Heath at 2:30pm and returning for another service in Bere Regis at 6:00pm. He then walked another four miles home. On Wednesday, 29 December 1830 all preachers working on the circuit had to lose a day's pay and walk nearly 16 miles to Weymouth for the quarterly Wesleyan meeting starting at 11.00am. They then walked home again after a 32-mile round trip. There was no money available to catch a ride on a passing horse-drawn coach and it is unlikely that either of the Loveless brothers had access to horses for the long journey. They would cover distance on foot, starting early – or the night before – and getting home late. Lay preachers also spent evenings after a full day's work in the fields studying and writing sermons based on Old and New Testament passages.

Plan for Wesleyan Preachers in the Weymouth Circuit on the Lord's Day for the period November 1829 – March 1830. George Loveless appears as number 8 on the list of travelling preachers visiting 19 different chapels scattered across farming communities between Bere Regis and Weymouth. (*Methodist Heritage*)

Moving around Dorset's country villages, however, brought the Loveless brothers into contact with a diverse range of folk; not just members of their congregations but fellow travellers they met and conversed with on their journeys on foot. Meeting new and old familiar faces exposed the brothers to a rich variety of information, opinions and news about the wider world. It is possible that while walking towards a village to preach at a service, they had heard about trade unions in London and the North of England from fellow travellers. They will have heard about how unions had been able to bring about improvements in the working conditions of tailors, cordwainers, flax dressers, woolcombers, stonemasons and hosts of other trades. George Loveless will have read about Robert Owen, the Welsh social reformer known as Britain's 'first Socialist' who was trying to form a combined union for all working classes called the Grand National Consolidated Trade Union, which in the early 1830s claimed a membership of around half a million people. Loveless would have used his time walking between one chapel and another considering how he, too, could form a Tolpiddle branch of a trade union and how to get in touch with Robert Owen. But how would he go about the task? That was the question ...

John Wesley (1703–91) was an Anglican cleric and theologian who, with his brother Charles and fellow cleric George Whitefield, founded Methodism. (*The Methodist Church at Central Hall*)

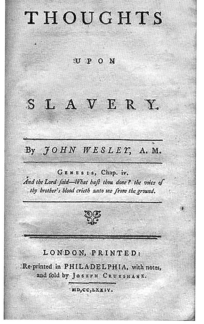

Title page of John Wesley's Thoughts Upon Slavery, 1778. (*Library of Congress*)

Chapter 3

Unity Is Strength!

1833/34

The farming men of Dorset have lately called a go,
And swear they'll have their wages rose before they reap or sow.
It's high time that working men should have it their own way
And for a fair day's labour, receive a fair day's pay.

George Loveless knew that if it were possible for a group of like-minded farm labourers to join him in some sort of fraternity and demonstrate their strength in numbers, and possibly even call a strike, landowning and farming employers might be convinced to take their request for fair wages more seriously. For effectiveness, however, Loveless needed committed people to sign up and knew that unity within numbers would provide members with the level of strength, influence and respect they needed to be heard. He wanted to use the fraternity as a platform from which his members could express grievances, gain moral and financial support and share commonly held beliefs.

Trade unions of one kind or another existed since biblical times. Loveless will have known that Chapter 5 of the Book of Exodus tells how Moses and Aaron met with Pharaoh to demand deliverance of Israelites from the bondage of slavery and tell him to 'Let my people go'. Pharaoh not only refused but punished the Israelites by telling his overseers: 'Ye shall no more give the people straw to make brick, as heretofore. Let them go and gather straw for themselves,' while still expecting them to produce the same quality bricks as before. The Israelites called the world's first industrial strike and Pharaoh quickly learned that river clay used to make wheat bricks was composed of fine particles which dried slowly. Adding straw 'opened up' the clay, allowing it to dry faster and fire more successfully. The nature of straw also added stability to clay bricks as wire mesh reinforces modern day concrete. Wheat bricks without straw cracked and crumbled easily, something that Loveless hoped might happen to Tolpiddle's landowners and farmers once his fraternity was formed.

Loveless probably did not know that in 1387 London's cordwainers – shoemakers who made fine soft leather shoes and other luxury footwear for the gentry – were in rebellion against 'overseers of the trade' and formed a permanent fraternity to represent their interests. Nine years later the serving-men of saddlers, known as 'yeomen' formed their own fraternity. Their masters, however, objected to a request for an increase in wages and the men walked away from their work benches until their masters offered a better deal.

Trade unions were declared legal in 1824. Previously British unions had been subject to severe repression but, nevertheless, became widespread in London, Manchester, and Birmingham. Once legality was won, vigorous attempts were made to promote the movement among different trades in all industries and promote working class influence on contemporary political issues. Unions were not, however, political organisations but economic movements formed to create better wages, benefits and working conditions for their members.

Unions were hated by factory and land owners, mine masters and those in charge of a hundred and one trades throughout Britain. Politicians and people in high places considered trades unions and their members as troublemakers out to exploit employers and threaten strikes if their demands were not met.

John Loveless, the older brother of George and James, was a flaxdresser who lived in the Dorset village of Burton Bradstock and was associated with the Leeds-based Flax Dressers Trade Union. George's other younger brother, Robert, also a flaxdresser, lived in London's Marylebone and, at John's request, provided his brothers with details of how to form a Tolpiddle union branch.

Sadly, as no copy of George Loveless' October 1833 letter to Robert Owen at the Grand National Consolidated Trade Union in London exists, this author can only speculate on its contents. Loveless would have first told Owen about the village of Tolpiddle and its population of 175 people (half of them children, mostly the sons and daughters of farm labourers). He would have explained the type of farming undertaken around the village, the crops cultivated and animals grazing there. He would have informed Owen about the landowners who leased their farmland to tenants who, in turn, hired labourers to work their land. Tenants made annual payments to landowners based on a percentage of the farm's income or made cash payments – or a combination of both. A tenant's rights over the leased land, farming accommodation and outbuildings were vague. In some parts of the country

Robert Owen, founder of the Grand National Consolidated Trade Union, which in 1834 had a membership of around half a million people. (*Thinkstock*)

tenants could be evicted on a whim; in others landowner and tenant signed a contract for a fixed number of years.

Loveless's letter would have outlined how the wages of Tolpiddle's farm labourers had been cut from ten shillings a week to starvation rates of seven weekly shillings – with a further threat to reduce the sum to six shillings. He would also have outlined how the workers had taken their plight to the local parson who, in turn, promised to make representations on their behalf to tenants and landowners. Owen would learn how Loveless had been elected to speak for the labourers at a special meeting in front of Frampton only to be told that farmers could pay whatever they liked to labourers. The parson's turncoat actions would also have been mentioned and how he and his fellow labourers were now feeding families on starvation diets of bread and potatoes. He would have asked for advice on how to start a union and requested a copy of union laws, rules and regulations. Loveless would then have thanked Owen in advance for the help he hoped to receive, re-read his letter, folded it, placed it in an envelope and taken it to Dorchester to catch the Royal Mail coach which would transport it to London, via Salisbury, in 16 hours.

George Loveless returned home to Tolpiddle and eagerly awaited a reply.

Part II

Either Hand or Heart

1833

When a 'bold peasantry' decays;
When want creeps in a thousand ways;
When labourers on farms struggling hard
Thro' toilsome years get no reward,
The Union will rescue – come what may;
Nor care they for the landlord's bray.

A written reply from Robert Owen's desk came back swiftly and George Loveless recalled that 'shortly afterwards two delegates from a trade society paid us a visit, formed a friendly society among the labourers and gave us directions on how to proceed. This was towards the end of October 1833.'

Everyone interested in joining the new Friendly Society of Agricultural Labourers was invited by word of mouth to attend a meeting in an upper room reached by climbing 10 wooden stairs to a room in Thomas Standfield's cottage overlooking the street. Forty farm labourers turned up and, while it was a tight squeeze to get everyone into the small candle-lit room measuring just 13ft x 17ft and directly underneath the thatched roof, the attendance demonstrated strong support for action within Tolpiddle. A small number of men from nearby Bere Regis also attended, including George Romaine, a young Wesleyan Methodist, who, like George and James Loveless, was also a farm labourer and lay preacher anxious to play his part in obtaining better wages for agricultural workers.

George first welcomed everyone to the first meeting of the union and introduced the two representatives from the Grand National Consolidated Trade Union in London. The names of the union men are unknown, but one of them stood up and told the meeting that trade unions had been lawful since July 1833 and thousands of men were now members. He said the government had given sanctions to the unions and had not, thus far, interfered in union matters. 'We have established unions for our protection here; we are given to understand that they are legal; we walk in procession in our metropolis [London] and neither police, magistrates, nor the ministers nor the judges of the land interfere with our operations. We recommend you do the same,' said the delegate.

Thomas Standfield's cottage, Tolpiddle – now known as Martyr's Cottage – where everyone wishing to join the Friendly Society of Agricultural Labourers met for the first time in an upper room in October 1833. (*Photograph: Alan Gallop*)

He then explained that for the union to work properly they had to follow a clear set of rules and regulations already in existence. These were read out to the company. The rules outlined how the union was to be run and that a grand committee of management had to be appointed of not less than seven men, including a secretary, who would report directly to the union's head office in London when required. The committee was to be democratically elected every three months comprising a president, vice-president, secretary, treasurer, conductor (to conduct initiation ceremonies), warden and outside and inside tilers (guardians) to protect the lodge from unwelcome spies and intruders. Before every meeting tilers were also required to 'go round and ascertain if any improper person be present'. As further protection against intrusion, all lodges would be given a secret password, to be provided by the Grand Lodge and which would be changed every three months. The first was to be: 'Either Hand or Heart,' a phrase based on the Book of Ecclesiastes 9:1 'For all this I considered in my *heart* even to declare all this that the righteous, and the wise, and their works, are in the *hand* of God.' No member would be admitted to the meeting without stating the correct password – or if they were drunk.

The society would also ask each member to pay a one-off joining fee of one shilling – the equivalent of nearly a day's pay – following initiation into the society plus one penny a week afterwards. In times of emergency the committee could also raise the weekly subscription. Accounts were to be made up monthly and any member not fully paid up was liable to a fine of eight pence but any member who was ill or out of employment was excused all subscriptions or fines. It was agreed that the society's Grand Lodge would be based at the Standfield house and similar lodges would be appointed in every local parish including Bere Regis, Charborough and Winterbourne Kingston. Loveless stated that 'no obscenity shall be tolerated in either songs or toasts and that no political or religious subjects be introduced during lodge hours.'

George Loveless then spelt out one of the society's principal objectives:

If any master attempts to reduce the wages of his workmen and if they are members of this order, they shall communicate the same to the secretary, in order that they may receive the support of the Grand Lodge; and in the meantime they shall use their utmost endeavours to finish the work they have in hand, if any, and shall assist each other, so they may leave the place altogether, and with as much promptitude as possible.

His next bold remark will have made some men in the upper room nervous:

If any member of this society renders himself obnoxious to his employer, solely on account of taking an active part in the affairs of this order, and if guilty of no violation or insult to his master, and be discharged from his employment solely in consequence thereof, either before or after the turn out, then the whole body of men at that place shall instantly leave the place, and no member of this society shall be allowed to take work at that place until such member be reinstated in his situation.

In other words they were to down tools and walk out on strike.

He told the meeting that, if any member were to divulge any secrets or violate its obligations, the name and a description

… of his person and his crime shall be immediately communicated to all lodges throughout the country; and if such person gets work at any place where a lodge is established, or where men belonging to this order are working, they shall decline to work with such an individual and instantly leave the place and receive the support of the Grand Lodge as if they were turned out against the reduction in wages.

Some members of the assembly sniggered when they heard that 'no member be allowed to eat, read, sleep, swear, bet wagers or use any obscene language during Lodge hours.'

He said that 'the word "brother" shall be used only during lodge hours.' Brother George also said that a box of three keys were to be kept 'wherein shall be deposited the Lodge's cash, books and regalia'. The keys were to be kept by the president, vice-president and warden.

So did trade unionism come to Tolpuddle that evening in October 1833.

A few days later the newly created Society wrote unsigned letters to labourers in local villages naming trustworthy men who could be relied on to distribute the information:

> Brethren, this will inform you that there is a possibility of getting a just remuneration for your labour without any violation of the law or bringing your person into any trouble. If men are willing to accept of what is offered, then labouring men may get two shillings or half a crown a day as easy as they now get one shilling only.
>
> Let men be united and the victory is gained, after men are united and strike for advance of wages they will be supported all the time they are staying at home from a certain fund provided for the purpose.
>
> Now will there be a danger of others undermining you, for you may take the most cowardly man in this kingdom, and let him be united, and he will stand firm as a rock.
>
> N.B.: Men are adopting this almost throughout the kingdom.

Chapter 4

Brothers All

1833/34

They tell us, my brothers, that sticks bound together
Are stronger in bundles than standing alone,
That the union gives strength to face bleak and foul weather
That all for each other brings each to his own.
'Tis true, as they say, but my brother remember
That union, though mighty, no tyrant shall be.
To make himself strong thus to fetter his neighbour,
And keep him in chains while his gaoler is free!
Then 'free and fair' be the motto we bear.
Freedom to labour wherever we may.
Freedom as brothers to bargain with others
For a fair day's work for a fair day's pay.

In October 1834, James Loveless travelled to Dorchester to visit an artist's shop run by John Whetham and his wife Frances in the town centre. He carried with him two rough sketches of a skeleton representing the Grim Reaper as a centrepiece holding a scythe in one hand and an hourglass in the other, symbols familiar to farm labourers representing their own hard lives and mortality. Above the skeleton's head the words 'Remember Thine End' had been written.

John Whetham was not present when James Loveless entered the shop so he spoke with Mrs. Whetham and placed the rough sketches onto the counter. He told her he wanted them to be reproduced as a large painting six feet high using dark and light colours to highlight different parts of the picture. Mrs. Whetham had never seen such a picture before and asked what it was for. James Loveless told her 'it is intended for a society'. He asked if the picture could be ready the following week and gave Mrs. Whetham his address before leaving the shop.

Mrs. Whetham showed the sketches to her husband when he returned. He examined them carefully trying to understand their meaning and thought they were distinctly odd. Being basically a sign writer who also painted pictures, he had never before been commissioned to paint such an illustration and was suspicious as to how it would be used and the trouble he might bring upon himself if the authorities discovered he was responsible for producing it. He decided not to go ahead with the painting before speaking in person to the man who had brought the sketches. He placed them under the counter and forgot all about them.

James Loveless returned to Dorchester the following week to pay for and collect the skeleton painting. Again Mr. Whetham was not present, but his wife told him he was having lunch at the nearby Antelope Hotel and Loveless went in search of him. The hotel was full of diners and it took several attempts to find Mr. Whetham. After introducing himself James Loveless asked the artist if his painting was ready. Mr. Whetham told him he had not even started work on it as he needed more information about the picture and how it would be used. James Loveless told him they were for a new secret society of which he was a member. Mr. Whetham said he could not make out the meaning of the designs and therefore could not produce the paintings. He was sorry to turn down such a commission as he could have charged up to five shillings for the piece.

A disappointed James Loveless returned to Dorchester empty handed – but somewhere along the line either he or his brother George managed to find someone willing to produce the painting exactly as they wanted it and in time for the first meeting of the Friendly Society of Agricultural Labourers.

o0o

After the society's opening meeting, the union met every evening after finishing work in the fields and barns. They debated and argued; they agreed and disagreed about a multitude of different issues facing farm labourers. They also initiated men into the society using the text of a ceremony originally produced for the Woolcombers and Weavers Union in Bradford, Yorkshire with its origins traceable back to the 1700s and early Freemasonry. It was given to them by the union visitors from London who told Loveless to adapt it for the Tolpiddle society's own circumstances. During initiation ceremonies, men wishing to be admitted to the union were required to be blindfolded, kneel and swear an ancient oath in front of the skeleton stating they would prove honest, faithful, just and true. They would be asked if their motives for joining the society were pure. Anyone who found they could not take on these demands was at liberty to leave.

A few days before Christmas 1833 union members arrived at the Standfield house to swear in more new members. Some were unable to attend that night including union secretary George Romaine and James Hammett who was not present for reasons best known to himself. Hammett's young brother John, however, was present and would give his older brother an account of what took place when he returned home later that evening. Also present was John Lock, the son of James Frampton's head gardener at his Moreton estate and Edward Legg, a farm labourer from Aftpiddle who had been brought to the meeting by James Brine. Both Lock and

This painting shows a skeleton, the Grim Reaper, holding a scythe in one hand and an hourglass in the other. The painting is larger than life-size and the Friendly Society of Agricultural Labourers used a similar one during their initiation ceremonies. New members were blindfolded and recited a secret 'oath of allegiance'. When the blindfold was removed the new member was presented with a shocking reminder of their own mortality and the damnation that awaited those who break their promises. (*The People's History Museum*)

Legg appeared nervous as they climbed the 10 stairs to the upper room where the lodge was assembled. They were not known to many in the assembly as they lived outside of Tolpiddle, but Brine assured the meeting that both labourers were sincere in wanting to join the union and could be relied on to keep its rules. But what nobody knew that night was that both Lock and Legg were spies recruited by Frampton to go to the meeting undercover to be sworn in and then report what had taken place in minute detail. It is not known how much they were paid for their services or how long they had been working undercover for Frampton. Their services might have been paid for in cash, with food or other favours.

The ceremony taking place that night was a mixture of the religious – including prayers, hymns and swearing oaths of allegiance on the bible – and a high degree of mummery, including passages spoken in (terrible) verse. The men were supposed to take what was being said seriously, but many must have secretly sniggered at some passages.

Principal union officers wore home-made surplices for initiation ceremonies. The upper room in John Standfield's cottage – the same room used for its first meeting – was illuminated by a single candle positioned in front of the skeleton. There was a knock on the door by an officer known as 'the outside Tyler', the name originally given to the doorkeeper of an inn. An 'inside Tyler' replied:

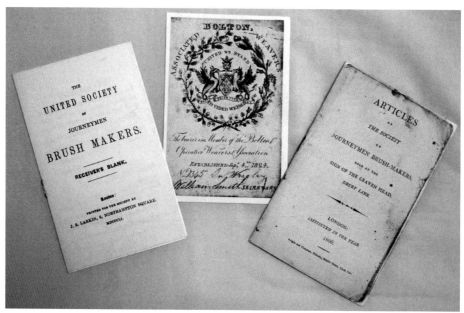

An example of three 19th century union documents given to members and similar to those produced by the Grand National Consolidated Trade Union for the Friendly Society of Agricultural Labourers: The United Society of Journeymen Brush Makers 1806 (left), the Bolton Operative Weavers Association 1824 (centre) and Articles of The Society of Journeymen Brush Makers 1806. (*Jackdaw – The Early Trade Unions*)

Who comes here to disturb the peace and harmony of this our most worthy and honourable order?

Voice from outside the door:

I am not come here to disturb the peace and harmony of this your most worthy and honourable order. I am a brother with strangers who wish to be admitted into your most worthy and honourable order.

Insider Tyler:

Most worthy President, Vice President, Secretary and brothers all, a brother stands at the door with strangers who wish to be admitted into this your most worthy and honourable order.

At this point the mummery part of the meeting commenced.

President:

In the name of the Lord, admit them.

The Principal Conductor then entered followed by blindfolded Lock and Legg. The assembly sings a hymn.

Principal Conductor:

Strangers, within our secret walls we have admitted you, hoping you will prove honest, faithful, just and true. If you cannot keep the secrets we require, go hence; you are at liberty to retire. Are you motives true?

Strangers:

Yes.

Principal Conductor:

Then, brethren, to initiate these strangers we will now precede, and our most worthy master may proceed to read.

The assembly sings a hymn.

Warden:

Stand, ye presumptuous mortals, strangers' steps I hear/ and I must know your trade and business here./ By my great power, there's nothing can from vengeance stay us,/ if you come here intending to betray us.

President:

Most worthy guardian of our sacred laws,/ they are farm labourers and wishful to protect the united cause.

Warden:

Then all is well.

Blindfolds are removed from the strangers' eyes and the men are placed opposite the skeleton.

President (pointing to the skeleton):

Strangers, mark well this shadow, which you see./ It is a faithful emblem of man's destiny./ Behold that head once filled with pregnant wit,/ these hollow holes once sparkling eyes did fit./ This empty mouth nor lips nor tongue contains,/ of a once well furnished head, see all that now remains/ The sting of death is sin – are we not sinners all?/ Then upon us one day the heavy stroke of death must fall.

Vice-President:

Strangers, hear me; and mark well what I say./ Be faithful to your trust or you may rue this day./ You are now within our secret walls, and I must know if you can keep a secret.

Strangers:

Yes.

Vice-President:

And will you do?

Strangers:

Yes.

Vice-President:

Then among us, you will shortly be entitled to the endearing name of brother,/ and what you hear or see here done, you must not disclose to any other;/ We are uniting to cultivate friendship, as well as to protect our trade,/ and due respect must to all our laws be paid./ Hoping you will prove faithful, and all encroachments on our rights withstand,/ as a token of your alliance – give me your hand./ And now shouldst thou ever prove deceitful,/ remember thy end, remember./ Guards, put these strangers into darkness,/ and conduct them to our most worthy master,/ to be further instructed in this our most worthy and honourable order.

The strangers are blindfolded again and made to walk several times around the room while members stamp on the floor with their feet. They are then led to a table, upon which the bible is placed. As the right hand of each is laid upon the sacred volume, bandages are removed and they take an oath swearing to support the brotherhood promising to never act in opposition to efforts supporting wages and assist in all lawful occasions to obtain fair remuneration for their labour. They state that if they fail to carry out these promises their souls will be plunged into an everlasting pit of misery.

President:

God save our noble King, William the Fourth let's sing. Brethren, ere we depart, let us join hand and heart in this our cause; may our next meeting be blest with sweet harmony, honour and secrecy in the Agricultural Labourer's cause. Amen.

Chapter 5

A Labourering Life

1830/34

A spade! A rake! A hoe!
A pickaxe or a bill!
A hook to reap, or a scythe to mow,
A flail or what ye will –
And here's a ready hand
To ply the needful tool,
And skill'd enough by lessons rough,
In labour's rugged school.

From The Lay of the Labourer *by Thomas Hood*

Living conditions experienced by labouring families in the 1830s were in primitive, appalling hovel-like dwellings built of mud and cob (a natural building material to make inexpensive building material for homes and barns) with compacted earth

Living conditions in labourers' cottages were primitive and their dwellings were built using mud, walls composed of road scrapings, chalk, straw and cob. (*Illustrated London News*)

on the ground floor covered with potato sacks and creaking floor boards on the upper level. The cottages were poorly thatched with the underside of the roof uncovered allowing rainwater to filer down onto the room below. The thatch in some cottages was so thinly laid that those in bed could stare up to see the stars through gaps in the roof. Many cottages were without windows apart from a square hole measuring 1ft x 1ft punched through one of the walls and without any glass or wooden shutters.

In September 1846, *The Times* produced a series of graphic articles about everyday life in Dorset's agricultural communities after a local correspondent had visited labourers' cottages and described dwellings as 'a horrible mode of existence'. Yet the writer was told by several people interviewed that 'the labourer does not complain. Where is the necessity for troubling yourself to alter his situation so long as he is satisfied?'

Farm labourers, however, did complain about their daily lot – but only among themselves with nobody else in earshot. The gentleman from *The Times* must have been very persuasive when asking farm labourers if he could visit their

> … hovels to which even Lear's daughters would have felt compunction in consigning him. He is a patient and much–enduring being, but his murmurs, if not loud, are sufficiently deep to make it evident that he is quite aware of the injustice of which he is the victim, and that he is not so dull as to be blind to the fact that custom and combination have fixed the reward of his daily toil at a miserable and insufficient sum, which can barely procure him the necessities, none of the comforts and decencies of life. In July when the beneficial result of his exertions is everywhere to be traced in the luxuriant crops with which the whole country teems, the reflection that he will be the last to feel the benefit of the forthcoming plenty is doubly painful. As a grey headed old labourer observed to me today, 'there will be plenty, if everybody could only get a share of it.'

The Times reported that the majority of labourers' cottages were tiny containing a single bedroom, connected to the living room below by a ladder, for large families of seven or more people which

> … produce instances of the most frightful depravity … and what is evident is the inevitable consequence of this disgusting and indiscriminate herding together of so many persons of both sexes into one common and confined sleeping apartment…The want of proper ventilation in these houses must be to the last degree detrimental to the health of the inhabitants; the atmosphere, especially in the sleeping apartments, to an unpractised nose is almost insupportable. It is worthy of remark that dishes, plates and other

Homes lived in by farm labourers were crowded and unpleasant. This picture shows a family of thirteen all living under the same roof; the oldest was the grandfather sitting in the corner and the youngest a baby in arms. (*The Graphic*)

articles of crockery, seem almost unknown; there is, however, the less need for them as bread forms the principal, and I believe the only kind of food which falls to the labourer's lot. In no single instance did I observe meat of any kind during my progress through the parish.

In a village near Tolpiddle, the same correspondent observed:

The cottages are built with mud walls composed of road scrapings, chalk and straw; the inundation is of stone or brick, and on this the mud wall is built in regular layers, each of which is allowed to dry and harden before another is put over it. Every dwelling is thatched as are also the garden walls; these are frequently built of the same cheap materials, the top being protected from the weather by a small roof of thatch, which extends a few inches over each side.

The writer's first observation on entering the village was:

… the total want of cleanliness which pervades it. A stream, composed of the matter which constantly escapes from pigsties and receptacles of filth, meanders down each street, being here and there collected into stranding pools, which lie festering and rotting in the sun so as to create wonder that the place is not the continual abode of pestilence – indeed the worst malignant fevers have raged here at different times. It may be sufficient to add for the present that the inside of the cottages in every respect corresponds with the external appearance of the place.

Another 'fruitful source of misery, as well as immorality' witnessed by that writer was:

… the great inadequacy of the number and sizes of the houses to the number of the population and the consequently crowded state of their habitations, which in Dorsetshire generally afford the most limited accommodation. It is by no means an uncommon thing for the whole family to sleep in the same room, without the slightest regard to age or sex, and without a curtain or the slightest attempt at separation between the beds. In one instance which came under my notice, a family consisting of nine persons occupied three beds in the same bedroom, which was the only one the house afforded. The eldest daughter is 23 years of age, the eldest son is 21. In some instances I have seen most ingenious and laudable attempts to effect a barrier between the sexes, but in general there does not appear to exist any anxiety on the subject; and indeed in most instances the size and form of the room and the number of beds required for the accommodation of the family, render all such attempt futile. It will easily be imagined that the nightly and promiscuous herding together of young people of both sexes is productive of the most demoralising effects, and it is no matter of wonder that there are more illegitimate children in this village than in any other village of equal size in Dorset. In case of a death in the family, should there be but one bedroom, the inmates of the house are compelled to pass their nights in the same room with the corpse until the time of burial.

Sanitary arrangements in labourers' cottages were very primitive. A privy was often situated at the bottom of a garden and shared between five or six households and used by over 30 people from a dozen cottages. The privy comprised a deep pit with wooden planks over it which was emptied every six months – usually Easter and Christmas – causing every door and window (when one could be found) in the neighbourhood to be sealed until the contents had been removed to a large pit on an empty piece of ground outside of the village and covered with soil. The outside of the privy was covered with planks of wood joined together at the top and taking the form of an upturned letter 'V.' It was popularly known as a 'Jericho' because, like the walls of Jericho in the biblical story, the privy's walls often collapsed in windy weather. Also outside was a water butt storing rainwater from the roof which was usually insufficient to meet the needs of a family. Water also had to be brought from a village pump or well and women carried it all the way home in buckets suspended from their shoulders by a homemade yoke. In addition to cooking and washing, water was also used for laundering and boiled over an open fire. Family clothes were washed in a tub and taken to a communal mangle where the owner could earn a few pennies by wringing it out.

Most labouring families barely subsisted, their wages were quickly consumed on rent (around one shilling weekly) and food. Families ate just one hot meal daily after men came home from the fields sitting around a rough wooden table; those who could not find a place ate their food sat on the floor. Much of the family income was spent buying bread, which cost 6d for a quartern loaf, made with 3½ lb (or ¼ stone) of wheaten flour. Bread was eaten with dripping and washed down with weak tea. On a good night an evening meal might consist of a little bacon with turnip tops, potatoes or anything else the family might grow in their small allotment, if they were lucky enough to have one.

During the two-week harvest season the cost of food was alleviated when women and children went to work with their men from sunrise to sunset haymaking and binding corn. Between jobs the women were allowed to go 'gleaning' – gathering ears of wheat using hand held wooden drag rakes which were similar in design to a garden rake but larger and with a split willow handle and teeth made from ash.

During the two-week harvest season women and children went to work with the men between sunrise and sunset haymaking and binding corn. (*Illustrated London News*)

Women working in the fields were allowed to go 'gleaning' – gathering ears of wheat using drag rakes – which could be taken home after threshing for grinding by a local miller. (*Illustrated London News*)

The drag rake also allowed hay to be dragged into lines so that men with pitchforks could load the hay cart without taking any unnecessary steps. Any 'gleaned' wheat left on the ground could be taken home and, after threshing, the grain was sent to a local miller for grinding; he would take some of the flour in payment and return the rest in a sack. Women were usually paid 6d per day and children 3d per day for harvesting work.

On some farms more generous landowners or tenant farmers began their first-day of harvest gathering with an early morning breakfast feast for workers going into the fields. At Northover Manor in Tolpiddle, the morning feast began with prayers of thanks for the harvest about to be brought in, followed by servings of cold fat bacon, boiled beans, fried potatoes, loaves of bread as big as bee-hives (and much the same shape) and as brown as the back of a farm worker's hands. The feast was washed down with ale or cider, but not enough to make labourers stagger out to the fields and, besides, there would be a break for more cider later in the day. Farm workers could also help themselves to a hunk of bread from the giant loaf and cut off a large chunk of cheese to wrap in their handkerchiefs and take out for a lunch to be eaten under the shade of a tree in a distant field. Harvest breakfasts were the only occasions that farm labourers and their families would sit together at a table covered with a cloth or eat food from china plates. The harvest breakfast would be the talk of the village for weeks afterwards.

Other employers would reward workers with a harvest supper once work in the fields was completed. Suppers would be a real feast consisting of roast beef and mutton followed by plum pies, washed down with copious quantities of ale or cider. The feast would be followed by 'turns' performed by individual musicians or singers known to have a good voice or musical skills and groups of singers who often sang saucy songs in unison or told lewd jokes to their audience of well-oiled farming men and women.

Most farm labourers were paid weekly on 'payday Friday' evenings. To collect their dues labourers lined up in front of a table placed in the farm yard during mild weather or inside a barn in autumn and winter. In Tolpuddle around 50 labourers employed on the 1,190 acres of farmland leased to Mrs. Northover stood in line before presenting themselves to a member of the tenant farmer's staff who looked for their names in a large ledger. The ledger listed the days and hours worked and calculated how much each labourer had earned. Anyone sick or needing time off lost pay for every day or hour they were absent. Once this had been verified, labourers were paid in cash, usually in one shilling pieces, which was carefully counted out onto the table to be picked up and deposited into a labourer's smock pocket. If there was any dispute regarding collecting a wage which might have fallen short of the amount expected, an Overseer representing Mrs. Northover – usually a solidly built fellow who stood no nonsense – was on hand to settle any complaint or query about what had been paid out. Whatever wage was collected did not go far. The cost of living for a farm labourer in Dorset in 1834 was high as the following list demonstrates:

Butter – 1s/2d per pound
Cheese – 5d per pound
Pot of meat dripping – ½d
Eggs – 1d each
Butcher's meat – 6d per pound
Eels – 3d per pound
Rabbits – 6d each
Geese – 3s/6d each
Ducks – 1s/- each

Fuel was also expensive. Coal was brought down from Newcastle to Wareham at a cost of 2s/6d per bushel which was too expensive for labouring families who used whatever they could forage locally to burn. Fruit, nuts and berries were considered fair game, including blackberries, gooseberries, elderberries, crab apples, hazel nuts, chestnuts, walnuts, wild raspberries and plums growing along a roadside. But woe betide anyone foolish enough to crawl under a hedge and trespass onto farmland owned by a landowner or tenant farmer in order to gather firewood or forage for food. The penalties were high and could include gaol sentences, transportation to a penal colony for seven years or even execution. Rabbits, hares or pigeons that could be snared along a public road or in the grounds of a labourer's cottage could, however, be kept by the captor for his cooking pot. If no meat could be found it was not unknown for labourers to catch a fox, skin it and cook it.

There was little left over from a labourer's wages at the end of a working week to buy articles needed in the home, including clothes. Extra money earned at harvest time went towards these items and clothes were handed down and worn until threadbare. Clothing once worn by older brothers and sisters was altered for smaller children. Women and children rarely wore shoes and children were never seen wearing caps or bonnets.

The men wore a smock – also known as a smock-frock or slop – as a protective outer garment. It had developed from a full shirt into a decorated form in which the fullness over the chest, back and sleeves was controlled by gatherings held in place by ornamental stitching. The smock was functional as well as decorative as it gave the garment shape and a certain elasticity allowing freedom of movement. Smocks were popular with ploughmen, waggoners, shepherds and pig farmers. They were also worn by gardeners, woodmen and game keepers. Tradesmen such as butchers, fishmongers, tailors, stonemasons, cider makers and brewery workers might also wear them. The garment was usually worn with a wide brimmed straw

Farm labourers wore a 'smock' as a protective outer garment. They were popular with ploughmen, waggoners, shepherds and pig farmers. (*Illustrated London News*)

hat with a fabric band around the juncture of the crown and the brim which helped keep its shape.

Most farm labourers owned two smocks. One was for everyday use in the fields and made from course twill – a type of textile weave with a pattern of diagonal parallel ribs – or calico coated in linseed oil to render it weatherproof. A ploughman like George Loveless would have worn a grey or black smock covering his shirt and the uppermost part of his trousers. It would have contained one or two large deep pockets in the front, one to carry any tools – such as a clasp knife – needed during his day in the fields and another to carry his lunch. A second smock, known as the 'best smock-frock', was worn on Sundays for church, special occasions, at weddings or funerals. This smock was usually made of coarse linen and decorated with embroidered patterns sewn onto the front, collar, shoulders and cuffs. These were usually white and often waxed. The stitches were often intricate with sheaves of corn, ploughs, rakes, pitchforks, hearts and flowers all worked into the finest details. The famous four words known to every countryman, 'God speed the plough' were embroidered onto the smock collar of many Dorsetshire ploughmen.

Like so much clothing worn by farming families, smocks were often handed down from grandfather to father and on to a son. A smock has been known to have been worn by five generations of one family. They were robustly made and, when cared for, could be worn for over eighty years. Buying a new smock, however, was expensive and a farm worker would have to save his pennies and shillings carefully to buy one from a shop in Dorchester or pay to have one made by a local smock maker. Either way the cost of a new smock could be up to £1/10s – three weeks wages – so saving for a new one could take some time.

Chapter 6

Speed the Plough

1834

You sons of Old England come list to my rhymes
And I'll sing unto you a short sketch of the times,
Concerning poor labourers you all must allow
Who work all the day at the tail of a plough.

On August 20, 1804 the population of the village of Tolpiddle numbered 289 souls – 145 males and 144 females. By 1834 the population had risen by a further 359, bringing the total to 648 persons. The various occupations resident in this growing village included a thatcher, tailor, farmers and farm labourers, pig dealers, a baker, a 'Poor House' for 10 people from three families, a Staymaker (or maker of stays and ladies' corsets), shepherds, carpenters, a shoemaker, a miller, carters, haymakers and the village vicar, the Reverend Dr. Thomas Warren who took up office in the 17th century church of St. John the Evangelist in 1805. He lived with

Rev. Thomas Warren, Tolpuddle's Anglican vicar, was not the only one in the village to wear a dog collar. His two dogs also wore brass dog collars on which their names had been inscribed in case they went missing or were stolen and needed to be identified. (*Duke's Auctioneers, Dorchester*)

his wife Jane in a large vicarage with nine bedrooms next to the church and was not the only one in the village to wear a dog collar. His two dogs also wore brass dog collars, inscribed: 'Rev. Thos. Warren – Tolpiddle' for identification if they went missing or were stolen from the vicarage.

There was no law that anyone had to go to Sunday church services, but Dr. Warren did his upmost to make it difficult for people who stayed away. An hour before services were due to begin, he sent out 'disciples' to walk around the village and knock on the doors of residents to remind them that Sunday matins would commence at 9:00am sharp and if they were not up, washed and dressed they had better move themselves. Once the congregation had arrived, an under-officer appointed by Petty Constable Brine and who could write and count, made a note of who was present – and who was not. The list would later be taken to Dr. Warren's vestry where names of absentees were recorded. 'Disciples' did not knock on the door of Tolpuddle's Wesleyan Methodists who had their own chapel in the village and needed no reminding that Sunday was a day of worship.

Services at St. John's, like many other Anglican churches across the country, were lengthy affairs in which congregations were expected to spend a great deal of time on their knees praying or on their feet singing hymns. The majority of Dr. Warren's congregation were farm workers who, for six days each week, rose at dawn. By Sunday most men were exhausted from their labours and used church services as an excuse for 'a quiet nod' in their pews, while kneeling for prayers or 'listening' to one of Dr. Warren's sermons with their eyes closed 'for better concentration'. Daily exposure to fresh air in the fields over their six working days made them drowsy as bats on the seventh and Dr. Warren made mental notes of anyone in the congregation heard snoring with whom he 'would have a few words' in the doorway as people left church.

Labourers had every right to be tired on Sundays. They worked long hours in hot sunshine, pouring rain, hail and snow, on both parched earth and muddy flooded fields. They had to be strong and fit throughout the year because, if they became unwell or had an accident and were unable to work, they lost all wages while absent which they could ill afford.

Farm labour was the largest employment sector in England until overtaken in 1871 by domestic service. The majority of farm workers were employed on a casual daily basis only when work was available. If a job was completed or bad weather prevented them from going into the fields they were sent home without pay. This might continue some days or even an entire season, particularly in winter, and caused severe hardship for both the labourer and his family.

A labourer needed to be more than just a farm hand; he had to be a Jack-of-all-trades. As well as working in fields and barns they needed to be armed with experience and knowledge of everything from digging ditches, planting crops and building fences to sheep washing, manuring and milking. It would also be helpful to

The Ploughman's Breakfast.

After an early start to their day, a ploughman and his helper pause from their work to enjoy a snack breakfast out in the field. (*Author's collection*)

the labourer, and his master, if he offered experience in carpentry, hewing and sawing, plastering, building, bricklaying, stone masonry, thatching, slating, tiling, joinery and blacksmithary. Not only would this knowledge help secure a job but it would also save the farmer money and eliminate any need to bring in outside tradesmen.

George Loveless was a master ploughman which meant that he offered years of experience working with farm horses and ploughing furrows of any length, width and depth on all types of land. By 1834 heavy horses had become the primary draft animal for agricultural use. Loveless would have worked with the same pair of horses for most of the year; a favourable arrangement as horses work more steadily under the guidance of the same driver than in the hands of different men. The ploughman also preferred working with familiar animals. Loveless would have agreed that a man and his horses needed to be acquainted before they could understand each other and, when the peculiarities of each party were mutually understood, their work improved.

He did not spend all of his time behind a plough and, when he and his fellow farm labourers were not needed in the fields, they were engaged in other skilled and unskilled jobs on the farm such as seed sowing, hoeing and weeding, mowing, spreading dung, harvesting, threshing after the harvest and hedging and ditching in winter. They also repaired barns, outhouses and the farmer's own house. They planted vegetables in the farmer's garden, cut grass with a scythe and generally made themselves useful at any job which might come their way. It was important to keep busy and dangerous to be seen standing around doing nothing in case they were sent home and lost a day's wages. They also needed to be versatile, strong and fit as the tools they used were generally heavy and the jobs tiring.

James Brine and James Hammett worked at different Tolpiddle farms in different capacities including field workers, shepherds, cattle men, dairy men or stewards.

George Loveless's working day began before daybreak at West Farm, a short walk from his home along the narrow street which ran through the village. His first job was to take animals to the horse pond in front of the barn for a drink. If the night had been freezing he also had to break the ice for the horses to reach the water. Horses leaving a warm steaming stable would not enjoy freezing water and, even if a horse trough had been available, it would be just as liable to freeze as the pond. Perhaps it never occurred to some farm owners to leave buckets of cold water overnight in stables where it would not freeze.

While men and horses were at the horse pond, other farm workers cleared the stable of dung and soiled litter made during the night and filled each stable with horse feed. Following their drink, horses were brought back to the stable for their first meal of the day – an allowance of corn. While the horses were feeding some farm workers could return home where their own meagre breakfast would be waiting.

West Farm, Tolpuddle, was one of the largest farm estates in the Tolpuddle area and employed George Loveless as a Master Ploughman, among many other jobs. (*Photograph: Alan Gallop*)

Back in the stable, horses were dressed, combed and harnessed to go into the fields where they worked until 12 noon when they returned to the stable for water and another feed of corn. The labourers either went home to eat or ate what they had brought in the pockets of their smocks. Most of West Farm's fields and meadows were located to the north of the village and farm yard; if ploughing was undertaken in one of the distant fields, such as the 25-acre Barn Close or the oddly named Nine Acre which actually measured eleven acres, it was not always practical to detach the plough and bring horses back to the stable to eat. On these occasions horses ate from nose-bags while their ploughman ate food wrapped in large handkerchiefs and drank water from a stone bottle. George Loveless, however, knew that horses should not be worked for seven or eight hours at a stretch and, when possible, returned them the stables to eat their corn and have a short rest while the men ate lunch. They were then ready to plough until sunset before returning home. The horses would have another drink from the pond after which any mud which had collected on their legs below the knees was washed off and dried by men using wisps of straw.

Farm horses usually had twice-weekly meals of mash, consisting either of steamed potatoes, boiled barley or oats mixed with bran and served into troughs. Work horses were fond of mash and, at around their meal times, ploughmen like George Loveless noticed that animals demonstrated signs of impatience. Getting to know their horses, their moods and their behaviour was something only experienced ploughman could achieve. Loveless knew that horses did not enjoy being confined to a stable for long periods, including Sundays, before becoming troublesome and when time or preaching duties allowed, he always looked in on the animals and made sure one of the farm boys took them out for a walk or allowed them to graze before returning them to the stable. When not pulling a plough horses were also hauling carts containing vegetables, supplies and equipment from and to the farm.

Loveless appreciated that the horse was an intelligent animal and always pleased to be in the company of men. He knew that when two or more people were standing together in conversation, a horse might approach them and listen to them talking. The horses recognised their own names and responded when called. They could distinguish the tones of farm workers' voices whether spoke in anger, encouragement or otherwise. Loveless would also have given his horses individual names and made sure they were sharp, emphatic and not exceeding two syllables in length. For geldings, popular horse names included Tom, Jolly, Ned, Tinker, Dobbin and Dragon and for mares Peg, Rose, Jess, Molly and Beauty.

Heavy draught horses used to pull his plough were chestnut coloured Suffolk Punch carthorses – good, strong and faithful workers with excellent constitutions, energy, and endurance. They were also used by coal merchants, distillers and brewers in towns and cities. The horses were traditionally docile with bright personalities and keen to form good relationships with their handlers.

Chestnut coloured Suffolk Punch carthorses were used at West Farm – good and faithful workers, showing fine examples of strength, constitution, energy and endurance. (*The Book of the Farm by Henry Stephens, 1844*)

SUFFOLK PUNCH.

Horses worked side-by-side in pairs to pull their ploughs. This was a complex operation and an experienced ploughman would understand both the overall operation of his equipment and the function of each individual part of the plough. To grow crops, soil had to be turned to bring nutrients to the surface. To do this Loveless would almost certainly have used a Rotherham swing plough, which Mrs. Northover would have purchased for around thirty shillings; this was constructed from wood with the mouldboard (the curved blade which turns over the furrow) and ploughshare (a horizontal pointed cutting blade) covered in iron plating. It was lighter than traditional ploughs and could easily be worked with a pair of carthorses to cut a furrow about seven inches deep on any kind of soil. It was the first plough to be widely built in factories and first to be commercially successful on farms across the country.

When pulled through a field, the plough cut horizontally into the soil. This released a rectangular strip of topsoil that was lifted and carried by the mouldboard up and over, so the strip of cut sod lifted and rolled over as the plough moved forward, dropping back to the ground upside down into the furrow and onto turned soil from a previous run down the field. Each gap in the ground where soil was lifted and moved was, and remained, a furrow. Swing ploughs greatly reduced the time needed to prepare a field, and thereby allowed a farmer to work a larger area of land. In addition to his duties with his horses in the field a ploughman would also be expected to know how to adjust the depth of his ploughshare to the working conditions of the day, adjust the seven key parts of the plough and fix them when needed.

Instead of using a bridle to direct the horses, Loveless used long trace chains especially made for horse pairs which were attached to horse collars, or yokes, and

A Rotherham Swing plough was lighter than traditional ploughs and could easily be worked with a pair of carthorses to cut a furrow about seven inches deep in any kind of soil. (*Author's collection*)

a crossbar in the horse's harness, known as the 'swingle tree', to which trace chains were attached to connect the horses to the plough.

On a fine day an experienced ploughman would take between eight and nine hours to plough an acre of farmland. In that time he and his horses would have walked around 11 miles. The horses needed few commands as they had ploughed the same fields many times before.

A 19th century woodcut, showing ploughmen using Suffolk Punch carthorses and a Rotherham Swing Plough to turn over the soil. (*Author's collection*)

To begin a day's field work, Loveless would have commanded his horses to 'walk on'. When he needed them to stop he would call 'whoa' or 'ho'. Once the team arrived at the end of a furrow, Loveless would have pulled either the left or right link chain to indicate which direction the horses needed to turn. Throughout ploughing he would call words of encouragement: 'Good girl Molly', 'steady now Tom' or 'turn right my darlin's' mainly re-assured the horses that he was still behind them.

As he held onto his stilt – wooden handles made from ash used to control the direction of the plough – Loveless would have used this time to mentally compose the sermons he would deliver the following Sunday. He would also contemplate how to improve life for his family and fellow farm labourers before returning the horses to the barn, washing them and bedding them down for the night. He would then go home to his wife and children.

This was the life lived by George Loveless and his fellow agricultural workers in the little village of Tolpuddle in 34th year of the 19th century, during the reign of King William IV. This is how they lived and scratched out a living from working the soil. It might not have been much, but they knew no better life. Like all oppressed people, however, they dreamt of improvement and asked for no more than fair wages to compensate their daily toil to help feed their starving families and put a leaking roof over their heads.

The skeleton at the plough. 'Those who owned and held the land believed that it belonged to the rich man only, that the poor man had no part nor lot in it, and had no sort of claim on society. They thought that when a labourer could no longer work, he had lost the right to live. Work was all they wanted from him. It was what he was made for, to labour and toil for his betters, without complaint, on a starvation wage. When no more work could be squeezed out of him, he was no better than a cumberer of other folk's ground, and the proper place for such as he was the churchyard.' (*From* The Painful Plough *by Roy Palmer*)

Chapter 7

The Dissenter

1818/34

The Wesleyan army in one are combined,
To war with the Devil, the foe of mankind:
Jehovah their Captain commands from the skies;
Death or victory their motto, and Heaven their prize.

It is not known when Methodism was established in Tolpiddle, but it was one of the first places in Dorset to have its own chapel. It all started in 1810 when the house of Thomas Loveless, father of George and James, was licenced as 'a dissenters' meeting house and a place of worship.' A 'dissenter' was regarded as a member of a religious body who, for one reason or another, become separated from the Anglican church or any other kind of protestant doctrine and did not recognise the supremacy of the established church. Any place of worship that did not follow the rules of the Church of England was required to be legally registered with the local authorities (the Registrar) and the local Bishop (in this case the Bishop of Bristol). Known as a Dissenter's Licence, a document authorizing George's father stated that his 'dwelling house' was 'set apart for the place of occasional public worship of Almighty God by a congregation of protestants called Methodists'.

Tolpiddle's Wesleyan Methodists were met with suspicion by many people in the village who failed to understand why dissenters could not attend the local church instead of crowding into someone's house for religious services. The 'dissenters' met in the Loveless home for regular services, bible study, Sunday schools and to give each other encouragement.

When the Loveless home became too small and the weather was fine the Wesleyan congregation moved onto the grassy heath under the old sycamore tree and held their services in the open air. The congregation was summoned by the sound of a horn. These open-air meetings angered people who looked upon the Methodist congregation as people not to be trusted. George Loveless, the peaceful ploughman, recalled that during the Swing riots of the early 1830s, he and his brother James discovered they had been accused of being involved in rick burning and machine wrecking. They were also accused of being smugglers and poachers. Loveless later wrote:

All this reporting, stabbing and slandering men was in the dark, behind the back, out of sight and well did the party know that there was no foundation for such foul and black assertions; and if there was ever an instance known in the space of 37 years which was my age when these slanders went abroad, I say, in any one instance, I stand chargeable for any misdemeanour or crime, I call upon James Frampton, Esq., magistrate, or his satellites or anyone else to stand out and declare it. Again, I challenge them to come forth and do it in a public manner, that the world may judge the case, and acquit me if innocent, or not let me escape with impunity if guilty. But the secret is this: I am from principle a dissenter, and by some in Tolpiddle it is considered as the sin of witchcraft; nay there is no forgiveness for it in this world nor that which is to come … and many a curious tale might be told of men that were persecuted, banished and not allowed to have employ if they entered the Wesleyan Chapel at Tolpiddle.

If working as a labourer on Tolpiddle's farms was not difficult enough, there is evidence that the village's Methodists faced 'bitter and unrelenting persecution' by their neighbours. In a letter to the *Morning Chronicle* sent by 'A. Wesleyan' and dated 2 April 1834 – the day that Charles Dickens joined the newspaper as a reporter – the correspondent spoke of attacks by 'violent mobs' and 'of the refusal of a clergyman to take his dead babe into the (Anglican) church, because it had been baptised by a Wesleyan minister'. He wrote of 'direct attempts to starve George Loveless and his family out of the village' and 'determined attempts to crush his sectarian spirit'. The writer, who was probably George Romaine, stated that attempts had been made to keep Loveless from preaching in one of Tolpuddle's neighbouring villages and that his only guilt, and that of his fellow Methodists, was 'inoffensive conduct, for diligence, for efforts to support themselves and their families and for general and good moral character'.

The writer said that Loveless and his fellow Methodists were

… guilty of one crime – a crime which is, I fear, in the estimation of certain persons in Dorsetshire, of far greater magnitude than any of those to which reference has been made. In this Protestant country they committed the great sin of reading their bible, of daring to think for themselves on what they read, of doing more. They had become members of the Wesleyan Methodist Society; a body of which now, in the estimation of some great men, is not the vilest in the world. But the climax – the head and the front of their offending – was this: George Loveless and one or two more became steady and useful preachers among the Wesleyan Methodists.

The writer challenged anyone reading the article to point out any evil act performed by Tolpiddle Methodists 'whether they were idle men, neglecters of their work, their families, whether they were poachers, frequenters of beer shops or were in any way persons of dishonest lives.'

The author failed to mention that many tenant farmers around Tolpiddle refused to give employment to Methodists and some shops refused to sell groceries to their wives. Becoming a Methodist in the 1830s meant that followers of John Wesley could expect a hard time: spat at and cursed upon, dismissed from their jobs, excluded from social life and ignored and rejected by people who ought to have known better. Fortunately George Loveless found courage, peace and composure in the midst of these frightening situations to set an example to members of his congregation and fellow farm labourers. He knew, or thought he knew, who could be trusted and went out of his way to avoid the rest.

Methodists were suspected by many of having radical tendencies even when their leaders went to pains to demonstrate their support for the Tory establishment. Within Methodism the both sides of the struggle between 'conservative' and broadly 'liberal' wings were convinced they were faithful to Wesley's principles and intentions.

By 1834, upwards of 400,000 people across England had become Methodists. The established Anglican order had become fearful of a radical challenge to its control. Methodism had been firmly planted in Dorset by the time Tolpiddle's congregation needed a place of their own to worship, so a search began for a suitable site on which to build a Wesleyan Chapel somewhere in the village.

They did not have to look far. A plot of empty ground 40ft x 30ft was available almost next to the Standfield family home. Two of the trustees appointed to govern the chapel were George Loveless, then aged 21, and Robert's son, Thomas Standfield. Others included the supervising minister for the Weymouth Methodist circuit, two maltsters (workmen specialising in the growing and harvesting of barley), two cordwainers (shoemakers), a confectioner, a blacksmith, a farmer, a carpenter and a draper. Apart from Loveless and Standfield the other trustees came from Methodist communities outside Tolpiddle.

The plan was to construct an unostentatious, non-authoritarian, simple rectangular chapel that offered simplicity of form and was neat and without any frippery that might distract the congregation from listening to a sermon. Like other barns and outhouses in Tolpiddle, it was built from pale brown cob, a natural building material made from subsoil (a mixture of small particles such as sand, silt and clay), straw and lime and mounted onto a brick and flint plinth. Cob was an ancient building material popular in the rural south-west of England where good building stone was hard to come by. Subsoil with heavy clay content was mixed with the straw, aggregate and water and trodden by workmen to provide a mix not too wet to collapse during construction or too dry to combine with other materials. Straw was important, providing connecting fibres across small cracks that naturally occur when cob dries out. The chapel probably had a slate roof and was thatched at a later date. It is almost certain that agricultural labourers in the congregation helped build the chapel in their limited spare time.

The chapel walls were around 2ft thick and, when completed, plastered to improve appearance and add to durability. They were then coated with a limewash finish to decorate and protect porous stone and lime-rendered surfaces. Limewash provided a breathable finish making it suitable for damp-prone walls by penetrating the surface.

Splayed windows were positioned at the front and back of the chapel and illuminated by rushlights, a type of candle formed by soaking dried pith from rush plants in fat or grease. These were cheaper than beeswax candles. Another window, set high in the north gable end wall, was designed to allow light to fall on the presumed position of the preacher.

The floor of the chapel's interior was probably covered in timber floorboards, although it might have been the same compacted earth which covered the floors in most of Tolpiddle labourer's cottages. Seating for the congregation faced north looking towards a central single-decker pulpit from where the whole service would have been conducted and the sermon preached. In front of the pulpit was a small railed space to accommodate a Communion table. South of this were box pews for chapel elders and beyond simple benching extending for the remaining length of the building. These would have been set out on an east-to-west alignment. The congregation would have entered the chapel through a doorway at the centre of the south facade.

The chapel opened its doors to the congregation for the first time on the evening of 13 October 1818 – nearly 80 years after John Wesley began preaching outdoors to crowds of working class men and women. Senior Methodists from parts of the Weymouth circuit accompanied by their wives and friends were present as guests of honour at its opening. No doubt the Loveless and Standfield families were

Methodism came to Tolpuddle in 1810 when the house of Thomas Loveless, father of George and James, was licensed as a 'dissenters meeting house' and place of worship. When the Loveless home became too small, the Wesleyan congregation moved to their own purpose-built chapel in 1818 and were issued with a 'dissenter's licence' allowing services in the building. (*Dorset History Centre*) present with the men having been given permission to leave work early to go home and change from their field clothes into their best frock smocks.

A terrible thing then happened; the *Salisbury Journal* reported:

> On Tuesday last, a Methodist chapel was opened in the village of Tolpuddle, Dorset. During the evening service, when the chapel was much overcrowded, some little disturbance was made on the outside, but the peace was soon restored. About 8-o-clock, when the Ministers and their friends were preparing to return, a mob of about 100 persons were found assembled near a chaise and another carriage, which were in attendance to convey them. These persons behaved in a most turbulent manner. A lady belonging to the Minister's party, before she could get to the chaise, was pushed down a bank into the road; the horses were much frightened by the tumult and noise, and the driver was for a considerable time unable to proceed. The ladies were under the necessity of walking a great distance, exposed to the most brutal insults. For more than two miles, in a very bad road, the drivers, horses and carriages were pelted with stones, mud, etc, the windows of the chaise were broken and even the side of the chaise was pierced by a stone: one lady who rode by the side of the driver had a severe blow on her head; and at Piddletown, two miles from Tolpiddle, the driver received a blow on his neck, of which he is now confined, and which, had it not been for a lace neckcloth, would have proved fatal. Mr. Bailey of The Golden Lion, Weymouth, to whom the chase belongs, has effected five guineas reward for a discovery of the offenders.

The Reverend William Worth, superintendent minister of the Weymouth Methodist circuit and a trustee of the Tolpiddle chapel, employed a solicitor and counsel and took four of the rioters to court. The accused were indicted based on witness statements and records stating that about 50 people or more were involved (not the 100 stated in the newspaper report), and they 'assembled in a riotous and tumultuous manner for a long space of time (that is to say) two hours'. One of the accused, an apprentice blacksmith from Tolpiddle called Thomas Way, was found to be age 14 and discharged. The other three – John Bullen, a carpenter, Francis Pearce, a yeoman and Thomas Way, a farm labourer – were found guilty and sentenced to pay a fine of £10 each and give security for their good behaviour for one year. They would be put in jail until the money was paid along with sureties at the cost of £25 each for their good behaviour.

Once regular services at the chapel were underway, George Loveless rehearsed his sermons from the back of his plough, using John Wesley's 'rules for preaching' written in 1749 as a guide on how to deliver them. Wesley wrote:

- Endeavour to be serious, weighty and solemn in your deportment before the congregation.
- Choose the plainest texts.

Tolpiddle's old Methodist chapel ceased being a place of worship over 150 years ago and has subsequently been used as a barn, stables and storage space for farm equipment. Today a small band of determined and professionally-minded people called Tolpuddle Old Chapel Trust are working hard to restore the building sympathetically for people of the village and anyone interested in the Martyrs' story. (*Top photograph by Alan Gallop/ bottom photograph by Tolpuddle Old Chapel Trust*)

- Take care not to ramble from your text, but keep close to it and make out what you undertake.
- Always suit your subject to the audience.
- Beware of allegorising or spiritualising too much.
- Take care of anything awkward or affected, either in your gesture or pronunciation.
- Tell each other if you observe anything of this kind.

Despite hostility towards Tolpiddle's Methodists, George and James Loveless, Thomas and John Standfield were comfortable in their faith which was soon to be challenged to the full in ways they had never envisaged. That time was coming very soon.

Chapter 8

The Squire

Our Squire, he has a private pew
He be nearer to God than yew.
In God's sight, each equals his brothers
But, Squire, he be more equal 'n others.
He pays Parson, Tom, Dick and Harry,
Says who works and who shall marry.
He, I muse, as I turn the sod,
Be even more like God 'n God.

James Frampton Esq. was a member of an old Dorset country landowning family and born in 1769 with a silver spoon in his mouth. As a child he lived on the 9,000 acre family estate which included Moreton House, described as 'elegant and well contrived' built from Portland stone and containing eight bedrooms, lounges, a library, a large dining room, a study and large kitchen where servants prepared meals for the Frampton family and their many guests. The mansion was surrounded by parkland and woodland.

He was educated at Winchester, founded in 1382 'for the supply of educated men dedicated to God and the public service', which he left at the age of 17 to move on to St. John's College, Cambridge where he graduated with a BA in 1791.

After university Frampton and his half-brother, Charlton Byam Woolaston, embarked on the Grand Tour – the traditional post-university trip around Europe for privileged young men. They visited Paris, Venice, Rome and Constantinople. In Paris they witnessed the indiscriminate bloodbath of the French Revolution breaking out around them. This included a significant episode

James Frampton JP., Magistrate, Squire and High Sheriff of Morton, landowner and the man primarily responsible for the arrest and transportation of the Tolpuddle Six. (*Dorset History Centre*)

North-West View of MORETON, the Seat of James Frampton Esqr.

Moreton House, home of James Frampton and his family, built from Portland stone, containing eight bedrooms, lounges, a library, large dining room, a study and kitchen where servants prepared lavish meals for the family and their guests. (*Top: Author's Collection, bottom: TUC*)

in French history in which King Louis XVI, Queen Marie Antoinette and their family attempted unsuccessfully to escape from Paris in order to initiate a counter revolution at the head of loyal troops. They escaped to the small town of Varennes-en-Argonne, 130 miles from Paris, where they were arrested after being recognized while making a dash to the nearest frontier point. Being in a country experiencing such turmoil had a profound effect on young Frampton. When he and Woolaston later arrived in Germany they were able to see the effects of the revolution with hundreds of French citizens fleeing there 'in tribes'. He wrote to his sister: 'I hope they will soon be able to do something against the uppermost party. For you must know that I am more of an *aristocrate* (sic) than ever.' What they had witnessed in France and Germany had frightened Frampton and Wollaston, who both knew that just such a revolution could easily cross the channel.

Back in Dorset, Frampton settled into his role as the Squire of Moreton. Another early duty was to fulfil the role of High Sheriff, an unpopular position for a young man of 24 involving much responsibility and no financial reward. A year later he was made a Justice of the Peace. He was also a magistrate for the next sixty years, seeing it as a natural extension of his duties as squire. In 1799 Frampton married Lady Harriet Strangways, daughter of the Earl of Ilchester, and through her aristocratic circle of contacts and friends exposed her husband to members of the royal family; she had been presented at court and the couple were to produce five children.

Frampton passionately believed in Church, Constitution, King and Country, maintenance of the status quo and that the class structure as it stood was sacrosanct. Although written in 1848 the second verse of the children's hymn *'All things bright and beautiful'* could have been written with him in mind: 'The rich man in his castle/The poor man at his gate/He made them high or lowly/And ordered their estate.'

Frampton was not a man to be confronted. Tenant farmers, members of his own staff working as servants indoors as well as labourers out of doors, tradespeople or anyone else who got in his way not only received the rough part of his tongue but often found themselves out of a job and a home. He could be irritable, vindictive, revengeful, petulant, fractious, outraged, imperious and vicious in his dealings with the lower classes – as six men from Tolpiddle were to discover to their cost. On the other hand he created paid apprenticeship schemes for young men seeking careers in agriculture and land management on the Moreton estate. He supported the church with generous contributions used for building and repairs and, in later years, paid for a small school to be built near his estate. His estate diary lists numerous cottages repaired or re-built and by 1845 he had provided them all with slate roofs instead of the usual thatch. There was even a Frampton family charity which created apprenticeships for Moreton children.

In addition to his Moreton fiefdom, Frampton also owned estates and properties in the parishes and hamlets of Affpiddle, Brianspiddle, Pallington, Tolpiddle,

Throop, Hurst and Wool. These included mansion houses, tenements, farm houses, dairies, cottages, a blacksmith's shop, barns, chalk and gravel pits, woods and plantations, mills, weirs and bridges. Land also included water meadows, arable and pasture land, asparagus beds, arable and heathland pastures. These properties were leased to tenants for periods between seven and twenty-one years. If a tenant died before the end of the lease, Frampton granted permission for the widow or oldest son to continue the lease to the end of its term.

Tenant farmers and land owners colluded to set rates of pay for farm labourers and consequently those in the area were all paid identical wages. In 1832 this weekly wage in South Dorset was just under ten shillings, but many tenant farmers found it difficult to maintain that figure throughout the year because of the high cost of leasing land, a series of harvest failures and cost of living increases. Tenant farmers, including Mrs Northover, consequently began reducing wages down to a meagre weekly sum of seven shillings for labourers. A further reduction to six weekly shillings was threatened. Frampton, no doubt, had input into wages paid and advised tenants to keep them as low as possible despite considerably higher wages paid to men working on his own estate. He wrote a letter in 1827 letter to the scientist, inventor and photography pioneer, William Fox Talbot, to advise how much a Head Gardener should be paid: 'He will come to you for twelve shillings a week and a house and garden....he may even ask a shilling or two more.' At the time he was advising tenant farmers to pay labourers far less for working longer hours without housing or rent subsidies. Mrs Northover, however, had the final say on the wages of her labourers. Although aware of the poverty in which her labouring families lived she was probably afraid to contradict Frampton's recommendations and, for a quiet life, gradually cut her own labourer's pay to the levels of paupers.

Away from his duties as a magistrate and Lord of the Manor of Moreton, Frampton enjoyed a fine social life in London and Dorset. He went on yachting excursions with Princess Charlotte Augusta of Wales, the only child of George, Prince of Wales, later to become King George IV. At a London dinner party he sat next to Henry Addington, 1st Viscount Sidmouth and wondered how 'anyone so very ponderous could ever have been Prime Minister'. He paid his respects to Charles X, the King of France who escaped to England after the outbreak of the 1830 French revolution. King George III gave Charles X a generous allowance and he and his mistress, Louise de Polaston, lived in exile at Lulworth Castle, 11 miles away from Moreton. Frampton's devotion to all things royal did not prevent him from 'depreciating the folly which led to their residence in England'.

Frampton's energy and independence never concealed his failure to grasp that men seeking fairer wages were driven to their desperate condition through near starvation. He never appreciated that labourers lived in appalling conditions and that their children, ill through lack of nourishment, often died. He could not imagine that wronged men would one day unite together to right their grievances. Landowners, as the natural guardians of law and order, could unite but union among labourers probably evoked the dreadful experiences he had witnessed on his Grand Tour. It never occurred to him that the best way to deal with grievance was to remedy it. He had the power and authority to do so and show mercy and understanding to his labourers and those of his tenant farmers. He never did and, once their grievances were expressed in rioting crowds and threats, he brought in police and militia as the natural instruments of authority against grievance. Always profoundly deferential to those few above his social station, Frampton never doubted his duty to control the many below it with an iron fist.

His first attempt to alert the Home Secretary, Lord Melbourne, that unions were forming in Dorset was sent from Moreton House on 30 January 1834:

My Lord,

I am requested by some of the Magistrates acting for the Divisions of Dorchester and Wareham in this County, and who are resident in this vicinity, to represent to your Lordship that they have received information from various quarters (of the authenticity of which they cannot entertain doubt) that Societies are forming among the Agricultural Labourers in parts of these Divisions, in which the labourers are induced to enter into combinations of a dangerous and alarming kind to which they are bound by oaths administered clandestinely. The information which the Justices have obtained as yet seems to apply to a few Parishes only, and more particularly to the Parish of Tolpiddle in the Division of Dorchester and Bere Regis in the Division of Wareham; in both of which Parishes nightly meetings have been held. As no specific proof of the time or place of these meetings or of the individuals forming them, have as yet reached the Justices so as to authorise them to take measures to interrupt the meetings or to notice the persons engaged in them; all they have been able to do at present has been to communicate with Trusty persons in the neighbourhood and by their means endeavour to trace the proceedings and identify the parties. But should they succeed in such steps they would still be under a difficulty in determining how to proceed so as to bring these parties concerned under the cognisance of the law: but feeling the very serious nature of the proceedings and the dangerous consequences which may ensure from their being allowed to spread and gain strength and consistency, they have thought themselves called upon to apprise your Lordship of these circumstances and to request your advice and co-operation in any further measures which it may be thought right to pursue.

I have the honour to be Your Lordship's most Obedient and Humble Servant, James Frampton – Justice of the Peace for the County of Dorset

He clearly wanted to make an example of the Tolpiddle men by being rid of them and making their wives, children and fellow union brothers to suffer. The letter was written early enough to catch the afternoon mail coach from Dorchester to London and be delivered at the Home Department in Whitehall the following morning. It was considered urgent enough to receive an immediate reply from Lord Melbourne's Permanent Under Secretary J. M. Phillips dated 31 January, 1834:

Sir,

I am directed by Viscount Melbourne to acknowledge receipt of your letter of the 30th instant.

Lord Melbourne thinks the Magistrates have acted wisely in employing trusty persons to endeavour to obtain information regarding the unlawful combinations which they believe to be forming along the labourers.

Lord Melbourne desires me to refer to the Mutiny Act of 1797 [for preventing taking or administering of unlawful oaths] which in cases of this description has been frequently resorted to with advantage. His Lordship thinks it is quite unnecessary to refer to Statutable provisions relative to the administration of Secret Oaths.

I have the honour to be, Sir, your Obedient Servant,

J. M. Phillipps.

Shortly after the exchange of letters, George Loveless and his fellow farm labourers were to discover they encountered in Frampton a man with a firmness of character, strong temperament and opinions. Frampton feared that trade unionism threatened the power base and wealth of the landed upper classes. Having witnessed the French Revolution, he was determined to suppress any sign of rebellion or opposition whatever the cause. The stage was being set for the tragedy that followed.

Chapter 9

The Caution

Saturday February 22, 1834

Says the master to me, is it true?
I am told your name on the books of the Union's enroll'd,
I can never allow that a workman of mine,
With wicked disturbances of peace should combine.
I give you fair warning, mind what you're about,
I shall put my foot on it and trample it out;
On which side your bread's buttered, now sure you can see,
So decide now at once for the union – or me.

By creating their own small union, the Tolpiddle men were acting within their rights; it was to require all the ingenuity of the Home Secretary and law officers of the crown to discover even a technical illegality in their conduct.

Long thought to be obsolete, the Mutiny Act of 1797 had originally been passed to crush a Royal Naval mutiny among discontented sailors and was carefully examined with a view to setting a trap for the Tolpiddle union. The mutiny centred on an anchorage in the Thames Estuary called the Nore where sailors, led by Richard Parker, a former officer who had been voted president of the fleet by the mutineers, wanted to end imprisonment, unequal pay, poor quality rations, and gain better leave entitlements. The mutineers wanted cruel or unpopular officers to be removed from ships and banned from serving on them again. They successfully blockaded London, stopping trade entering and leaving Britain's busiest port.

The mutiny was, however, hijacked by radical delegates to an unofficial Fleet Parliament whose intransigence and bid for a mini social revolution hardened the stance of the Government and Lords of the Admiralty. Cut off from food and racked by internal dissent, the mutiny dissolved with ships slipping their cables and deserting the cause. Parker and his co-conspirators faced swift justice from a vengeful Admiralty and, after a brief trial, were hanged for treason and piracy.

The Mutiny Act was considered to provide the best case for breaking the Tolpiddle union and severely punishing its members. Dissolution of the union would not be enough; its ringleaders needed to be subjected to a punishment sufficiently exemplary to deter others from ever having anything to do with unions.

Lord Melbourne and James Frampton considered the matter and proceedings were undertaken against the union men for using an oath at their initiation ceremonies – as Richard Parker and his mutineers had sworn similar oaths between themselves to ensure that their planned mutiny remained secret.

No prior warnings that secret oath taking at Tolpiddle union meetings were illegal was given until the morning of Saturday 22 February, 1834 when notices from local magistrates were posted across Tolpiddle and neighbouring villages stating that

> … mischievous and designing persons have been endeavouring to induce labourers in various parishes to attend meetings and to enter into illegal societies or unions to which they bind themselves by unlawful oaths, administered secretly by persons concealed, who artfully deceive the ignorant and unwary. We the undersigned Justices think it our duty to give this public notice and caution that all persons may know the danger they incur by entering into such societies. [Any person] who shall induce or endeavour to persuade any other person to become a member of such a society will become GUILTY OF FELONY AND BE LIABLE TO BE TRANSPORTED FOR SEVEN YEARS.

The caution was signed by Frampton, his son Henry, his step-brother Charles Wollaston and other local magistrates. George Loveless saw a copy of the notice pinned to a tree on his way to work. He carefully read it, unpinned it and put it into his smock pocket. Over the next 24 hours he shared it among his fellow union members. From this point onwards they were all expecting trouble of some kind to come knocking on their doors and two days later exactly that happened.

CAUTION. 9

WHEREAS it has been represented to us from several quarters, that mischievous and designing Persons have been for some time past, endeavouring to induce, and have induced, many Labourers in various Parishes in this County, to attend Meetings, and to enter into Illegal Societies or Unions, to which they bind themselves by unlawful oaths, administered secretly by Persons concealed, who artfully deceive the ignorant and unwary,—WE, the undersigned Justices think it our duty to give this PUBLIC NOTICE and CAUTION, that all Persons may know the danger they incur by entering into such Societies.

ANY PERSON who shall become a Member of such a Society, or take any Oath, or assent to any Test or Declaration not authorized by Law—

Any Person who shall administer, or be present at, or consenting to the administering or taking any Unlawful Oath, or who shall cause such Oath to be administered, although not actually present at the time—

Any Person who shall not reveal or discover any Illegal Oath which may have been administered, or any Illegal Act done or to be done—

Any Person who shall induce, or endeavour to persuade any other Person to become a Member of such Societies,

WILL BECOME

Guilty of Felony,

AND BE LIABLE TO BE

Transported for Seven Years.

ANY PERSON who shall be compelled to take such an Oath, unless he shall declare the same within four days, together with the whole of what he shall know touching the same, will be liable to the same Penalty.

Any Person who shall directly or indirectly maintain correspondence or intercourse with such Society, will be deemed Guilty of an Unlawful Combination and Confederacy, and on Conviction before one Justice, on the Oath of one Witness, be liable to a Penalty of TWENTY POUNDS, or to be committed to the Common Gaol or House of Correction, for THREE CALENDAR MONTHS; or if proceeded against by Indictment, may be CONVICTED OF FELONY, and be TRANSPORTED FOR SEVEN YEARS.

Any Person who shall knowingly permit any Meeting of any such Society to be held in any House, Building, or other Place, shall for the first offence be liable to the Penalty of FIVE POUNDS; and for every other offence committed after Conviction, be deemed Guilty of such Unlawful Combination and Confederacy, and on Conviction before one Justice, on the Oath of one Witness, be liable to a Penalty of TWENTY POUNDS, or to Commitment in the Common Gaol or House of Correction, FOR THREE CALENDAR MONTHS; or if proceeded against by Indictment may be

CONVICTED OF FELONY,

And Transported for SEVEN YEARS.

COUNTY OF DORSET,
Dorchester Division

February 23d. 1834.

C. B. WOLLASTON,
JAMES FRAMPTON,
WILLIAM ENGLAND,
THOS. DADE,
JNO. MORTON COLSON.

HENRY FRAMPTON,
RICHD. TUCKER STEWARD,
WILLIAM R. CHURCHILL,
AUGUSTUS FOSTER.

G. CLARK, PRINTER, CORNHILL, DORCHESTER.

On the morning of Saturday 22 February, 1834, notices were pasted across Tolpuddle and neighbouring villages by local magistrates warning that anyone inducing or trying to persuade any other person to become a member of a society (trade union) will 'become guilty of felony and liable to be transported for seven years'. (*Jackdaw – The Early Trade Unions*)

Part III

The House of Correction

Monday 24 February–14 March, 1834

Young men of every station, that dwell within this nation,
Pray hear my lamentation – a sad and mournful tale,
Concerning six fine young men that were lately confined
And heavily bound in irons in Dorchester jail.

His Majesty's United Gaol and House of Correction at Dorchester looked as grim from outside as it was inside. The county prison, controlled by a small committee of men under the Chairmanship of Henry Frampton, had been built 40 years before George Loveless and his fellow labourers were escorted there by Petty Constable Brine. It held over 500 prisoners and the forbidding iron gates at the front of the prison were only a short walk away from Mr. Wollaston's comfortable home. Here the Petty Constable said goodbye to his prisoners and handed them to John Cox, a turnkey, waiting at the gate.

The men were led inside and treated like guilty felons, stripped of their clothes and searched. In the pocket of George Loveless' work smock Cox found a copy of the magistrate's notice threatening to punish with seven years transportation any man who swore a secret oath. They also found a note from a friend and a small key. Cox confiscated the items and had received instructions that anything found in their clothing was to be immediately delivered to Frampton. Their heads were then close cropped like common criminals before being locked together in a dismal room, not a cell, where they remained for six days until 24 February.

Their personal details were carefully noted in the prison register. These showed they all shared the same 'crime' of administering an illegal oath. Along with other agricultural workers, the register also revealed that the men had scars on their hands and faces, the result of their work with scythes and billhooks – traditional tools used on farms for cutting material such as shrubs and branches. In each case the register records that all the men were committed to prison by James Frampton, Esq. and listed them as follows:

James Brine, age 20, from Tolpiddle, a labourer and single man living with his widowed mother and four siblings, whose crime was administering an illegal oath. He is 5ft 5¾ inches tall with very dark brown hair, grey eyes, a sallow complexion with a large cut extending from the forehead through the eyebrow into the eyelid on the right side of his face and the mark of a scar on the left cheek which appears alongside a little sunk-long nose.

James Hammett, age 22, from Tolpiddle. He is 5ft 7¼ inches tall with dark brown hair, a fair complexion and blue eyes. He works as a labourer, is married with one child and has a cut diagonally on the right side of the forehead and a pock mark on the right cheek bone.

Thomas Standfield, age 44, from Tolpiddle. He is 5ft 6¼ inches tall with a dimpled chin, rather swarthy complexion, dark hazel eyes and black hair streaked with gray. He works as a labourer and is married with five children aged five to 21.

John Standfield, age 21, from Tolpiddle. He is 5ft 8¼ inches tall with dark brown hair, dark hazel eyes, a mole on the right corner of the right eyebrow, a mole on the middle of the right cheek, a cut diagonally on the middle of the upper lip, a mole under the right end of the bottom lip and a dimpled chin.

George Loveless, age 37, from Tolpiddle. He is married with three children aged five to nine years. He is 5ft 5 inches tall with dark brown hair, dark grey eyes and a swarthy complexion. [There were no further remarks about Loveless and no mention of his red whiskers, low forehead, small dimpled

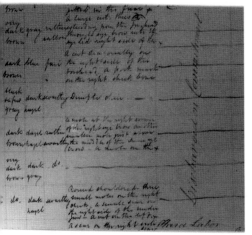

Dorchester gaol records for the six Tolpuddle men. (*Tolpuddle Martyrs Museum*)

chin and the small scar on his upper lip that was to be noted on prison records soon to be taken on board a transportation ship.]

James Loveless, age 25, from Tolpiddle. He is 5ft 7½ inches tall with dark brown eyes, dark hazel hair, a swarthy complexion, round shoulders, three moles on his right cheek, a small scar on the right side of the under jaw and a cut on the left side of the left hand. He is married with two children aged three years and 14 months.

On the last day of their prison confinement, the men were escorted to another part of the jail where a bench of magistrates awaited them with James Frampton at its head. Those also sitting around a long table included Charlton Byam Woolaston, Henry Frampton and a group of local clergymen. It was clear to the Tolpiddle men that none of the magistrates – or clergymen – had any love for agricultural labourers misguided enough to join a trade union, particularly when four of them were known Methodist dissenters. To their surprise, Edward Legg, the spy sent by Frampton to join the union and observe secret oaths taken at the initiation ceremony, was also present. Legg was asked to identify the Tolpiddle men and state their names. He then made a sworn statement to the gathering about the union initiation ceremony he had attended at John Standfield's house which, Loveless later recalled, 'differed considerably to his first statement'. Legg had almost certainly been rehearsed by Frampton and Woolaston and told exactly what to say to the court when the time came. The six men were then fully committed to be tried at the next assizes. At no stage was it mentioned by James Hammett or Edward Legg that Hammett had not been present at the oath taking ceremony and it had been his brother John who had attended.

Loveless later wrote: 'Directly after we were put back [into the prison room], a Mr. Young, an attorney employed on our behalf, called me into the conversation room, and, among other things, inquired if I would promise the magistrates to have no more to do with the union and, if so, they would let me go home to my wife and family. I said, "I do not understand you." "Why," said he, "give them information concerning the union, who else belongs to it, and promise you will have no more to do with it." "Do you mean to say I am to betray my companions?" "That is just it," said he. "No, I would rather undergo any punishment,"' Loveless told Young.

The same day the men were sent to the 'high jail', another part of the prison containing cells, where they remained until the start of the assizes on March 18. Loveless remembered: 'I had never seen the inside of a jail cell before, but now I began to feel it disagreeable company, close confinement, bad bread and what is worse, hard and cold lodging, a small straw bed on the flags, or else an iron bedstead – "and this," said I to my companions, "is our fare for striving to live honest".'

The men were visited by the Revd. Dacre Clemetson, chaplain to the jail. But instead of providing them with spiritual comfort he poured

> ... a volley of instruction in our ears, mixed up, however, in the cup of abuse. After upbraiding and taunting us with being discontented and idle, and wishing to ruin our master, he proceeded to tell us that we were better off than our masters, and that the government had made use of every possible means for economy and retrenchment to make all comfortable.
>
> He inquired if I could point out anything more that might be done to increase the comfort of the labourer. I told him I thought I could; and began to assure him our object was not to ruin the master. And as to being worse off than ourselves, I could not believe it, while I saw them keep a number of horses for no other purpose than to chase the hare and the fox. And besides, I thought gentlemen wearing the clerical livery, like himself, might do with a little less salary. 'Is this how you mean to do it?' said he. 'That is one way I have been thinking of, sir.' 'I hope the Court will favour you, but I think they will not; for I believe they mean to make an example of you.' And saying this, he left us.

Confined to the comfortless jail until the morning of March 15, the men were later moved down the road to 'the high jail' or the Crown Court of the Shire Hall, a building dating from 1796, where they were 'ushered down some steps into a miserable dungeon with only a glimmering light; and to make it more disagreeable, some wet and green brushwood was served for firing. The smoke of this place, together with its natural dampness, amounted to nearly suffocation; and in this most dreadful situation we passed three whole days.'

A line of cells – six on one side of a passageway and four on the other – were located beneath the Crown Court and took the form of individual black boxes 3ft 6ins wide x 6ft long. Without light or sanitation these were extremely claustrophobic. They were positioned along a narrow corridor leading from the gaoler's room and each cell fitted with a 'Judas hole' – a peep hole through which the gaoler could hold up his lantern to see what the prisoners might be up to on the other side of the door. The only bedding in the cells was straw scattered on the floor.

Occasionally prisoners were allowed into the small square gaoler's room which contained the only fireplace in the prison. The 'wet and green brushwood' used as fuel filled the room with acrid smoke which poured from a fireplace that provided hardly any heat. Because there were no windows in the prison and the only opening to the outside world was the single door through which prisoners passed to reach the cells, the smoke lingered for hours causing inmates to cough, heave and be physically sick.

These were the miserable conditions the six farm labourers from Tolpiddle endured before their trial. They were allowed no visitors and not permitted to write letters to their loved ones. Accordingly they were unaware how their families were finding money for food, how they were being treated by the rest of Tolpiddle's citizens and where they might turn to for assistance.

The outlook was bleak indeed.

Chapter 10

The Trial

Friday, 14 March–Wednesday, 19 March 1834

As I walked through the streets of old Dorchester,
I heard six wretched men to say,
Farewell our dearest wives and children,
We can with you no longer stay,
In agony and broken hearted,
We are compelled behind to leave
Our native lands, our friends and kindred,
For our awful fate to grieve.

The interior of the Crown Court was constructed entirely from wood – the panelled walls, the floor, the galleries and steps leading up to them, the box where prisoners stood before the bench with a wooden staircase leading to the cells below and a steeply raked gallery from where the public watched the proceedings. An area on both sides where magistrates and jury members sat was also wooden as was the high platform on which was mounted a table and an elaborate seat for the Judge. Above the judge was an arched canopy under which the royal arms of King George III (the monarch when the court was first opened) was displayed.

Entrance to Dorchester's Crown Court.
Today it looks exactly the same as in 1834.
(*Photograph: Alan Gallop*)

On 14 March 1834 an inexperienced judge, the Honourable Mr. Justice Baron John Williams, swept into Dorchester from Salisbury in his official horse-drawn carriage accompanied by the Honourable Sir John Bosanquet and an armed 'cavalcade of javelin men'.

On 14 March 1834 an inexperienced judge the Honourable Mr. Justice Baron John Williams, swept into Dorchester in his official horse-drawn carriage to attend the Dorchester Assizes. (*TUC*)

Justice Williams was described as 'under middle height with no striking quality either about his face or figure. He is thin in the face and slender in person. His complexion has something of ruddiness about it. He has an aquiline nose and sharp eyes. The muscles of his face are generally in full play; sometimes they move so rapidly, and in such a way as to cause an involuntary smile on the part of the beholder.'

The Dorchester Assizes would mark the first time Judge Williams had presided over an Assize. For many years he had been a Whig MP and had been rewarded for his work by being appointed a judge and made a Baron of the Exchequer less than a month before coming to Dorchester. He was probably suffering from stage fright as he entered the court determined to prove himself as a judge. He was known to be a prickly character and a passionate man who allowed no personal feelings to enter his life. Williams was devoted to the Prime Minster, Earl Grey and his Whig Party which was identified with Britain's great aristocratic families and wealthy merchants.

After attending a Divine Service at Dorchester's St. Peter's Church, Bosanquet headed off in the direction of the lower court of *Nisi Prius* (a term used to denote all legal actions tried before judges of the King's Bench Division), while Judge Williams entered the Crown Court to try the case of the King v George Loveless and Others which would follow over the next few days.

The Dorchester Assizes was the first time that The Honourable Mr. Justice Baron John Williams had presided over a trial. (*Dorset Life*)

On 15 March the 23 carefully selected members of the Grand Jury were sworn in and it was unanimously agreed that the case be remitted for trial. Members of the Grand Jury, who would help decide the fate of the six unfortunate men from Tolpiddle, included local magistrates and prominent people – all close colleagues of James Frampton. The Grand Jury consisted of Frampton himself, his son Henry and Charles Woolaston while its foreman was to be William Ponsonby, the brother-in-law of Home Secretary, Lord Melbourne. In other words, a cosy little cache of 'gentlemen' with minds predetermined as to the outcome of the case. Other members of the Grand Jury, all local land owners, were also briefed in advance as to the result they were expected to support. They were named as Henry Banks, Thomas Bower, Humphrey Weld, Benjamin Lester, John Michel, Thomas Horlock, John Bragge, William Banks, William Hanam, James Heming, John Lethbridge, Richard Steward, Samuel Cox, John Hussey, George Loftus, James Fyler, George Thompson, Jacob Augustus and Thomas Badger.

A handful of 'witnesses', handpicked by Frampton and Woolaston to give testimony, was also present. Before their court appearance each had been rigorously rehearsed on what to say by newly ennobled Sir Edward Gambier, acting as Counsel for the Prosecution at the trial. He even wrote down what they needed to say and instructed them to become familiar with the text by the time they were called to testify on the following Monday. These 'witness statements' are clearly not in words or phrases normally used by farmers or shopkeepers.

At the request of Mr. George Butt, Counsel for the labourers' defence, various written testimonies supporting the six men were submitted to the Grand Jury and Judge for consideration. One came from an un-named 'principal farmer from the village of Tolpiddle' stating 'that the Loveless brothers were the last men in the parish that he should believe would have been guilty of wrong'. The testimony added that 'in the neighbourhood where they live numerous signatures can be obtained to corroborate this statement'. Mrs. Susannah Northover also wrote a note to the judge providing character witnesses for four labourers working for her. She said that George Loveless, James Loveless, Thomas Standfield and John Standfield 'have been agricultural labourers of mine for many years. I most willingly comply with your request and now state that they are all honest and industrious men. Not one of the individuals has been accused of the slightest breach of the law. All persons acquainted with the characters say that more honest, peaceable and industrious men were not to be found in the county of Dorset.'

Another testimony was submitted in writing from – of all people – the Rev. Dr. Thomas Warren, the man who had sworn to do everything in his power to obtain better wages for labourers from their masters and then went back on his word. He stated that he had known the prisoners for the last twenty years and they were 'honest, industrious, hard working men'. He added: 'I have never known a charge against them but for the present.' The testaments were handed to Judge Williams who imperiously cast them aside stating that he 'could not attend to them as they had not been handed in sooner.'

In his address to the assembled gathering, Judge Williams was openly hostile towards the prisoners and informed the carefully selected jury that trades unions and everything about them were evil. In defence Mr. Butt said that the Tolpiddle six had been seeking only to provide a fund for workers to draw on in time of need. As the only person in the room on the side of the Tolpiddle men his words sounded hopeless.

The manacled prisoners were brought up from the cells to stand before the Grand Jury in the private room. According to Loveless:

The whole proceedings were characterized by a shameful disregard of justice and decency; the most unfair means were resorted to in order to frame an indictment against us. The Grand Jury appeared to ransack heaven and earth to get some clue against us, but in vain: our characters were investigated from our infancy to the then present moment; our masters were inquired to know if we were not idle, or attended public houses, or some other fault in us;

The judge's raised platform and desk beneath an arched canopy under which the royal arms of King George III was displayed, as viewed from the Grand Jury's balcony. (*Photograph: Alan Gallop*)

The Judge's view of the court, including the box in which the six prisoners stood throughout the proceedings. (*Photograph: Alan Gallop*)

and much as they were opposed to us, they had common honesty enough to declare that we were good labouring servants, and that they had never heard of any complaint against us; and when nothing whatever could be racked together, the unjust and cruel judge, ordered us to be tried for mutiny and conspiracy, under the Mutiny Act of 1797.

Loveless further pondered:

There is no danger but we shall be found guilty, as we have a special jury for the purpose, selected from among those who are most unfriendly towards us – the Grand Jury, landowners, the petty jury, land renters. Under such a charge from such a quarter, self-interest alone would induce them to say 'Guilty!'

o0o

A long line of people queued outside the court on the morning of Monday, 17 March hoping to bag a seat in the public gallery. Word had got around that this was going to be one hell of a trial to witness and more people turned up hoping to be admitted than there was space inside the court. Those lucky enough to find a place to sit had come armed with bags of food and bottles of drink to consume noisily during the trial.

The wives of George and James Loveless, James Hammett, John and James Standfield along with the mother of James Brine also travelled to Dorchester attempting to see their husbands and son and witness their trial. They had obtained a magistrate's order allowing them access to the jail but were refused entry to the cells. All the women had applied for Parish Relief, small sums of money administered by the Anglican Church in Tolpiddle to help needy families pay for food and rent. Their requests had been rejected. Through a Methodist friend (George Romaine, perhaps?), a letter was sent to Frampton pleading for mercy on the wives and children of the Tolpiddle men but he refused to order Parish Relief Officers to grant funds to the families, stating:

> No person could be considered entitled to receive parochial relief who could afford to pay a shilling on entering and a penny a week afterwards to support the union, which would thus, in fact, be maintained by the money of the parish and as none of these persons (the Tolpiddle men) have ever in any way acknowledged their error or expressed any sorrow at having joined the unions, we have seen no occasion for altering our opinions.

In desperation the Tolpiddle women contacted Charles Woolaston to complain about his half-brother's severity, outlining their distress and begging him to use his influence to help them secure relief. When they received no answer the ladies personally knocked on Wollaston's front door in Dorchester. On appearing he sternly refused to provide help. They tried to explain that they had repeatedly applied to parish officers for relief but were refused aid of any kind. Showing no sympathy for the tearful ladies Woolaston shook his fist in the direction of Mrs. Standfield and said: 'You shall suffer want; you shall have no mercy because you ought to have known better to have allowed such meetings to have been held in your house.'

The women realised that a cruel combination had been formed between magistrates to afflict their husbands and starve their families. They were told: 'Go to your Union club and see if they will assist you now.'

It is not known if any Tolpiddle families were present in court to witness the proceedings. Had they attended and found seats in the public gallery, they would not have been permitted to show themselves to their husbands who, once they appeared in the dock, had their backs to the public and were under orders to look straight ahead in the direction of the judge and not turn around. They might, however, have snatched a quick glance in the direction of the public gallery at the end of the day as they turned to walk down the wooden steps leading back to the cells. If so George Loveless never mentioned it in his later writings.

The petty jury – or trial jury – consisted of 12 jurors who were all farmers or millers. They were named as J. Moroan, J. Tucker, M. Galpin, E. Bennett, S. Harris, J. Case, E. Duffett, T. Cox, W. Booby, H. Bryant, G. Tulk and W. Bullen. It was their job to hear evidence in the trial and decide on the innocence or guilt of the defendants. After listening to witnesses and lawyers, they would then retire to reach a verdict. One jury member, a linedraper (a dealer in linen) from Bere Reis called Job Bridle, was turned out of the jury box because he was not a farmer and had occasionally heard George Loveless preach in the Methodist Chapel he attended. Thus was the kind of people selected to serve on the petty jury – tenant farmers, employers of labouring men whose work they had exploited, whose wages they had cut and who had joined a trade union.

The court was brought to order by a clerk who asked those present to rise for Mr. Justice Williams who appeared wearing a traditional full-bottom horse-hair wig and a furred scarlet robe with a matching hood and mantle. Underneath, he wore breeches with stockings and buckled shoes. He looked around the crowded court room before issuing an instruction to bring up the prisoners.

The six men appeared in the dock one after another; unwashed, unshaven, dirty and dressed in the same work clothes they had been wearing when they were arrested a few days before. The dock was hardly big enough for six adult men, but George Loveless found himself in the centre with the remaining five men squeezed together behind him.

The judge asked how the men pleaded and Counsel for the Defence, Mr. Derbyshire, stood up and said in a loud and clear voice: 'Not guilty, m' lord.' There was cheering from the public gallery. A charge was then read out and those in attendance heard that the men

> … feloniously and unlawfully did administer and cause to be administered unto one Edward Legg a certain oath and engagement purporting and then and there intended to bind the said Edward Legg not to inform or give evidence against any associate confederate or other person of and belonging to a certain unlawful combination and confederacy before that time formed and entered into by the said George Loveless, James Loveless, James Brine, James Hammett, Thomas Standfield and John Standfield and diverse others ill disposed persons and which said oath and engagement was then and there taken by the said Edward Legg against the peace of our said Lord the King, his crown and dignity against the form of the Statute in that case made and …

So it went on through a further eleven counts by which time onlookers in the public gallery, who had probably never been to any kind of trial before, began to become restless and started talking loudly to each other causing the judge to bang his gavel onto the sound block to bring silence back to the court.

The judge asked Sir Edward Gambier, Learned Counsel for the Prosecution, to open the case. He directed the attention of the jury to the Mutiny Act of 1797 pronouncing that to be an unlawful combination or confederacy which imposes an oath unauthorised by law 'and any person guilty of the offence might be prosecuted for a misdemeanour'. He then called his first witness to the stand.

John Lock, the son of Frampton's head gardener at his Moreton estate took the stand and told the court:

I went one or two days before Christmas to Tolpiddle. I know the prisoner James Brine; I saw him at Tolpiddle on the day in question. He took me to a house oppose Thomas Standfield's and asked me to go, but I would not. I went away down the street. About a fortnight or three weeks after that I saw Brine at Mr. Brine's [no relation] barn in Aftpiddle. I was then at work. He asked me to go with him to Tolpiddle. The prisoner James Hammett was then with him; it was in the evening when I was about to leave work. I agreed to go with them and on the way met four other men – Edward Legg, Richard Percy, Henry Courtney and Elias Riggs. As we walked along one of the men asked whether there would not be something to pay; he was answered that there would be a shilling to pay on entering and a penny a week afterwards. On arriving at Tolpiddle we went into a room into which John Standfield came; two of the prisoners at the bar, James Loveless and George Loveless passed through a passage and one of the prisoners asked if we were ready to have our eyes blindfolded. We said yes. We then, all five of us, bound our handkerchiefs around our eyes and we were then led by a person through a passage into another room on the same floor. On getting into that room a paper was read out to us, but I do not recollect any of the words that were read. After that we knelt down on being desired to do so. Something else was then read to us, the voice which read appeared to be the same. I don't know what the reading was about but I think it was some part of the bible. We then got up, turned ourselves around and took the bandage from our eyes on being desired to do so. A light was on in the room. I saw in the corner of the room something – a picture, I think – which had the appearance of a skeleton. On looking at that picture, James Loveless said: 'Remember your end.' We were then desired to blind our eyes again and to kneel down. The same voice read again something which I don't remember. We were afterwards desired to kiss a book; our eyes were then unblinded. I then saw all the six prisoners present, some of them were sitting some standing. James Loveless had then a different dress (smock) on from what he now has on, more like a surplice than a smock-frock. The rules were then named to us, I think by George Loveless; I did not know the exact meaning of the rules; something was said about a shilling on entering the society and a penny a week afterwards to support the men out of work – those who had struck – till their masters had raised their wages. I know the meaning of the word 'strike,' – it is to stop work; I don't recollect that I heard the word used that night when I was blindfolded. We were told that when we intended to strike we need not name it to our masters, because they would have a letter sent to them acquainting them of it. I did not pay a shilling at the time of my entering the society. I paid it in the course of two or three weeks afterwards. I gave it to George Loveless. I don't know what became if it afterwards.

Lock stood down and was replaced by Edward Legg. In a halting voice he told the court:

I live at Aftpiddle and I am a labourer. I saw Brine and Hammett about Christmas last in the evening between six and seven o-clock. I was in my house at that time. They knocked at the window and said they wished to see me. I went out and Brine asked me to go with them. I asked where and they said Tolpiddle. I asked what they were going there for – whether they wished to swear me for anything. I said I had heard that there was some swearing in of people at Tolpiddle but I did not know what it was about. James Brine upon this observed that they wished to see how many men they could assemble together. I asked the names of the persons they were going to swear. He mentioned the names of three persons – Percy, Courtney and another. We all went to Tolpiddle and on arrival there we went to Thomas Standfield's house. Brine and Hammett conducted us. We all went upstairs into a room; Thomas Standfield, John Standfield and the two Lovelesses, John and James were present. I don't remember what was said in the first place; but after some time had elapsed, we were asked if we were ready and on our saying 'yes' we blinded our eyes with our handkerchiefs. I believe that all of the Aftpiddle men were blinded.

   We went from that room through a passage into another room. When we got into the last mentioned room something was read to us while we were blinded. I don't know whose voice it was that read to us, nor do I know what it was about. After the reading we were desired to kneel down and something was said to us, but I don't remember what. It was something concerning wages, something about striking for wages, that we were to strike when others did, or something to that effect. They said that they intended to strike and we might do the same if we liked, that our master would have notice of it by means of a letter. We were told that we should have to pay a shilling on entrance and a penny a week afterwards. While we were blinded a book was given to us which we kissed. I repeated some words after some person – I don't know the person – before I kissed the book. It was something about our souls, something about eternity, something about our souls being plunged into eternity if we did not keep the secret, if we disclosed anything that we heard and that was done there. The other Aftpiddle men repeated the same words as myself on their knees. I think it was James Loveless who read to us, but I am not certain. After rising from my knees and on the bandage being removed from my eyes, I observed James Loveless, George Loveless, Thomas Standfield, John Standfield, James Hammett and James Brine and the Aftpiddle men all standing near me. James Loveless had on something like a surplice. A book was on the table and from its size I think must have been a bible. I saw a picture in the room which represented death. The words 'society' and 'brothers' were used after we had been sworn.

Cross-examined by Mr. Butt, Legg said that he knew all the prisoners and 'they are hard working men and I never heard a word against any of them. I did not know Hammett before the summer previous to the last.' At this point Legg could have volunteered that the man in the dock known as James Hammett was not the man he had seen at Standfield's house but was another man. But he failed to do so.

Commenting on testimonies given by Legg and Lock, the National Co-operative Trade Union and Equitable Labour Exchange newspaper *The Crisis* later commented: 'Their characters are of the very worst description. The magistrates are acting a most cruel part in the business.'

Next to be examined was Mrs. Frances Whetham, wife of John Whetham, the Dorchester-based journeyman painter and art shop owner from who James Loveless had attempted to order a picture of a skeleton to be drawn for use in the union's initiation ceremonies. She said:

The prisoner James Loveless came to my husband's shop sometime last year and said he wanted something painted; he said he had the design and he then produced two papers which he left with me, and which I afterwards destroyed. One of the papers represented death and the other a skeleton. Loveless said the ground of the painting must be dark and their height was to be six feet. Over the head of death, Loveless said he wished to have painted 'Remember Thine End.' He said it was intended for a society but more than this he would not mention. He came to the shop sometime in October and he said he should want the picture on the Monday following. He left his address: 'J. Loveless, Tolpiddle.' My husband saw the designs and I destroyed them in about two months after Loveless left them with me. My husband did not execute any part of the paintings.

Onto the stand came Mrs. Whetham's husband John who said:

James Loveless came to me sometime afterwards when I was at the Antelope Hotel (a coaching inn in the centre of Dorchester) where he asked me if the paintings were done. I said no, I could not make out the meaning of the designs. I then asked him for what the paintings were wanted. He replied they were for a society – a society of their own which was a secret of theirs. I said I could not undertake to execute the painting.

John Cox, a turnkey at Dorchester County Jail said he remembered George Loveless coming to the jail on February 25. 'I found in his pockets two printed papers, a letter and a key.' (These were handed to Cox to confirm they were the items confiscated). He continued:

When I took the key from the prisoner he asked me to return it to him. I told him I could not let him have it again. He then begged me to take particular care of it. On looking at one of the papers, the prisoner said that was the cause of his being there. I gave the papers to the Governor of the jail, Mr. Robert Andrews.'

Cox made way for the next witness, John Toomer, an employee of James Frampton who confirmed he had received the key to the box from Frampton and went to the Loveless house to find it, open it and remove the contents, including two books; one listed the names of men already signed into the union alongside the organisation's rules and regulations and another contained a record of subscriptions paid and their amount. The books were taken to Frampton for examination. At last he had the names of every man who had become a member of the union since it began and the union's financial records. He wondered how farm labourers who had complained about their meagre wages could afford to pay an entrance fee of 1s and a weekly contribution of 1d.

While in possession of the books, Frampton had also noted the union's 24 General Laws – or rules – which included orders that if masters attempted to reduce members' wages they must leave their work and walk away in support of another member being discharged for being signed to the union. Members were also instructed to decline work with anyone divulging union secrets. The books included the union's 12 Bye Laws covering everything from Lodge opening times, the correct use of passwords at meetings, rules about smoking, eating, reading, sleeping swearing or betting (none was allowed during meetings), that the name 'brother' was to be used by one member speaking to another, the election and make up of union officers and so on – all sensible, legal and inoffensive rules designed to keep order during meetings.

Speeches were then made for the defence by Messrs Butt and Derbyshire who argued that the mysterious Act of 1797 was confined to cases of mutiny and sedition; that the Tolpiddle union was perfectly legal and properly constituted and that no oath within the meaning of the Statute had been administered. At the conclusion of the speeches the judge inquired if the defendants had anything to say. George Loveless immediately passed him a 'short defence' in writing on which he had jotted the following words (it is unknown how Loveless obtained paper and pencil in order to scribble the note):

> My Lord, if we have violated any law, it was not done intentionally; we have injured no man's reputation, character, person or property: we were uniting together to preserve ourselves, our wives and our children, from utter degradation and starvation. We challenge any man or number of men to prove that we have acted, or intended to act, different from the above statement.

The note was passed up to the judge who quickly read it and then asked Loveless if he wished it to be read out to the jury. On receiving an affirmative reply, the judge mumbled the words to the jury in such a rapid and inaudible fashion that Loveless himself could not understand it. The crowd in the public gallery also made a fuss, letting it be known that they, too, did not hear what was contained in Loveless's message. There was much hammering of the gavel hitting the woodblock until silence returned to the court.

With evidence concluded, it now fell to the judge and jury to play their decisive parts in the drama. He told the jury at portentous length that they must satisfy themselves as to the illegality of the oath that Legg had taken and which had been administered by other members of the society:

> The precise formality of the oath is not under inquiry, but the Act of Parliament refers to an oath fixing an obligation on a party to whom it is administered. To sustain and prove this charge you must be satisfied that the oath administered to Legg was to bind him not to divulge the secrets of the society; if so, it will come within the meaning of the Act. It is also a question whether the dress of James Loveless, which resembled a clergyman's surplice, was not intended to give a degree of solemnity and additional force to the proceedings. The representation of a skeleton and death's head seems also to have been intended to strike awe on the minds of the persons to whom the oath was administered. In taking the oath, mention was made of the 'soul and eternity' and if you are satisfied that the oath was intended as an obligation on the conscience of the person taking it, it clearly comes within the meaning of the Act which I have mentioned to you.
>
> From the evidence of Mr and Mrs Whetham, it appears on the confession of one of the prisoners himself, who applied to them for two paintings, that the Society to which he belonged was a secret one, and he did not choose to divulge anything more to Mr. Whetham than that he wanted a representation of death, six feet high and a skeleton with a scythe in the right of hand.

Now it is for you to consider whether these things were not intended to strike awe on the beholders. The skeleton having a scythe was, it is supposed, intended to represent 'time' which mows down everything before him. This, with the exception of the scythe was a rather unusual emblem, for 'Time' as you must well-know, is generally represented by an old man, bald behind and having a tuft of hair in front, which has led to the proverbial expression of taking 'Time' by the forelock.

His Lordship remarked on the rules of the society, which spoke of the violation of an obligation, evidently referring to the oath which was administered by the prisoners; and that such a violation would be deemed by the society as a crime. His Lordship also read from a book belonging to the society the names of several people – including the prisoners – who had contributed to its funds. On hearing this, several men in the public gallery cleared their throats and looked down at their feet when their names were mentioned.

He then said something amazing to the prisoners:

The object of all legal punishment is not altogether with a view of operating on the offenders themselves, it is also for the sake of offering an example and warning, and accordingly, the offence of which you have been convicted, after evidence that was perfectly satisfactory, the crime, to a conviction of which that evidence had led, is of that description that the security of the country and the maintenance of the laws on the upholding of which the welfare of this country depends, make it necessary for me to pass on to you the sentence required by those laws.

I will now leave it to the jury to draw their conclusions from these facts and the whole chain of evidence which has been repeated to them.

Judge Williams had spoken to the jury as if the men on trial had committed murder, arson or treason instead of innocently swearing an oath that they had no idea illegal. Whatever sentence was imposed it was surely to be a lenient one; a few more days in jail at best and a flogging at worst.

The jury retired and five minutes later returned with their verdict: 'GUILTY!' There was a great intake of breath from the public gallery and angry voices were raised as Judge Williams got up and left the court without looking at who was making the din. Mr Derbyshire leapt to his feet to declare that 'a great number of persons will be dissatisfied and I shall be for one.'

The prisoners were hastily ushered down the steps back to their cells below. It would be another 36 miserable and despairing hours before they would know their sentence, but between them they already had made up their minds what their awful fate was to be.

Chapter 11

The Sentence

Wednesday 19 March, 1834

Now you gallant lads of England, just listen unto me,
It's the last song I shall pen in my own country,
For I have received my sentence as you shall understand
I'm transported for seven years, my boys, into some foreign land.

In the 36 hours since they last stood in the prisoner's dock, the six men had time to think about and discuss what had taken place at their trial. So, according to the judge, they had not really committed any sort of crime, yet were to be made an example for threatening the security of England. How, they wondered, had a handful of farm labourers living a hand-to-mouth existence in a tiny Dorset village, managed to threaten the security of the country's 14 million citizens? With a few minor exceptions, the only people they knew lived in Tolpiddle and its neighbouring villages – and they had never threatened any friends, neighbours or even those persecuting them for their religious beliefs. So how could this be taken as a threat to the entire country? And if they were to be punished as an example, who exactly would benefit from such a sentence?

None of the Tolpiddle Six were stupid. Although the judge had not said so in as many words, they knew that the real reason for their imprisonment and pending sentence had nothing to do with taking an oath, which they had no idea was illegal, but because they were members of a trade union where trade unionism was despised and feared by land owners. This had nothing to do with threatening the security of England, but threatening the pockets of landowners and their tenants who wanted their labourers to remember their lowly place in society – and to remain there. Being 'dissenters' cannot have helped, either, although this was never mentioned at the trial; Methodism was legal yet despised by many in and around Dorchester. They could not understand much said by the judge. Although they could all read and write his legal jargon was a totally alien language.

They all, perhaps with the exception of James Hammett, spent time in the cells singing hymns and saying prayers for the care of their families and for strength and courage to face whatever was coming their way – and for a speedy re-union with their wives and children.

On Wednesday, 19 March the manacled prisoners were again paraded back up the wooden steps to stand before the judge to hear their sentence. Daylight pouring through the two large windows behind the public gallery hurt their eyes and. after two days in the dark and gloom of the cells, they needed a few moments to get used to the light.

Judge Williams gave the prisoners in the dock a long hard look and took a deep breath before telling them:

> I have noted from your plea that you had not intended to harm anybody by your actions. What your intentions were can only be known to yourselves. There have been cases whose effect on public security was such that an example had to be made, whatever the intentions of the participants. Your offence comes into this category because you had withdrawn yourselves from the recognition of the law and kept your conduct private and secret from the rest of the world. I therefore state that you and each of you be transported to such places beyond the seas as His Majesty's Council in their discretion shall see fit for the term of seven years.

And with a bang of his gavel, the case was closed.

Pandemonium ensued. Five of the six men stood frozen in shock at the monstrous sentence. George Loveless, however, pulled a sheet of paper from his smock on which two verses had been scrawled:

> *God is our guide, from field, from wave,*
> *From plough, from anvil, and from loom;*
> *We come, our country's rights to save,*
> *And speak a tyrant faction's doom.*
> *We will raise the watchword, liberty,*
> *We will, we will, we will be free!*
> *God is our guide! No swords we draw.*
> *We kindle not war's battle fires:*
> *By reason, union, justice, law,*
> *We claim the birth-right of our sires:*
> *We raise the watch-word, liberty,*
> *We will, we will, we will be free!!!*

Before a prison guard could snatch the paper from Loveless's hands, he had screwed it into a ball and tossed it into the crowd. Unfortunately it was seized by a prison guard who carried the ball of paper back to the judge. By all accounts, after reading it Judge Williams remarked that writing such words was a crime of no less magnitude than high treason.

The Song of Freedom
to the tune Madrid

Music: William Matthew

The original words of '*We Will be Free*' which George Loveless hurriedly scribbled down were not composed by him but were part of a song originally named '*The Gathering of the Unions*' by George De Bosco Attwood and first appeared in Hodgson's Song-Book for 1833, 'a collection of upwards of 100 popular favourite and entirely new songs and none in this collection can offend the chastest ear.' The version here, known as *The Song of Freedom*, includes music by William Matthew. Methodist Heritage.

Some accounts state that George Loveless had scribbled the words of the hymn down while standing in the dock with his fellow prisoners. With both wrists manacled to other prisoners this was highly unlikely. Most probably he would have written it in the lonely 36 hours he and his fellows were incarcerated awaiting sentence. Goodness knows where he found a pencil and piece of paper he used to scribble it somewhere out of sight of the jailer. He never claimed that the words were his own – and they were not. The two scribbled stanzas were part of a hymn originally named 'The Gathering of the Unions' by George De Bosco Attwood, the son of Thomas Attwood who founded the Political Union for the Protection of Public Rights in Birmingham in 1830. After being put to music in 1832, two years before his arrest, 'The Gathering of the Unions' was sung on 7 May of that year at a great meeting on Newhall Hill, Birmingham, during the run up to the Great Reform Act. Known today as 'The Tolpuddle Hymn' or 'The Song of Freedom', Loveless probably came across 'The Gathering of the Unions' in Hodgson's Song-Book for 1833, 'a collection of upwards of 100 popular favourite and entirely new songs and none in this collection can offend the chastest ear.' Perhaps it had also been included in an early Wesleyan Methodist hymn book or distributed to trade unions by the Grand National Consolidated Trade Union. For many years the tune used for the hymn was 'Madrid', by William Matthew, although it is not the original tune. Today it exists in a setting composed by Dr. George Frederick Brockless, a well-known organist and orchestral conductor in the 1940s.

The original song began as follows and was followed by the two other verses written down by Loveless:

> *Lo! We answer, see we come*
> *Quick, at Freedom's holy call,*
> *We come, we come, we come, we come,*
> *To do the glorious work of all*
> *And hark! We raise from sea to sea*
> *The sacred watchword, Liberty!*

oOo

Anyone from Tolpiddle and its surrounding villages who had been a member of the Friendly Society of Agricultural Labourers was rightly fearful. There were over forty such men who waited for a knock on their cottage doors from the Petty Police Constable and expected to be marched to Dorchester jail and tried in court like their six colleagues. Some single men were driven to flee the area while married men with children feared eviction from their homes and jobs if they were known to have become union members. They knew that a book containing the names of union members was in the spiteful hands of James Frampton and were certain he would instruct farmers leasing his land to dismiss anyone with names recorded in it.

Frampton himself wrote to Lord Melbourne on 19 March 1834 informing that it was 'probable that at this time of year when farmers generally make new agreements with their labourers, they will show a great unwillingness to employ those who are known to have belonged to the union'.

In a later letter to Under Secretary of State, Lord Howick, Frampton commented that he

... particularly recommended to the farmers (who have expressed themselves most willing to follow my advice) that every encouragement should be given to those labourers who did not join the union by increasing their wages and placing them all in the most profitable work, so that they may feel the advantage of their good conduct by making a marked difference between them and the unionists, and on no account at present to make any addition to wages of the latter, lest it should have the slightest appearance of being done by fear ... In some cases the wages are low, but some of the unionists were in constant regular work, and earning the best wages ... and whatever complaints the labourers of Tolpiddle may at any time have had occasion to make against the farmers, there can be no doubt but that for several years the farmers have had to deal with a very troublesome, irritating and difficult set of people.

Chapter 12

The Hulks

5 April–25 May, 1834

As we sailed down the coastline on the 25th of May,
Every ship that we passed, we heard the sailors say,
There goes a ship of clever lads about to withstand
Punishment for crimes in Van Dieman's Land.

Almost as soon as the prisoners were returned to their cells, George Loveless fell ill; he had spent 36 hour locked in an unsanitary cell without any ventilation and air filled with acrid and suffocating smoke pouring from a fireplace burning damp wood. He found it difficult to breathe, his chest was tight and he was feverish and dizzy. After two days he felt no better and, having asked to see a doctor, he was taken to the prison hospital. He remembered:

> As soon as I entered I had to cope with a new antagonist, Dr. Arden, surgeon of the hospital. I told him I was too ill for conversation and requested him to allow me to go to bed; but he appeared so angry as not to regard what I said. At length I threw myself on a bed and answered his questions, until he was very mild and after this he manifested the greatest possible kindness and attention towards me until I left the prison. I told him they could hang me with as much justice as transport me for what I had done.

On 27 March, while Loveless was still in hospital, the other five Tolpiddle men were hurried outside and, with their hands and legs manacled to the prison gates, they awaited a coach taking them to Portsmouth. There they were to serve part of their sentence toiling on convict hulks anchored in the harbour before boarding transportation ships bound for Australia. They were not permitted to visit George Loveless in the hospital before leaving but were sure he would be joining them once he felt stronger.

Loveless was not informed that that his comrades would soon be on the high seas on route to Botany Bay while he would be spending at least a month on a convict hulk before being taken to a place 700 miles away from them in a place known as Van Diemen's Land – the toughest, roughest, most gruelling part of the Australian penal system.

The real reason for hurrying the men onto prison hulks and transportation was the government's fear that delay might result in an appeal which could prevent the deportations. Some politicians were ready and willing to call for an appeal but had to wait for an opportunity to lodge one on an already long list of issues to be addressed by parliament. The sooner they were on the high seas the better was uppermost in the minds of those working at Lord Melbourne's Home Department.

On Wednesday, 2 April Loveless was informed that he had an important visitor. He hoped it might be his wife but no less a dignitary than Mr. Charlton Byam Woolaston strode into the hospital. He was polite, said he had heard how ill Loveless was and asked if he was feeling any better. Loveless thanked him and said he was feeling much better than shortly after he arrived at the prison. Woolaston sighed and said he was sorry to see a man like Loveless in such a situation. He added: 'But it is your own fault, you are now suffering for your own stubbornness and obstinacy; you have such a proud spirit, you would not pay attention to the cautions of the magistrates; but would rather hearken to idle fellows that were going about the country, who now have deceived you.' Loveless replied that he had not been deceived by anyone and he did not know of anyone like those that Woolaston had described. 'Yes you do,' snapped Woolaston, 'for you have hearkened to them rather than pay attention to the magistrates' cautions; for I am certain you saw them, one of them being found on your person when you went to prison.' Woolaston must have been referring to the letter from George Romaine found in Loveless's smock and confiscated following his arrest.

Loveless asked: 'Is Mr. Woolaston in his right mind?' 'What do you mean?' asked the magistrate. 'The circumstance concerning which the witnesses swore against us, took place on the 9th of December and the magistrate's cautions did not appear till the 21st February following; so we have been tried for what took place at least nine weeks before the cautions had existence; and yet you say that I paid no attention to the magistrates, but listened to idle fellows going about the country; within three days after the cautions appeared I was in the body of the gaol.' 'Ah, it's no use talking to you,' said Woolaston angrily as he marched towards the door. Loveless said as a parting shot: 'No sir, unless you talk more reasonable.'

Later the same day Loveless was informed by Dr. Arden that his five companions had left the prison and were on their way to Portsmouth to join a convict ship. There was no time to catch up with them and he had to wait until Saturday, 5 April before he was told to prepare for a journey of his own. With leg irons clasping his ankles, Loveless was led from the prison to a waiting coach. This was the first fresh air he had breathed for over two weeks and he took deep breaths before climbing on board.

He was to ride on the outside of the coach on one of the upper seats next to passenger luggage and exposed to the elements. His leg irons were fastened to the coach, making it impossible for the prisoner to attempt an escape. He was accompanied by the clerk of the prison, Mr. Glinister, who rode on the inside of the coach. As the horse drawn carriage passed through Dorchester and out towards the open countryside, passers-by would only have known that the man sitting on top of the coach was a prisoner on his way to punishment if they had seen the shackles securing him to the vehicle.

The coach stopped at Salisbury to water the horses and allow passengers to stretch their legs. Glinister asked Loveless if he wanted his legs to be freed as he needed to walk through part of the town 'and the rattling of the chains would cause people to be looking after you'. When told that he would be chained up again as soon as he re-joined the coach, Loveless refused 'as I was not ashamed to wear the chains, conscious of my innocence'.

The coach rumbled on through the afternoon and early evening; it reached Portsmouth around 9.00pm and Loveless was 'given up' into the charge of officers from the wooden convict hulk *York* who removed his chains. Convict hulks were decommissioned and retired wooden ships that prison authorities used as floating prisons. A 'convict hulk' was not to be confused with a convict ship. A 'hulk' was a ship that was afloat, but, because of its age, was not seaworthy; convict ships

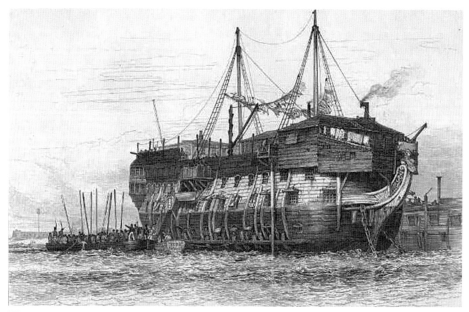

The prison hulk 'York' had once been a 90-gun three decked square rigged ship but by 1819 had been sold to the Convict Establishment to serve as a prison hulk at Portsmouth. (*National Library of Australia*)

were seaworthy vessels which transported convicted prisoners from their place of conviction to a place of banishment.

On both hulks and convict ships prisoners were never free of the iron manacles around their ankles which clanked and rattled at every moment. The prisoners'

Prison hulks laying off shore in Portsmouth harbour. (*Creative Commons Attribution-ShareAlike*)

bodies, clothing, beds and the very walls of the hulks were infested with vermin. Sickness was always present; scrofula – a tubercular infection of the lymph nodes in the neck – consumption, scurvy, cholera, dysentery and smallpox swept through the hulks like unstoppable waves over the side. Death came as a welcome release for many older and infirm convicts. Frequent arbitrary punishments could include a reduction of rations, an increase in the weight of leg irons and floggings of unspeakable severity.

The *York* had once been a smart 90-gun, 1,743 ton, three decked square rigged ship but was now without guns, masts or sails. She was launched 1807 and had served in the West Indies where she was involved in the bold capture of the island stronghold of Martinique. Her Napoleonic war continued in the Mediterranean Squadron off Toulon before she returned to Portsmouth 1819 to be sold to the Convict Establishment to serve as a convict hulk. The hulks were originally intended for temporary use only but overflowing prisons ashore caused their use to extend for over 70 years.

Embarking on the *York*, anchored on the Gosport side of Portsmouth Harbour, was a demoralising affair for a simple ploughman not used to mingling with 500 other callous and mocking forgers, housebreakers, thieves, cracksmen, footpads, pimps, poachers, murders and rapists. Lads who had rarely left their native village found such a society unspeakably alien and terrible. Prisoners had to climb laboriously up a steep gangplank leading from the jetty to the main deck to be stripped of their clothes, with buckets of cold water thrown over them, issued with slops – unappetizing watery food – re-chained with heavy duty shackles around each ankle and an iron chain between them allowing them to hobble a mere six

A line of prison hulks in Portsmouth Harbour. By 1834 England's prisons were full to bursting so convicts sentenced to transportation were sent to rotting decommissioned naval ships until they were transferred to prison ships bound for Botany Bay and Van Diemen's Land. (*Picture by Ambrose-Louis Garneray. National Maritime Museum, London*)

inches at any one time. Most were then sent down to the lowest deck of the hulk – the darkest and most foul part of the ship reeking with the stench of urine, sewage, vomit and rotting vegetation.

Loveless 'was struck with astonishment' at what he saw on deck:

> The clanking of chains and of so many men being stripped. When ordered to put on the hulk livery – a course grey jacket and breeches – and to attend on the smith (blacksmith) to have fetters riveted on my legs, for a moment I began to sink down, until the first mate, Mr. Nicholson, told me I was to go into No.2 ward, middle deck, one of the best and quietest wards on the ship, by the Captain's order, in consequence of a good character he had received with me from prison.

Although Loveless was sent to 'the quiet' part of the ship, he was forbidden to talk to anyone although 'they could not stop my ears from hearing others'. In a letter to his wife, Loveless told her:

> One day as I was in the gun wharf assisting in weighing some old iron, I overheard two gentlemen that were standing by, talking. One said to the other that O'Connor [a prominent Irish-born Chartist MP for County Cork who spoke against the Tolpuddle sentences] had done all he could for the trade unions, but the government was determined to transport them, and so they ought.

Loveless was unaware of what had happened to his fellow labourers apart from knowing that they were certainly not on board the *York*. So where were they?

His brother James, the two Standfields, Hammett and Brine had been deposited onto the *Leviathan*, a former 74 gun warship originally launched in Chatham 1790 but now floating with two broken masts and a large wooden 'shed' built onto the top deck providing extra convict accommodation. The ship had fought at the Battle of Trafalgar and was converted into a convict hulk in 1816.

It mattered little what hulk you were assigned to. In all of them life was brutal, tough, regimented and cruel. A contemporary wrote of life on the *Leviathan*: 'At three o'clock [in the morning] cooks are let up to boil the prisoners' breakfast. Food composed of a very coarse kind of barley boiled up with soup made from meat given to the convicts every alternate day. The dietary of the hulk, exclusive of meat and barley soup, was, three days in each week, a portion of a mysterious semi-petrification, very much akin to chalk both in taste and durability.' Cheese was also distributed 'too big to swallow and too hard to bite'. For breakfast and supper, when meat was not allowed, each man received a pint of barley boiled in water. A pound of very black unpalatable bread also formed the daily allowance of each man, with a pint of very bad vinegar, better known on the hulks as 'table beer.'

On Saturday evenings prisoners had to go to the upper deck to take a bath in which, two or three at a time, they were soaked and scrubbed by the wardens with long-handled brushes. On Sundays all hands were called and mustered to sweep the decks after which prisoners returned to their wards for breakfast. At nine they were mustered in divisions on the main deck for inspection and examination of their clothing to make sure they were clean and in proper repair. Divine service was performed by a chaplain once every Sunday.

The Tolpiddle men remained on the prison hulk until 29 March when they were ordered on deck to be examined before being dispatched overseas. After examination, new irons were riveted onto their ankles. Then, with around 100

Adieu, adieu my native land, by an unknown artist and showing manacled prisoners about to be taken out to a transportation ship bound for Van Diemen's Land. (*Tasmanian Archive and Heritage Office*)

Black-eyed Sue and Sweet Poll of Plymouth. A pair of heavily shackled criminals bid farewell to their battered prostitute sweethearts while an official with a gun in his belt sternly points towards their prison ship waiting at anchor. (*Trustees of the British Museum*)

other prisoners, they were taken by lighter – a flat-bottomed barge used to transfer goods and passengers to and from moored ships – out onto Plymouth Sound to join the convict ship *Surrey* which would soon be taking them to Australia. Already on board were 100 other men from the *Leviathan* but no sign of George Loveless. They were unaware that Loveless was to be transported elsewhere from Portsmouth and far away from his fellow farm labourers in a bid to prevent them from 'bringing their dirty union ways to the other side of the world'.

Australia had become a dumping ground for the refuse of Britain's prisons by the late 18th century. But in 1834 coastal areas originally set up as convict stations were fast becoming the epicentre of a new nation, populated by vigorous 'free' settlers who created farms out of parched earth, grazing land out of eucalyptus groves, commercial industries to match those left behind in England and ports and wharfs for loading and unloading cargo from the 'old world' for citizens of the 'new world'. Avenues of elegant and imposing buildings had begun to appear on the horizon alongside smart houses and business premises. Sheep dotted the landscape and men started to sow wheat and prospect for minerals including copper, silver, lead, iron, marble and opals. Building work was undertaken by convicts and prisoners who had served their term and decided to stay on after their sentences to launch their own construction and mercantile trading businesses.

o0o

It was a matter of urgency that all six Tolpiddle men be transferred from the hulks to transportation ships and kicked out of the country as fast as possible. Lord Melbourne was aware of a strong undercurrent of discontent among working men and certain politicians demanding the prisoners be set free before they were on the high seas when it would be too late to return them. Their deportation to the penal colonies was ordered without further delays.

The *Surrey* was a triple mast square rigged ship with copper sheathing around her lower quarters to protect her from the corrosive effects of salt water. Her eleven passages to Australia gave her one of the longest careers as a convict transport. Under the command of Charles Kemp, the *Surrey* would be carrying 260 male passengers including five men from Tolpiddle. The journey was expected to take up to 115 days and, hopefully be uneventful, unlike the *Surrey's* first trip to Australia in 1814 when a raging fever among its crew and prisoners followed killings of her Master, first mate and forty prisoners.

On Friday, 14 April 1834, the *Surrey* weighed anchor and headed west down the English Channel towards Land's End and the choppy waters of the Atlantic Ocean.

Two weeks after arriving on the *York*, Loveless was still waiting to be transported. He was permitted to write a letter to his wife, Betsy, in reply to a message she had sent a few days before. The letter demonstrates Loveless's wonderful courage, his strong and unflinching spirit, despite the sham of a trial, an unfair judgement, incarceration and falling ill inside the prison.

My dear wife,

I received your kind letter this day (April 20) and it gave me great satisfaction to hear that you were all well – as it created in my heart gratitude to the God of all our mercies that you are favoured with kind friends to supply your wants, for I consider the kindness shown to my wife and children as shown to me.

My health is gradually improving, but it is still weakly. I have been at Portsmouth a fortnight, during which time I have been employed in the Gun Wharf. I have not heard of my companions since my arrival here; whether they are gone from this country, or still staying in Plymouth. And it is all uncertain to me when I shall leave this place.

If my companions are gone from Plymouth in the Bay (Botany Bay) ship, in all probability I shall not see them again, as the next Bay ship will be destined

The *Surrey* was a triple mast square rigged ship which had one of the longest careers as a convict transporter, making 11 round-trip passages to Australia. In 1834 it carried 260 male passengers including five farm labourers from Tolpuddle. (*National Library of Australia*)

for another port – the last was destined for Sidney (sic) and I think the next for Hobart Town. However, be as it may – all is well. WE SEE ONLY THE BEGINNING; NOT THE END. I doubt not but it will work together for good; though I am suffering as an Innocent Man. I feel no disposition to complain. I can say: 'It is the Lord, let him do what seemeth him good!'

Though painful at present, 'Twill cease before long, And then, O how pleasant, The Conqueror's song!' [from *Be Gone Unbelief, My Saviour is Near*' by the Rev. John Newton, sailor and clergyman (1725-1807) who also wrote Amazing Grace.]

You say many friends want to send me some money, if I could receive it. The regulations of this ship are that I can receive no money for my present use, nor provisions of any kind. It can be put into the care of Mr. Kirkham, our commander, and then it would be forthcoming at my leaving this ship, at any time, or for any place.

You enquire if it would be prudent for you to come and see me? I see no imprudence whatever, were it not for the expense of the journey. Were it not for this, I would like to see you and brother William before I leave. You can see me on Sunday only – I leave it to you whether you come or not.

I hope you will answer this shortly. I know you too well to say 'take care of the children'. Give my love to each of them – Father – to Dinniah and her children; John Mitchell, Mr. Sansom and all friends.

I am not afraid but that God, whose I am and whom I endeavour to serve, will at length deliver me, for 'He that is for us, is more than all against us.'

From your loving and affectionate husband,

G. Loveless – Prisoner 5366

Loveless went to work with a gun wharf party along a jetty next to the *York* hulk. He spent six weeks manhandling cannons, cannon balls and gunpowder until, on the morning of Saturday, 17 May he was instructed to prepare himself for a voyage across the world to Van Diemen's Land. He would be sailing on the 447-ton ship *William Metcalf* which would carry 121 prisoners from Portsmouth in addition to a further 120 miserable convicts who had boarded in Woolwich – 51 of them to serve life sentences in the colony. The ship was scheduled to sail on 25 May.

Before departing, he dashed off another quick note to Betsy:

Spithead, May 24th, 1834: I thank you, my dear wife, for the kind attention you have ever paid me, and you may safely rely upon it that as long as I live it will be my constant endeavour to return that kindness in every possible way, and hope to send to you as soon as we reach our place of destiny, and that I shall never forget the promise made at the altar: and though we may part awhile, I shall consider myself under the same obligations and though living in your immediate presence. Be satisfied, my dear Betsy, on my account. Depend upon it, it will work together for good, and we shall yet rejoice together. I hope you will pay particular attention to the morals and spiritual interests of the children. Don't send me any money to distress yourself; I shall do well, for He who is Lord of the winds and waves will be my support in life and death.

In the afternoon of 25 May, the *William Metcalf* weighed anchor and was soon passing The Needles with a fresh leading breeze behind. The following evening they passed Land's End and headed out into the Atlantic. Loveless was assigned

... a small bed, pillow and blanket which would have contributed greatly to our comfort, had there been room sufficient to have laid on them, but we could not. A berth of about five feet six inches square was all that was allowed for six men to occupy day and night, with the exception of four hours we were allowed daily on deck, two hours in the forenoon and two hours in the afternoon for air. For nearly ten weeks in fourteen I was not able to lie down at length to take rest. But what then? I was a prisoner, and there is no pity. 'You have no business here, so you must take it as it comes, for better, for worse,' is the consolation you get when you complain.

Part IV

The Voyage

25 May–4 September, 1834

In Dorset I was born, near Dorchester town did dwell,
I loved my wife and family and that you know full well,
For starting a trade union has caused me to be
A Transport from my native land across the raging seas.

It would take 111 days for the *William Metcalf* to sail the 15,226 miles from Portsmouth to Hobart Town, the largest and most remote settlement in the penal colony of Van Dieman's Land, crossing two large oceans and making stops at five ports on route. They were to experience raging storms, gale force tempests, scorching sunshine and becalmed seas.

At daybreak on the morning of 10 June the prisoners saw rocks known as The Deserters off the south-east tip of Madeira, 1,484miles from Portsmouth. The following day they sailed past The Salvages, a cluster of treacherous rocks between the Madeiras and the Canary Islands. Four days later the *William Metcalf* anchored in Santa Cruz, Tenerife where they re-stocked the ship with fresh water and victuals, including a plentiful quantity of pumpkins and onions. Live poultry was loaded for the senior officers along with locally produced wine and brandy for the Captain's cupboard.

The ship then turned into a southerly direction for the 1,013 mile voyage to the Cape Verde Islands. By now the weather was extremely hot, and nowhere more so than in the unventilated areas below decks. Eleven days later the *William Metcalf* crossed the Equator and was half way through the 2,940 mile journey to Rio de Janeiro. Once there the crew sent out a long boat over the side to buy sugar, coffee, rum, port wine, rice, tapioca, tobacco and other victuals, mostly for the officers and crew. Meals for convicts were almost the same every day; basic rations included rough bread or ship's biscuit-bread, porridge and grain and vegetable broth with meat of some kind or another thrown in every other day. If lucky, prisoners were occasionally given pieces of fruit taken on board at one of the tropical ports where oranges and limes could be bought for 6d a hundred and eaten while standing on deck gazing at Rio's vast granite and quartz mountains raising high into the sky from the sea.

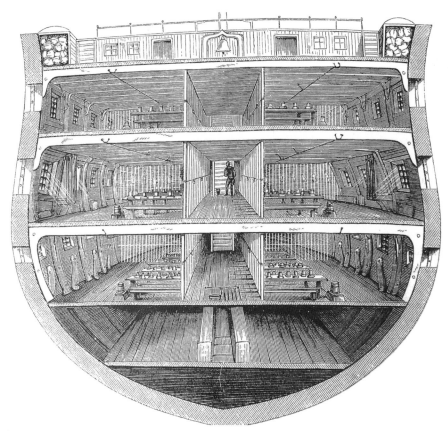

Sectional view of a convict ship showing six separate large cell arrangements which ran the full length of the ship from stem to stern and running off three central passageways. Prisoners lived behind barred walls and slept and ate their food in these cells. The bottom section shows the bilge compartment where the two sides of the ship meet at the keel. This was the most unpleasant part of the ship where many prisoners were sent as a punishment for making trouble and where many died of dysentery. (*Illustrated London News*)

The *William Metcalf's* passage continued a further 3,763 miles across the Atlantic towards the Cape of Good Hope on a voyage lasting four weeks, much of it in rough seas and with waves reaching up to 80ft high causing seasickness among convicts, crew members and officers alike. On 25 August the ship cast anchor in Table Bay next to vessels from many different nations. Once convicts were allowed on deck for fresh air they saw 'the table land' which stands behind the town, a black and dreary looking mountain, flat on top and over eleven hundred yards in height. Violent gusts of wind blowing from it raised unpleasant clouds of dust to make walking on deck next to impossible.

While the ship lay at anchor in Table Bay, Loveless fell ill on 31 August with 'acute pains in his right shoulder' – the result of being unable to lie down properly to sleep in the crowded cell and after being thrown against the ship's bulkhead

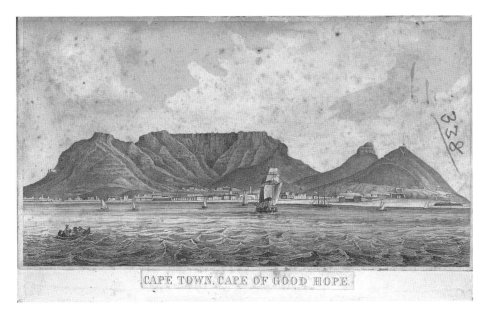

CAPE TOWN, CAPE OF GOOD HOPE.

The convict ship *William Metcalf* dropped anchor in Table Bay on 25 August 1834 next to vessels from many different nations. Violent gusts of wind blowing down from Table Mountain created so much dust that work on the deck was impossible. (*Cape Town Partnership*)

during a violent storm. The ship's surgeon-superintendent, Dr. Evans, gave Loveless a daily course of embrocation, rubbing his shoulder twice-daily with liniments and lotions. He also pulled the prisoner from his on-deck duties and for the next eleven days moved him from his crowded cell to more comfortable 'quarters' which allowed him to lie down properly on a horse-hair mattress and

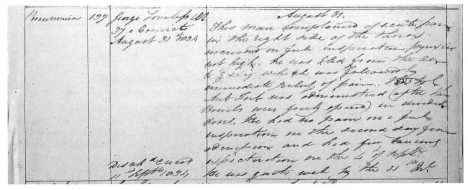

While the ship lay at anchor in Table Bay, Loveless fell ill on 31 August with 'acute pains in his right shoulder'. He later developed pneumonia, but the ship's medical log records that 'by September 11th the prisoner was feeling much better and stronger' and was returned to his horrid cell and sent back to work swabbing the *William Metcalf*'s decks. (*Convict Records – State library of Queensland*)

recover from his aches and pains. Loveless later developed pneumonia, but Dr. Evans' log records that 'by September 11th the prisoner was feeling much better and stronger' and was later returned to his horrid cell and sent back to work swabbing the *William Metcalf's* decks.

oOo

Discipline on board the *William Metcalf* was severe and anyone causing trouble – arguing with an officer, fighting with another prisoner, being un-cooperative with a member of the crew, stealing or showing violence to anyone else on board – was

Two single sheet 'Political Drama' wood engraved cartoons published by George Drake of Houghton Street, London, during the period when the public and some politicians were calling for a return of the Tolpiddle men.

Political drama No 32 shows the Dorchester labourers kneeling for mercy before King William IV and reminding him that his Coronation oath pledged he would 'temper justice with mercy.' They plea: 'We have committed no moral sin against God or man. Forget not, Sire, that millions of your sacred Majesty's loyal subjects are bound by oaths in their different societies to protect themselves from unjust encroachments on their rights? Are not these, Royal Sir, as culpable as ourselves....O King, we only bound ourselves for the just protection of our miserable earnings....Oh Sire, have mercy on poor humanity.' The King replies: 'Guards, turn the slaves out. They must be transported. My duty to the capitalists, landholders, the Tories and my nine hundred and ninety nine cousins demand it.' (*Link Tasmania*)

severely punished with a brutal flogging or deprived of rations and left to starve in the bilges, the lowest and filthiest part of the ship. These punishments were designed to break the spirits of rebellious prisoners (if travelling half way across the world in a convict ship was not bad enough). Prisoners were sometimes chained flat out onto the deck next to a cauldron of hot coals out of which a branding iron could be seen. Once the prisoner had been secured by his wrists and ankles, the red hot branding iron would be removed and placed on his open palms and left for a full five seconds. He would be marked for life. Prisoners who had been flogged with a knotted cat-o'nine-tails took their punishment on the top deck of the ship. The victim was given twenty-four hours in which to make his own cat and locked in leg-irons on the upper deck while awaiting punishment. Once the cat was made, the boatswain cut out all but the best nine tails. If the task was not completed in time the punishment was increased. Following his lashing, he was thrown into a

Political drama No. 33 shows John Bull (left) pushing a rowing boat carrying ten politicians out into choppy waters. A flag on the bow tells us that the boat full of politicians is bound for Botany Bay. Two oarsmen guide the boat towards a convict ship from which a returning boat carries the six Tolpiddle men, five of whom are standing and raising their hats while cheering 'Huzza! Huzza!! Huzza!!! One more cheer: Huzza!!!!' Among the politicians are caricatures of Lord Melbourne who exclaims 'Oh that I had done justice while in my power!', the Duke of Wellington, Chancellor of the Exchequer, Viscount Althorp and Secretary of State for War and the Colonies, Lord Glenelg who moans 'Oh, this is my reward for my arduous and disinterested service in the cause of God and my country.' The cartoon muses that the men in the boat should be on board the hulks in place of 'these unfortunate men.' (*Link Tasmania*)

wooden bath filled with salt water, known as a brine bath, which was supposed to help his wounds heal faster, but must have been double the agony for the poor felon as the salt water ate into his open wounds. The beaten prisoner must have cried out long and loud following this vicious sentence.

The *William Metcalf* had hardly cleared the southern African coast when a south-east wind set in and continued to blow for several days knocking three or four days from the ship's long journey to Van Diemen's Land. Crossing the entire Indian Ocean from west to east was the longest part of the journey and, thanks to a succession of fair winds and pleasant weather, a crew member in the crow's nest was able to call 'land ahoy' by 3 September after the final 6,223 miles of the voyage. After their long confinement the convicts were overjoyed by the change of scenery but fear filled their hearts as they had no idea what brutalities lay in store on dry land. While cruising along the Van Diemen's shoreline they cast many an anxious eye towards a land which consisted of tree-covered hills as far as the eye could see. By the following morning the ship had entered Storm Bay and a favourable wind carried them 30 miles up the River Derwent through the night to Hobart Town. At half-past six on the morning of 4 September 1834 they were met by a pilot boat after a gruelling voyage from Portsmouth of 111 monotonous days and uncomfortable nights. The pilot led the *William Metcalf* to its mooring place at ten o'clock. It dropped anchor and government officials came on board to examine the prisoners one by one, taking full particulars of their names, ages, occupations and sentences; a detailed description of each man was carefully recorded in a large ledger.

The voyage was over but it would be another eight days before convicts left the ship. Two hundred and forty prisoners had boarded *William Metcalf* in England and twenty-four perished on route from a variety of sickness including scurvy, cholera and other fevers. Several also died from broken hearts and knowledge that they were unlikely to ever see their families again. At sea the dead were wrapped in blankets and sewed into hammocks along with three 18lb cannonballs to help carry the bodies down to the sea bed. A few words from the ship's parson was their last farewell – no reading from the bible, no prayers, only a scribbled note of the day they died entered into the ship's log to be included in a letter home to their families after the voyage.

Chapter 13

Prisoner 848

Winter/Spring 1834/35

The first day that we landed upon that fatal shore,
The planters they came round us, full twenty score or more.
They ranked us up like horses and sold us out of hand,
They yoked us unto ploughs, my boys, to plough Van Dieman's Land.

Authorities in Van Diemen's Land had been informed that one of the so-called Dorchester Labourers was on board the convict ship and should be identified at once to be brought before the Assistant Police Magistrate and Muster Master, Mr. Thomas Mason. A constable came for Loveless to take him to the police office near the port and told him that he had been allocated the prison number 848 for the duration of his stay and that sometimes this is how he would be addressed.

It took Prisoner 848 some time to re-adjust to walking – or shuffling – on dry land once again and the manacles still clamped around his ankle did not help matters. At the police office Mason was waiting, impatiently pacing up and down. He did not invite the prisoner to sit down. Within minutes of setting foot on dry land for the first time in many weeks the hectoring inquisition he experienced from Dorset magistrates began all over again. Mason began asking 'questions about my father, mother, brothers, sisters, wife and children' before the following exchange took place:

Mason: What is all this about unions? You think of doing great things, I suppose; now tell me what you meant.

Loveless: We meant nothing more, sir, than uniting together to keep up the price of labour and to support each other in the time of need.

Mason: Now I know this to be false; there is some secret design of conspiracy at the bottom, is there not?

Loveless: No sir, quite the reverse; for every man that is a member of the union is under an obligation not to violate the laws.

Mason: Yes; surely I know you mean they are bound not to break any of their own laws.

Loveless: I mean they are under an obligation not to violate the laws of their country.

Mason: I do not believe anything you say about it, there is so much secrecy belonging to it. Now what is that secret sign or signal which the unions knew when to meet all over England at the same time?

Loveless: I do not know of what you are talking, sir.

Mason: You daring fellow, Prisoner 848, you will tell me so again: do not you know that they did meet all over the kingdom at once!

Loveless: I know of no such thing as their having secret signs or signals to know when to meet; I never heard of such a thing before.

Mason: Where were you when they made such a noise then? Be careful in what you say.

Loveless: I understood the union had public meetings at different places, but I was at the *York* hulk, Portsmouth at the time.

Mason: It is no matter where you were, you are one of them Prisoner 848, and you know all about it, and if you do not tell me here and now all and everything about them, I will report you to the Governor, you shall be taken on shore and we shall give you a second trial, and you shall be severely punished; now what are those secrets you are so backward in revealing?

Loveless: I have none to tell, sir.

Mason (getting excited and raising his voice): Now you pretend from a scrupulous conscience you cannot reveal the secret to me; if you have taken an oath not to reveal it, you are sinning against God and man, until you break that oath, and if you still refuse to tell me you shall be severely punished Prisoner 848.

Loveless: I am in your hands, and am ready to and willing to undergo any suffering you shall think proper to inflict upon me rather than say I know anything, when in reality do not.

Mason: That will do. I will report you to the Governor, and you shall be punished 848.

o0o

In 1934, one-hundred years after George Loveless was interrogated by Assistant Police Magistrate Thomas Mason, a long forgotten document was discovered in the Tasmanian Government Archives dated September 5, 1834. The document, headlined 'A Statement by G. Loveless' (which reads more like a confession), relates how 'two delegates whose name I did not know' came from London to meet Tolpiddle's labourers wishing to join the new union. Presumably the delegates were the same two men sent by Robert Owen's Grand National Consolidated Trade Union to explain how the union was to function. Loveless is reported to have said that:

> About 40 others met at the home of Thomas Standfield where a form was read out, of which I could not recall the words but the purpose of which was that all who entered the union should never attempt to violate any law of the Kingdom, that whenever we met together no political or religious subject should be introduced and that we should endeavour to support each other to the best of our abilities whenever we were required on all just and lawful occasions.

The statement also said that Loveless spoke of 'a book' being brought forward and read from, but nobody was allowed to look into it. 'The names of God and Jesus Christ were introduced into the declaration, but in what way I cannot tell: the best I can remember was that it was a sort of prayer calling on God to keep us steadfast in what we had engaged.' He said that the union password was 'Either Hand or Heart' and was to be used on entering lodges. A fund was to be established by each man subscribing a penny or twopence weekly from which they were 'to receive assistance should we be at any time in distress or out of work from our master wanting to reduce our wages – it was understood that we were not to submit to any reduction in wages.'

Loveless explained that three particular men present at the meeting were not tried with the other six men 'presumably because they were the magistrate's own neighbours'. Here Loveless is probably referring to Edward Legg and John Lock who were acting as James Frampton's 'spies.' 'We all wore bandages over our eyes from the time the meeting commenced until it finished. I inquired what was the reason of that and they told me that the mode of initiating members was taken from the Freemasons. I was not aware at the time that I was committing any offence, but I am now convinced that I was deceived by the delegates into committing a breach of the law.'

Loveless was obviously and understandably attempting to be economical with the truth here. He probably did not believe the two 'delegates' had deceived him and his brothers into breaking the law. It is, however, likely that the 'delegates' themselves were as unaware as the Tolpiddle men that swearing an oath could be considered a crime. It is unlikely that a Christian man like Loveless could not remember what was said when words from 'the book' were read out and God and Jesus Christ were mentioned; similarly improbable is that everyone in the room

Lieutenant-General Sir George
Arthur, Governor of Van
Diemen's Land (1823–1837).

GOVERNOR ARTHUR.

was blindfolded with bandages. Only the eyes of men about to be initiated into the union were usually covered.

Van Diemen Land's Lieutenant Governor, George Arthur, dispatched the Loveless 'confession' back to London for the urgent attention of Lord John Russell who rapidly drew the conclusion that the Tolpiddle men were not after all responsible for the 'ritual' performed at the union ceremony – one reason for the severity of their sentences – which was all the fault of 'the union delegates'. In a note attached to the document, Governor Arthur wrote: 'If this statement is to be credited, it is evident that he (Loveless) and his companions have ignorantly become the victims of more artful men.'

From this point George Loveless was no longer suspected of being engaged in a dangerous conspiracy and, after he had worked for a week chained to a road gang, Governor Arthur put him to work on the government farm.

Another result was that Lord John Russell himself had changed his views about the Loveless brothers whom he had hitherto regarded as prime offenders. It was this document that largely influenced him to yield to agitation in England supporting the release of the Dorchester labourers. Letter from George Loveless to his brother James, Port of Hobart, 10 September 1834:

My dear brother,

We left Portsmouth Sunday May 25 about 4 o'clock in the afternoon and arrived safe in this harbour Wednesday September 3, a voyage of 111 days.

'I was examined before the Magistrate yesterday who threatened me with punishment if I did not tell them by what sign the 'trade union' could assemble in bodies all over the Kingdom at once. I know of no such sign and therefore cannot tell. Fear not brother, he that is for me is more than all that is against me. We expect to go on shore tomorrow or the day after. Then there will be the prospect of thanking God from being separated from the company I have been in for the last fourteen weeks.

The convicts were finally disembarked later that day to attend an open-air divine service performed under a giant gum tree by the Chaplain of the penal settlement. The crowd also included the crew and troops from a nearby barracks and, towards the back, Loveless noticed a small number of natives standing some distance away listening intently to the hymns and prayers. They were almost naked, with just a brief loin cloth around their waist, and carried a long spear; many stood balanced on one leg propped upon the other. For most of the congregation recently arrived in Van Dieman's Land, including George Loveless, this was the first time they had ever set eyes on a non-white person.

This new land, populated by thugs, thieves, convicts and strange natives was supposed to be Loveless's home for the next seven years. To him it was not as beautiful as the hills, valleys and fields of home in Dorset and he was homesick for his wife, children, congregation, union 'brothers', fellow farm labourers and his team of cart horses. He was, however, determined to 'make a go of it' in this distant land on the far side of the world. He knew he had come to a tough place; a place where men murdered each other in order to be hanged as a way out of the hell they could no longer bear, where punishments were often indistinguishable from torture, where groups of men attempted an escape by disappearing into the

Hobart viewed from the Government Farm to which George Loveless was assigned after leaving a chain gang building new roads for the fast growing town. (*Tasmanian Government*)

parched bush in groups in the hope that one or two of them might make their way to freedom by devouring their comrades and where lone children of ten were sentenced for stealing a handkerchief and committed suicide as a way of escaping from the sexual predators that surrounded them. Yet, this was a penal system created and imposed by men of gentle and refined manners back in England; men sitting in velvet armchairs sipping fine sherry that conversed with each other in the language of liberty and justice and had recently put down the abominations of the slave trade. These sentences were imposed from a belief that, as the poor were becoming poorer, only a system of severe punishment that was becoming more brutal each year could deter them from crime.

o0o

At daybreak on Friday, 12 September the convicts were woken and told to go onto the top deck to be landed and escorted to the prison barracks. Later that day, still manacled, they were marshalled into the prison yard for inspection by Governor Arthur in the company of the bullying examining magistrate Mason who identified Loveless as 'Prisoner 848 – one of the trades union men'. Mason told the Governor he had already interviewed the prisoner but wanted to arrange another session. Instead, the Governor did some interrogating of his own:

Governor (to Loveless): What a fool you must have been for having anything to do with such things; what object had you in mind for doing so?

Loveless: The motives by which we were influenced were to prevent our wives and families from being utterly degraded and starved.

Governor (outranged): Poh, poh, no such thing! What? Cannot labouring men live by their labour?

Loveless: Not always now, sir.

Governor: I mean good labouring men. Surely they can live comfortable?

Loveless: No sir, times have been in England when labour was well rewarded, but it is not so now; there is many a good willing workman that cannot get employed at all, and others get so little for their labour, that it is impossible for them to live if they have families.

Governor (getting angry again): But you know that you did very wrong, do you not?

Loveless: I had no idea whatever that I was violating any law.

Governor (stamping his feet): But you must know that you have broken the laws, or how came you here?

Hobart, with Mt. Wellington in the background. (*TUC*)

Loveless: By some means or other I was sent here; but I cannot see how a man can break a law before he knows that such a law is in existence.

Governor: You might as well say you have done very wrong and that you acknowledge it and are sorry for it.

Loveless: I cannot do this, sir, until I see it.

On Saturday, 13 September a constable asked for Loveless to be brought out of his cell again and marched him to the police office. On arrival he was taken to a private room where waiting for him was none other than Mr. Mason and a clerk. Mason asked Loveless if he remembered the conversation they had had a few days before. Loveless said that he did. 'Go ahead and repeat it, Prisoner 848,' said Mason. Slowly the convict relayed the story of his village union, his arrest, court appearance and sentence to seven years transportation which the clerk carefully entered into his ledger. Mason then stood up and pushed his face to within an inch of Loveless's and said: 'Go on, reveal your secret to me – NOW!' Without flinching Loveless replied that he had already told him everything that he knew. 'But think now,' said Mason, 'is there something you have not told yet?' Wearily, Loveless replied that he had told him everything adding 'it appears that you know more about it than I do.'

Mason went back to his chair, sat down and looked hard at the prisoner before him: 'Well I have to tell you that you was ordered for severe punishment; you were to work in irons on the roads; but in consequence of the conversation you had with the governor yesterday, his mind is disposed in your favour; he won't allow you to go where you was assigned; he intends to take you to work on his farm.'

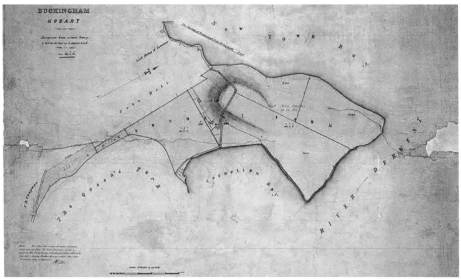

Map of Hobart and the Government Farm where George Loveless was employed as a stockman. (*Archives Office of Tasmania*)

Before being transported to the farm, Loveless was put onto a chain gang building new roads in the growing town of Hobart. There was much to do building the colony of Van Diemen's Land. Convicts with skills were in high demand and assigned to wealthy landowners who treated them well. Convicts without special skills were relegated to road gangs. Doing time with the notorious chain gang was not a normal experience for convicts. The gang was an 1826 colonial innovation designed to break the spirit of those who were insolent or questioned authority. Men were made to break rocks and dig ditches with their ankles chained together; the greater the punishment, the shorter their chain. The pain was excruciating but the threat of the chain gang helped to keep convicts in line.

In the penal settlement of Van Diemen's Land, the overwhelming majority of convicts were assigned to work for property owners who had been granted land across the island and were prepared to pay £1 per head for a convict worker. Before being taken away to work, suitable convicts were brought onto the barracks parade ground and potential masters escorted out to look them over. Convict names were written on a list along with their ages and details about their employment history before being transported. Therefore, a blacksmith could easily be found in one of the many smithies in and around Hobart Town and there was always work for a carpenter or bricklayer. Convict workers wore rough clothing patterned with arrows to show they were government-issue. Their rations were more generous than those served in prison and many convicts later married, settled down and raised families once their prison term was over. There were no bars on their windows and they lived in cottages or out-houses instead of cells.

While the colonial labour market was reliant on convict skills, prisoners received no pay. Carpenters, masons, bricklayers, mechanics, blacksmiths, sawyers, wheelwrights and coopers were particularly valued. Their masters' reliance on their practical abilities gave skilled convicts more power in any bargaining for indulgences. Minor transgressions, such as drunkenness, were often tolerated for fear that magistrates would reassign an accused convict to another property.

Convicts without skills were relegated to work gangs building roads and bridges that connected settlements across the island. The stereotypical image of the convict held true on the chain gang. The penal system was based on a belief that harsh punishment was the key to reforming criminal classes. Under Governor Arthur's authority, chain gangs were introduced as a punishment. The system was invented especially for convicts who dared to be insolent or question authority. The method was found to be effective in curbing recalcitrant behaviour and became an integral part of the punishment system. Soldiers, rather than convict overseers, guarded chain gangs. 'Never were men better worked, better flogged and better managed that they were in the gang,' said a social commentator at the time.

Men working on chain gangs received the following daily rations: 1¼lb bread, a handful of vegetables or one extra loaf of bread, ¼ pint oatmeal, ½lb vegetables, 1lb fresh or salt meat, or 10oz of pork along with ½oz salt and ½oz soap.

Only a small proportion of convicts actually ended up in chain gangs. The majority went into government service if they had suitable skills or were assigned to free settlers as labourers or domestics (often not even locked up at night). Under the new probation system introduced in 1840 men worked in gangs on public works for two years before being allowed to work for wages.

Loveless recalled working 'on the roads with the chain gang in the day and slept in the barracks at night, without a bed or covering; whether any was allowed for me I cannot say, I had none.'

oOo

Penal colonies were expected to provide a degree of 'moral and religious instruction through the medium of sincere and devoted men placed there for the purpose by the government,' wrote James Blackhouse, a missionary and botanist from Yorkshire who spent six years from 1832 visiting prisons in Australia and Van Dieman's Land. Blackhouse discovered that many colonial chaplains in Hobart strongly objected to voluntary Christian philanthropy designed to provide spiritual comfort to prisoners. In 1834 he heard that 'there were strong objections to the labours of a Wesleyan Minister who was a prisoner in Hobart Town and offered to gratuitously visit some of the prisoners weekly without interfering with the duties of chaplains, by whom he was refused.' Unfortunately Blackhouse, who published 'A Narrative of a Visit to the Australian Colonies' about his prison visits to penal colonies in 1843, failed to mention the name of the Wesleyan minister. Could he have been referring to Prisoner 848 George Loveless, the Wesleyan Methodist lay preacher from Tolpiddle, Dorset? Loveless himself never mentioned anything in his later writings about how he went about meeting his own spiritual needs while a prisoner, let alone meeting those of other convicts. There is no doubt that his personal faith remained strong throughout his incarceration, but strange that he never recorded this part of his life and how, and if, he had ever been refused a chance to provide spiritual comfort to other prisoners. If the Wesleyan in question was George Loveless could it be he was prevented from undertaking spiritual calls on other prisoners because he was that wretched union man who refused to reveal the secret oath by which other union men could be called together to bring insurrection upon their masters? Sadly we will never know.

o0o

Fortunately for Loveless, his time working on a chain gang lasted for just over one week and on 22 September he was sent to the government domain farm. The farm was created in an area of Hobart called Cornelian Bay and three miles from town. It was staffed by 30 'trustworthy' convicts with agricultural skills whose leg shackles were removed and whose work was managed by a team of overseers. The farm supplied fresh vegetables, milk and other produce to the residents of Hobart and the town's public institutions including the hospital and jail. A good crop of wheat was produced each year making the farm the colony's major agricultural enterprise and the largest area under cultivation in Van Diemen's Land; by 1834 it comprised 120 acres including 60 acres under crop, 23 acres of which wheat was grown and a further 13 acres under barley.

Most of the colony's livestock was owned by the government and the farm was home to 153 head of cattle and 301 sheep. Buildings on the estate consisted of a dwelling house, barn, cow shed, a piggery, fowl and pigeon houses, a blacksmith's shop, two stalled stables and various ramshackle huts where labourers slept. There were no iron bars or metal doors to keep the prisoners in but high fences surrounded the entire farm both to contain prisoners and exclude wild animals.

An early writer described scenery surrounding the government farm area as:

... most romantic, and will well repay the traveller for the fatigue of his journey. Among the most beautiful places may be mentioned the village of New Town, distant about three miles from Hobart Town, consisting chiefly of gentlemen's houses and properties, well cleared, cultivated, and laid out into gardens and meadows: it is on the bank of the River Derwent, the views of which at this spot are quite charming. This place reminds one of a quiet English village, and it only requires a spire to render the illusion complete.

Loveless was employed at the farm as a stockman and shepherd and he lodged in one of the huts put aside for prisoners on the estate where he found the level of comfort to be as bad as the prison barracks. He recalled:

A small brick building with a tin roof and chimney was George Loveless' home at Government Farm, Hobart. (*On The Convict Trail*)

Eight men, with only five beds, so, of course, the newcomer must go without; and this was my portion until some of the older hands got into trouble and I was entitled to a bed having been longer at the farm than the others…[The hut he slept in] was not of the best: in fine weather we could lie in bed and view the stars, in foul weather feel the wind and the rain; and this added greatly to increase those rheumatic pains which were first brought on by cold irons round the legs and hard lying – and which, in all probability will be my companions until I reach the tomb.

We are now going to leave Prisoner 848 here for the time being to tend his sheep and cattle while we take a look at what was happening back in England in a bid to release the Tolpuddle Six from their sentences at the other end of the world.

A plaque commemorating George Loveless' achievements in Van Diemen's Land was unveiled jointly by the Methodist Conference and Unions Tasmania in 1970. It was originally affixed to the exterior of the Trades Hall building in Davey Street and is now preserved by Unions Tasmania at their North Hobart premises. (*Heritage People, Tasmania*)

Part V

A Shocking Perversion of Justice

April–May 1834

Adieu to you judges and juries,
You justices and bailiffs also,
Seven years you have transported my true-love,
Seven years he's transported you know.

The Tolpiddle men, still on the high seas bound for penal settlements in New South Wales and Van Diemen's Land, were unaware that in their absence scores of meetings and demonstrations were taking place up and down the country denouncing their trial and the severity of their sentences. Numerous editorials were printed in newspapers for and against the sentences. In April 1834 *The Pioneer; or Grand National Consolidated Trades' Union Magazine* said that working people in general – and the Tolpiddle Six in particular – had been intimidated by capitalists, land owners, other men of property, magistrates and judges. It asked:

Why has the cruel, the unjustifiable sentence of transportation been carried into effect against inoffensive beings, so blameless as those victims in

A convict gang go to work on building a new road in Sydney. (*Australian National Archives*)

equity and even in regular law? The answer is plain: it has been done to intimidate us, brethren; and it has been done under the intimidation of capitalists, land-owners, and other men of property, to whom the ministers and the parliament are compelled to be subservient. The present system of government, and the present order of society, cannot be maintained without intimidation on their part. What is their standing army – what is their well-organized police? Are not these instruments of intimidation? And how do they intimidate? Is it not by threats of worse than brutal force? Is it not by a strictly disciplined – a perfected system of murder? Look at the science that they enlisted in the cause of intimidation – listen to the honourable appellations, and view the splendour of apparel, by which their system of intimidating violence is rendered glorious and seductive! When their forces move, blood is shed, and the widow, surrounded by orphans, mourns amid its triumphs. They fill graves, and they boast that they have restored peace. Ours is a very different movement, brethren! Our firm but pacific ranks come forth not to destroy, but to reprove, to enlighten, and to convince! We will not wound the bodies of even our most obstinate enemies; but we will wound and subdue the consciences of those who, proud of the power they at present possess, make the forms of justice a mockery to us, and banish us as felons for the pretended crime of striving, by unity, to maintain the hireling price of our labour. Yes; they who thus, in their cowardly pride of trembling authority, have done this evil – verily, I say unto you, brethren, they must and shall repent!

The meetings, demonstrations and editorials galvanised Robert Owen's Grand National Consolidated Trade Union into action. A Grand Meeting of the Working Classes was arranged for 24 March 1834 and 10,000 people assembled to petition the House of Commons to ask King William IV to suspend the sentence. It also requested that a committee be established to examine the principles and objects of trade unions, which they believed 'were not only just but most praiseworthy'.

The radical MP for Oldham, William Cobbett, presented the petition to Parliament, but it was ordered to lie on the table. Meanwhile a provisional committee was established who met regularly at The Red Lion Tavern, York Street, in St. James Square to arrange demonstrations throughout the country to protest and memorialise the King to remit the sentence. It appealed to all to assist the Committee 'in affording relief to the wives and families of the Dorchester labourers'. Meetings were held across the country at which people contributed money to assist the labourers' families. The radical newspaper *The Pioneer* announced on 12 April 1834 that contributions to relieve distressed families of the Tolpiddle Men had started to arrive from all parts of the country supplemented by contributions from trade unions representing paper stainers, coach painters, trimmers, silk weavers, silk hatters, gardeners, shipwrights, jointers, cordwainers, journeyman tailors, wheelers and brush makers.

Another public meeting was held in London at the Institute, Charlotte Street and appointed a deputation to present a petition to the Home Secretary, Lord Melbourne, 'beseeching the King to exercise his prerogative of mercy, and remit the sentence'. They also wanted Melbourne to understand that he had all too eagerly accepted the blunder of an inexperienced judge. The meeting agreed that a delegation, headed by Dr. Arthur Wade, a Chartist and Church of England clergyman, would call on Melbourne to speak with him in person. Over 12,000 people wanted to join the delegation, but it was agreed that the authorities might deem this 'a breach of the peace' and only a handful accompanied it. According to the trade union and equitable labour exchange newspaper, *The Crisis*:

> Melbourne received the delegation 'in the most affable manner and told them he would take an early opportunity of presenting the material to His Majesty and promised that the execution of the sentence should be stayed until His Majesty's pleasure was known. He also made several enquiries respecting the objects of the unionists and seemed very much affected at the circumstances of 12,000 persons who hoped to attend the deputation but were dissuaded from doing so.'

The petition was duly laid before the king, who turned his back on it and refused any action.

This agitation reflected itself more and more in a changed attitude by MPs who had originally been hostile to demands for the prisoners' return. John Hardy, MP for Bradford had stood up in parliament on 26 March and called trade unions 'a curse'. By 14 April he had changed his views and stated he 'could see no objections to workmen entering into combinations to better their conditions'. Irish political leader Daniel O'Connell, MP for Dublin City, started out as an anti-unionist but by April had declared in favour of shortening the Tolpiddle men's sentences. He also demanded to know why, if trade unions were acting illegally by taking an oath, Freemasons, Orange Lodges, Oddfellows and various other organisations with MPs in their membership were allowed to go scot-free. The little known Society of the Horseman's World was another fraternal society which operated from the 18th through to the 20th centuries. Its members, drawn from those working with horses, passed through a ritual initiation ceremony and swore oaths known only to themselves and people working in agriculture; they appeared, however, to escape the investigations about secret oaths which later did affect Orange Orders, Freemasons and Oddfellows.

A petition signed by over 7,000 people from Kingston-on-Hull was presented in the House of Commons by Liberal politician William Hutt who roundly asserted that the Tolpiddle men had not been punished for taking a secret oath 'but for having been members of a trade union'. Irish Chartist leader Fergus O'Connor told the House that 'the men who should be on board the convict ships in place of the Dorsetshire Labourers were the Prime Minister, the Lord Chancellor and Secretary for the Colonies.' Radical MP for Leeds, Major Aubrey Beauclerk, presented a petition to the House pleading that there 'ought not to be one law for the rich and another for the poor'. Parliamentary radical, Joseph Hume, MP for Middlesex stood up on the floor of the House and earnestly exhorted that parliament should redress 'the cruel and unjust act that had been perpetrated'. John Roebuck, the Independent MP for Bath, argued that the law the Tolpiddle men were

William Cobbett, MP for Oldham, was one of many parliamentarians who presented petitions to the House of Commons calling for a return of the Tolpiddle men. (*National Portrait Gallery*)

supposed to have broken 'was so obscure that many lawyers are in ignorance of its existence. Half the legal profession think the sentence is not legal and all will acknowledge that the law has been most severely administered.' Roebuck accused the government of 'hurrying the men off to transportation to prevent the general expression of public sympathy from having any effect in their favour.'

But the mother of parliaments failed to be impressed with these speeches and petition after petition was left to 'to lay on the table'. The government, far from remitting the punishment, refused to even recognise that it was excessive and left the unfortunate labourers to proceed to their penal exile. Agitation, however, continued and grew steadily in volume attracting more people who realised that a shocking perversion of justice had taken place. On 17 April an advertisement on page four of *The Times* informed readers:

> Dorchester Labourers – A public meeting will be held at the Crown and Anchor Tavern in The Strand tomorrow at 7 o'clock in the evening to Petition the King on behalf of the Six Agricultural Labourers recently convicted at Dorchester. Issued by Colonel Sir George De Lacey Evans, MP.

The Times was present at the meeting and reported that long before admission time 'the great room of the tavern was crowded to suffocation' with over 3,000 people gathering. Those who failed to get into the room crowded onto stairs, inside passageways and spilled onto the street outside. At the meeting the charismatic Irish nationalist leader Daniel O'Connell remarked that he was 'glad to see so numerous, so respectable and so imposing a meeting as the one he had the honour of addressing'. He added: 'As a lawyer I have the gravest of doubts about the legality of the conviction and I am determined that my object is not to be defeated by such tricks....I am decidedly of the opinion that the government has made an error in sending these innocent men out of the country before an appeal could be made to the court of the King's Bench and I think it is their duty to send an express after these people and bring them back to their homes.'

O'Connell stated that Judge Baron Williams had contended that he had no alternative but to sentence the men to seven years transportation once they had been found guilty. He thundered: 'He might, in his discretion, have affixed the sentence at any length from one day to seven years but he thought fit to inflict the highest penalty.' John Roebuck, MP said that 'speaking as a lawyer I can confirm that the men were not only morally but legally innocent.' Roebuck expressed astonishment at the news that the government had sent the men away 'in such indecent haste to New South Wales'. He added: 'It would have been more decent to have allowed them to remain in this country in order that their case might have been argued in the House of Commons or in the Court of King's Bench.' Lord Melbourne responded with a statement from his office expressing an opinion that 'the law, in this case, has been most properly applied' and the sentence carried out 'with special celerity'.

Masonic and Orange lodges across the country went into panic expecting to be raided by police constables at any time and their members arrested for swearing illegal oaths. The first to abolish secret oaths was the Masonic Grand Lodge of Scotland; its former Grand Master, the 5th Duke of Gordon (described in *The Times* as 'the most hated and unpopular man in all England') put an end to all oath taking on Masonic premises. He was swiftly followed by the Board of the Independent Order of Oddfellows whose Chairman, Thomas Armitt, wrote the following letter to the editor of the *Manchester Guardian:*

> Sir, I can inform you that previous to the committal of the Dorchester Unionists, an oath was administered to every new initiated member, of course without the knowledge that such an act was illegal; but at the first annual general meeting of the order after that occurrence, a law was passed forbidding the administration of an oath, either at the initiation of a new member or at any subsequent period; and no such oath in any shape is now taken.

After decades of secret oath taking, no one from the Masonic or Oddfellows orders was arrested, cautioned, fined or even challenged. The only people to fall foul of the 'illegal act' was six poor agricultural labourers from an obscure Dorset village who, merely hoping to improve their wages in return for their labour, were arrested and sent to the other side of the world for uttering secret oaths at their initiation ceremonies. They had committed no crime but paid the price and were chained to hardened criminals. Such was British law in the fourth decade of the nineteenth century when self-important land owners could stamp on the lower classes and punish anyone who did not please them or had the audacity to ask for more money.

Chapter 14

A Petition to the King

Monday April 21, 1834

March! March! Comrades in Freedom now,
On let us march to the music of Order!
All the nation from cowmen to ploughmen
Are united in their cry to 'bring home the labourers' – now!

The Grand National Consolidated Trades Union proved to have a wider influence than the government expected. The whole machinery of the organisation was turned over to the preparation of further petitions to parliament, arranging more public mass meetings and creating waves of sympathy for the Tolpiddle men. *The Times* wrote leader after leader condemning further petitioning and rabble-rousing meetings.

By 1834 London's Copenhagen Fields was a popular venue for radical demonstrations and agitation. Protest meetings were attended by crowds of over 100,000 and rioting often followed. *The Times* referred to the area as 'the old rendezvous of disturbance'. On Monday, 21 April in Copenhagen Fields – close to where King's Cross station now stands – members of London-based trade unions began assembling early in the morning 'in very large numbers to express their feelings on the case of the Dorchester Labourers, and to adopt a form of petition to the King for remission of the terrible sentence passed on them,' wrote *The True Sun*, a pro-Whig evening newspaper. 'This meeting, so great in point of numbers, was characterised by propriety and peacefulness of bearing and yet by the same fixed, rigid and uncompromising determination to persevere in the accomplishment of their object.'

A green plaque in honour of the Tolpuddle Martyrs and those who fought for their release by marching from Copenhagen Fields was recently unveiled. (*London Borough of Islington*)

The Grand National Consolidated Trades Union hired London's Copenhagen Fields from where a gigantic procession through London's streets carried a petition with 800,000 signatories to Lord Melbourne calling for the return of the Tolpuddle Men. (*Jackdaw – The Early Trade Unions*)

Robert Owen had officially rented Copenhagen Fields so a gigantic procession could take place on private, union hired property free of police intervention. Owen made an appointment to see Lord Melbourne to give him full advance details of his intentions and the route the procession would take. Melbourne, naturally, disapproved of the plan but received Owen 'with his accustomed courtesy' and told him he would be at the office from 11:00am to 5:00pm on the day. Melbourne was already acquainted with the case through his brother-in-law, William Ponsonby, who lived in Dorset and had been foreman of the grand jury which sentenced the Tolpiddle men to transportation for seven years.

London's Chief Magistrate, Frederick Roe, had 2,500 copies of a poster printed and displayed all over London directed at:

... the great number of persons who intend to assemble on Monday 21st April with the intention of accompanying in procession and array, through the streets of the Metropolis, with a Deputation to present to the Secretary of State a petition addressed to the King and Whereas such a Meeting and such Proceedings are highly improper and objectionable, calculated to excite terror in the minds of the peaceable and well disposed Inhabitants of the Metropolis, and may prove dangerous to the public peace as well as to the individuals enjoyed in them: The Magistrates of the Police Officers hereby warn all classes of His Majesty's subjects of the danger to which they will expose themselves by attending such a meeting, or taking any part in such proceedings. The Magistrates also enjoin Masters to prevent their Apprentices, Workers and Servants from being present at such a meeting.

Owen and members of the Central Committee visited the Metropolitan Police to furnish them with details of the procession and assure them that the protest would be peaceful and not troublesome. The police told Owen they had instructions to protect both the procession and property of people watching from pavements. Melbourne, however, drafted in detachments of Lancers, the Queen's Bays and the Royals plus eight battalions of infantry and 'twenty nine pieces of ordinance' from Woolwich barracks. Their job was to 'stand discreetly out of sight in readiness in case of emergency'. Five thousand extra special constables were drafted in alongside 2,812 policemen to be stationed through all parts of the city. A special guard was also posted outside the Bank of England.

On the morning of the march, the Whiggish *Morning Chronicle* told its readers that 'the march's intent can only be to intimidate and overawe the legal authorities by an ostentatious display of physical force.' This did not deter thousands of people turning out to witness the demonstration. The exact number who turned out to protest that day depends on which newspaper you read at the time. The *Times* calculated that 35,000 people were involved while *The True Sun's* estimate was that 200,000 individuals had assembled. The latter figure may well have been true if spectators on the streets are included.

At the centre of the demonstration a huge petition signed by 800,000 people from across the country was to be carried through London's streets by twelve bearers to Lord Melbourne's Home Department in a special light wagon festooned with blue and red calico. On top of the wagon was an ornate iron frame containing the petition mounted on a wooden spool.

By 8:00am roads leading to Copenhagen Fields were packed with members of different union lodges all wearing crimson ribbons, including tailors 'distinguished by the jauntiness of their appearance', blacksmiths and metal workers 'a little dingy', coal-heavers 'in their frocks and fan-tails', and silk weavers whose appearance 'told a tale of squalid misery which every man must regret to know exists'.

Each union had its own place on either side of the dirt road that ran down the centre of Copenhagen Fields and each placed banners prominently so latecomers could find their way to where their brothers were positioned. Thirty-five banners on top of long poles were on show fluttering in the wind on this bright spring day. By 9:00am the field was full of people and *The Times* reported that the scene 'was most imposing; the utmost decorum prevailed and the *coup d'oeil* [the look] was most striking, inasmuch as it bore so strong a semblance of military array, discipline and good order'.

A rocket was fired into the air at 9:30am signalling the procession to start. In front were horsemen, including one bearing the portly figure of Joseph Hume wearing a top hat and riding a white horse. This was followed by the Central Committee of the Metropolitan Trades Union, including tin plate workers, masons, carpenters, plasterers, bricklayers, masons' labourers, cordwainers, wood sawyers, blacksmiths, glassblowers, silk hatters, leather workers, tailors, gold beaters and farriers. They were followed by twelve bearers carrying the petition and delegation members who were to present it to Lord Melbourne. Among these were Robert Owen and the corpulent figure of Dr. Arthur Wade 'chaplain to the Metropolitan Trades Unions' who wore his best clerical robes and the scarlet hood of a Doctor of Divinity.

The procession followed with the crowd marching five and six abreast with military precision on a pre-arranged route from Copenhagen Fields through to Russell Square into Tottenham Court Road, along Oxford Street, down Regent Street into Waterloo Place, along Pall Mall to Charing Cross into Whitehall and then to the Home Department. They marched in total silence, never uttering a word and looking straight ahead. London's streets were lined with tens of thousands of people and shops and businesses came to a standstill. The procession was greeted by cheers from spectators in the streets and leaning out of upstairs windows. When, however, they noticed the procession was marching in silence, they, too, fell silent and the only sound to be heard was boots, shoes and horse's hooves tramping down the road. Said *The Times*: 'The unionists themselves seemed anxious not only to maintain order themselves, but to set an example of peace, discipline and decorum to the bystanders.' A number of Members of both Houses of Parliament were spotted in the crowds witnessing 'with astonishment the peaceable conduct of the unionists'.

Robert Owen and his horse left the procession at Tottenham Court Road and took a short-cut to Whitehall to be at the Home Department before the rest of the procession arrived. Earlier that morning Owen had received a written message from Melbourne stating that following much thought he was not prepared to receive any deputation backed by an army of supporters on the grounds that it would appear that he did so under duress. Owen hoped to persuade the indifferent Melbourne otherwise, but on arrival at the Home Department he was refused entry and told he would not be granted an audience with anyone. Meanwhile the huge procession advanced closer.

Owen insisted that he be admitted into Melbourne's presence and eventually Viscount Henry Howick, Melbourne's Under Secretary of State came to the door just as the deputation was approaching. A deputation member said they wished to have an audience with Lord Melbourne; Viscount Henry replied that, despite being in the building, he was unable to receive them. He said he could not receive the petition because there was such a large body men accompanying it. He informed them that Melbourne had seen a copy of the petition at his recent meeting with Owen 'and did not disapprove of the language of it and that if the petition should be presented on another day, and in a becoming manner, he would receive it and lay it before the King.' Howick then dismissed the deputation 'politely but decisively'. Melbourne witnessed all of this while watching secretly from a discreet front window at the Home Department and quietly sent word down to the petition bearers that they may, if they wished, leave by the back door and procure a coach to convey the petition away without anyone noticing.

The procession continued to march down Whitehall and across Westminster Bridge towards a vacant piece of ground opposite Bethlehem Hospital and on to Kennington Common where it peacefully dispersed. A few days later *The Pioneer* wrote: 'Last Monday was a day in Britain's history which long will be remembered; for labour put its hat upon its head and walked towards the throne. It is most gratifying to add that not the slightest appearance of disorder was witnessed during the whole day.'

The following day *The Times* wrote: 'The procession of trades unions yesterday passed off, thank God, without the slightest approach to disturbance. For this the metropolis is no doubt indebted partly to the seasonable and earnest warnings of the daily press.'

The massive petition was finally accepted by the Home Department without any fuss a few days later and on 28 April the Central Committee received what the *True Sun* said was 'another of those evasive and unmeaning answers....The King has not yet been pleased to issue any commands thereupon.' The reason is probably because the King had not even bothered to read the petition's contents. Had he done so he would have read:

To the King's most excellent Majesty:-

The petition of the undersigned, humbly sheweth that six men named James Loveless, George Loveless, Thomas Standfield, John Standfield, James Hammett and James Brine, all common agricultural labourers, or farm servants, has been convicted at Dorchester of administering an illegal oath. That –

The said six men, with others, were members of a Trade Club or Society, called the Friendly Society of Agricultural Labourers –

The object of the Society was to maintain the wages of farm servants –

The rules of the Society are similar to other Trade Societies and do not violate any law –

Many Societies, composed of highly respectable, honourable and dignified persons, have similar rules –

Your Petitioners do not, however, approve of any Society, whether it be called Agricultural or Freemason, or any other name whatever, which has any secret proceedings –

Your Majesty's Petitioners are of the opinion that Clubs or Societies of Farm Servants, free from all secret proceedings, would be the means of diffusing improvement among a class of your Majesty's subjects who are greatly in need of information, and would tend to put an end to incendiary fires –

The large number of such fires, and the immense destruction of property during the last four years, would not have taken place, had farm servants been congregated in Clubs, as tradesmen and mechanics have been –

Words of the oath administered by the six poor, uninstructed men, if made one of the articles of the Club, would not, however improper, be a violation of any law –

The poor, ignorant, unfortunate men who have been convicted, declared upon their trial, in writing, that if they had done anything in violation of the Act of Parliament, it was quite unintentional –

There is a wide difference between the conduct of these poor ignorant men who did not intentionally break any law and those hardened miscreants whose practice is knowingly to break the laws continually –

The sentence of seven years transportation is the same as is frequently passed on atrocious criminals for the commission of crimes of great enormity –

Under the late regulations, transportation has been made a very severe punishment in our penal colonies, to which none ought to be subjected but those whose habits are inimical to civilised society, and your Majesty's Petitioners believe that the recently ordered severity is intended for such persons, and not for men who may have committed and offence in ignorance –

The punishment of transportation is greatly too severe for farm servants, who have not become demoralised reckless criminals –

The horrible sufferings of the farm servants, criminals as they were, were not intended to be inflicted; and it is to save these men, whose conduct is much less criminal, and scarcely more than venial, from such horrible sufferings, that your Majesty's Petitioners now pray for mercy.

Your Majesty's Petitioners are satisfied that a remission of further punishment, with suitable admonition and caution, will greatly tend to put an end to all illegal proceedings, secrecy and oaths in Trade Societies to produce a better understanding between labourers and their employees, and put an end to all attempts to fire stacks and barns, the prevalence of which your Majesty's Petitioners do most deeply deplore.

Your Majesty's Petitioners therefore most humbly pray, that for these reasons, and that because the conviction of the six unfortunate men is the first which has recently taken place, that your Majesty will be pleased to remit the sentence passed on these men, causing such admonition to be given, as may be honourable to your Majesty's Government, merciful to the poor men and tend to the well-being of the whole of your Majesty's subjects.

And your Petitioners will ever pray.

o0o

The authorship of this bloated document is unknown; it might even have been prepared by 'a committee' whose members each had a hand in constructing its overblown contents. It is little wonder that the King took his time to read it; in fact he probably failed to read it but instructed one of his minions to do so and make recommendations. Whatever the King's involvement, the petition failed and a great many more petitions, demonstrations, speeches, debates and newspaper articles would be needed before the Tolpiddle men were finally brought home.

Chapter 15

Botany Bay

1834–1837

Come all you young fellows wherever you be,
Who delight in a song; join in chorus with me,
I will sing you a new song, which was made the other day
Concerning five poor lads sent to Botany Bay.

In August 1786 a decision was made to send a colonisation party of convicts, military and civilian personnel to Botany Bay under the command of Admiral Arthur Phillip who was to be Governor of the new colony. The six convict ships held 775 convicts and a further 645 people including officials, crew members, marines and their families joined the convoy. In all, eleven naval ships were sent on what became known as the First Fleet which was accompanied by a further two naval escorts and three provisioning ships. The fleet sailed from Portsmouth on 13 May 1787 and arrived at Botany Bay on 20 January 1788.

It soon became clear that it would be impossible to establish a colony at Botany Bay due to 'the openness of this bay, and dampness of the soil, by which people would probably be rendered unhealthy'. Admiral Phillip decided to examine Port Jackson, another bay a few miles north, mentioned by Captain Cook in his 1770 journal as a possible alternative.

Here Admiral Phillip stumbled upon one of the finest harbours in the world 'in which a thousand sails of the line might ride in perfect security'. Different coves around the harbour were examined and preference given to one which offered fresh spring water and where ships could anchor so close to the shore that quays could be built at which the largest vessels in the fleet could unload. The cove was about half a mile in length, and a quarter of a mile across the entrance. It was named Sydney Cove in honour of Thomas Townshend, 1st Viscount Sydney, President of the Committee on Trade and Foreign Plantations under Prime Minster William Pitt the Younger.

Here the first permanent European colony on the Australian continent was established and named New South Wales. Food shortages initially caused a high mortality rate among the new arrivals. Ships only carried sufficient provisions for settlers until they could establish their own agriculture in the region. Unfortunately, with insufficient skilled farmers and domestic livestock, the colony waited on the arrival of the Second Fleet which disastrously provided little help when it arrived in June 1790 with a cargo of sick and dying convicts.

All but one of the Tolpiddle men wrote of their hardships under the hands of prison staff, overseers and farm owners when they reached the new colony. The exception was James Hammett who was always the odd fellow in the group and, perhaps, could not write but could certainly read. In Australia the four others recorded their stories about the life and hard times of a convict in New South Wales.

John and Thomas Standfield's Story:

On 27 March 1834, and following 'our mock trial and harsh sentence,' John Standfield, his father Thomas, James Hammett, James Brine and James Loveless were ironed together at Dorchester prison and taken to a waiting coach. They were told they were to be taken to Portsmouth where they arrived in front of the convict hulk *York* at eight o'clock that night. Their Dorchester irons were removed and fresh manacles fitted to their ankles. They spent two days on the *York* before being transferred to the *Surrey* bound for Botany Bay which weighed anchor on 31 March with 200 convicts on board and sailed from Portsmouth to Plymouth to collect a further sixty men before departing for New South Wales on 11 April.

John Standfield recalled:

I then began to feel the misery of transportation – confined down with a number of the most degraded and wretched criminals, each man having to contend with his fellow or be trodden under foot. The rations, which were served daily, were of the worst quality and very deficient in quantity owing to the peculations indulged in by those officers whose duty it is to attend to that department. In addition to this, the crowded state of the vessel, rendering it impossible for prisoners to lie down at full length to sleep, the noxious state of the atmosphere and the badness and saltiness of the provisions, induced disease and suffering which it is impossible to describe. Added to this, in the case of myself and brethren, the agonising reflection that we had done nothing deserving this punishment and the consciousness that our families, thus suddenly deprived of their protectors and a stigma affixed to our names, would probably be thrown unpitied and friendless upon the world.

John Standfield mentions nothing in his recollections about the perils of the outbound voyage or the ports visited on route. His next entry states that after

THE LANDING of the CONVICTS at BOTANY BAY

Transported convicts landed at Botany Bay after a long voyage. (*From Captain Watkin Tench's* A Narrative of the Expedition to Botany Bay)

a voyage lasting over 100 days the *Surrey* arrived in Sydney of 17 August and on 4 September they were taken ashore and marched four-a-breast to Hyde Park Barracks 'where we found about 300 (what they called) old hands – men, if possible, worse than those with whom we had already been associated'.

The Tolpiddle men had already been assigned to their respective masters before coming ashore and three hours after arriving in the barracks John Standfield was summoned by a messenger to proceed to his master. The following day his father and James Loveless were also sent for and as John ran to say goodbye to them 'my little bundle of necessities was stolen from me'.

He later recalled:

I went to the clerk's office and after much entreaty he gave me directions where I might find my father. I was then forwarded to my master, Mr. Richard Jones MLC [Member of the Legislative Council] in Sydney, in which place I remained for five days before sending me to the *Sophia Jane* steam-boat to proceed to one of his farms on the Hunter's River, called Balwarra [it was, in fact, named Bolwarra] 150 miles from Sydney; and on the following day I arrived at my journey's end, being a farm three miles from the rising town of Maitland.

This large estate and country house had been acquired by Richard Jones – a wealthy merchant, whale fishery owner and importer of Saxon sheep. He founded The Bank of Australia in 1826, was president of The Bank of New South Wales in 1828 and appointed to the Legislative Council in 1829.

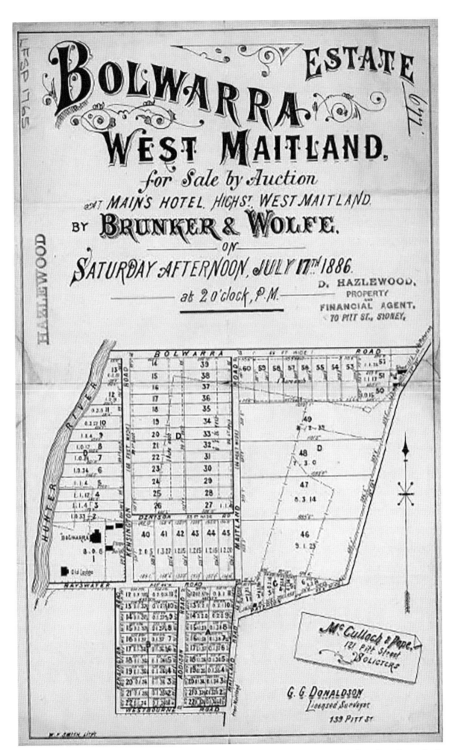

A map of Bolwarra Estate, owned by wealthy merchant Richard Jones, 150 miles from Sydney. (*National Library of Australia*)

The *Sophia Jane* steamboat transported James Loveless from Sydney to Bolwarra to work at Richard Jones' property. (*Painting by Dickson Gregory, courtesy of the State Library of Victoria*)

Mr. Jones' Bolwarra property was described by a visitor as:

> ... a well cultivated farm that is beautifully situated, one that would answer the pretensions of a respectable family. It possesses an extensive water frontage to the silvery waters of the Hunter River and a much more extensive frontage along the public high roads towards Paterson. All the cleared land is fenced in (containing 60 different fields of various sizes), and the estate has been opened to Mr. Jones' taste and improvement. A snug shingled house, with two rooms and a store stands in the grounds. The soil is rich, alluvial flooded land.

After Standfield had been at the farm for three weeks he was given permission to visit his father who was working alone on another farm three miles away on the Williams River. When he arrived he was told his father was 'somewhere in the bush' tending a flock of sheep. It took a few hours to locate him and when he stumbled across Thomas Standfield by accident, he 'found him in great distress'. Thomas related to his son some of the sufferings he had gone through in a vast landscape where it was like standing on the edge of the world looking into another. Thomas Standfield was now working as a shepherd with a flock of six hundred sheep which he had to lead into the bush several miles away from the farm owner. The bush was an immense forest of trees and brushwood with clear spots onto which sheep were driven. It was not unknown for newly arrived prisoners working as shepherds to become lost in the outback and to mislay their sheep. This could last for several days during which time they faced danger from aborigines and hunger. They were provided with a single day's rations when out with the sheep. On their return, sheep were counted by an overseer and any found missing resulted in the poor shepherd being flogged. The great quantity of sheep, however, made counting them impossible; if any went missing or were stolen by natives the overseer would have been none the wiser.

The next time John Standfield saw his father 'he was then a dreadful spectacle, covered with sores from head to foot and weak and helpless and a child.' Young Standfield went to inspect the place where his father slept, a tiny wooden hut 6ft by 18ins known as a 'watch box' containing a small bed and one blanket, a place where he 'could lie and gaze upon the starry heavens, where the wind blew in at one end and out of the other, with nothing to ward off the peltings of the pitiless storm'. Inside the 'comforts' of the watch box he encountered an infestation of blowflies and the stink of hides. Standfield senior had, furthermore, to walk four miles every night for his rations.

A visitor to the bush in the Maitland area in the 1830s said that life in the outback 'could have a hallucinatory strangeness for men fresh from England'. He said that convict quarters in the bush, similar to that housing Thomas Standfield, were a cross between a zoo and an Irish cabin with

> ... a multitude of noisy parrots, intended for sale; pet kangaroos and opossums, and a wide variety of kangaroo dogs, greyhounds and sheepdogs; on the fire was a huge boiler filled with the flesh of kangaroo, and close by were suspended the hind quarters of another of these animals. In one corner was a large pan of milk; in another a number of skins partially dried; while a few feet from the ground were the filthy bed-places or cribs of the people themselves.

Standfield junior visited his father at regular intervals for nine months until Thomas was moved to another station on the Williams River 30 miles away. John's overseer would not permit his best worker to go so far from Balwarra 'thinking it too great an indulgence'.

On 25 January 1836 young Standfield was sitting in his hut trying to devise a plan by which he could get to see his father when a constable appeared in the doorway. He said he had orders to move him to Maitland to be joined by his father. When he arrived orders were given that he should be sent to the lock-up – a small room used as a prison in a small town, in which criminals could be kept for a short time – where he lay that day and the following night. Next morning he asked the jail keeper to let him go to the court house to find out what was to become of him and to ask for some food. The keeper said he was not due to be fed as there were stated periods for prisoners to receive food and clothing – periods known as 'dues'. He would, therefore, have to wait until he had been in the lock-up for two days before being fed. When the time arrived for him to visit the court house, he was escorted by two constables. On arrival he found his father waiting under the charge of his own constable. The magistrate would not give the men any further information and sent them back to the lock-up for a further two nights with a little bread and water but no beds or blankets.

Early on the second day orders were given for Standfield and son to get ready to board a steamer to Newcastle 100 miles away. They were joined by eight other prisoners and chained two-a-breast. John asked for food for his father and himself but was told they would be provided with something on arrival. They asked when might that be but received no answer. Once on the steam boat John asked if his father could be unlocked from his chains but the constable refused. They remained in that state until they reached Newcastle where they were taken from the boat and marched to jail 'and examined in the usual form'. John asked for food only to be told 'you ought to have got that where you came from'. The Standfields were now exhausted. They were locked in jail for three days and nights before being taken on another steamer to Sydney. They were given mamony meal (Indian corn) for breakfast and told they would be given dinner at the end of their journey. By this time John Standfield was beginning to lose his temper. A constable appeared and tried to put handcuffs on his wrists. Standfield stood up and told him very firmly where to put his handcuffs and demanded to be informed why he and his father were locked in irons. He asked the constable if he was aware they had not committed any crime and could conduct themselves properly without being handcuffed. The jailor was taken aback and muttered something about not seeing any necessity to lock them in irons 'but I must act in accordance with my directions'. He was then handcuffed to his father and a stranger.

On the rough crossing to Sydney all the prisoners were sick 'but not one of our hands was loosened to help ourselves'. They arrived in Sydney at nine o'clock in the evening and marched to the common jail in George Street. After a week of starvation, cold, hungry and without beds or blankets, they were locked up to lie on cold flagstones for two nights.

Some 100 convicted criminals were in the same jail waiting to receive judgement from the Criminal Court. On the second morning all were allowed out into the courtyard and arranged in uniform order and twenty men were picked at random to attend court that day; Thomas and John Standfield were two of them. The 'lucky' twenty men were chained and handcuffed together and marched through Sydney's streets 'like a lot of wild beasts'. But instead of going to the courthouse, the Standfields were taken to Hyde Park Barracks and put into the watch house

– a place where people under arrest were held in custody. Their request for food was refused and they remained in the watch house for two days and nights. In desperation John demanded to see the barracks superintendent who, much to their surprise, appeared outside their cell. 'Sir, do you know the reason of our being confined in this miserable place, as we are not criminals?' he asked. 'I am determined to go out, and if we are not released I shall seek for further redress.' Next morning they were permitted to breathe fresh air in the barrack-yard.

For ten days the Standfields had not been able to wash, shave, change their clothing, sleep on a bed with a blanket, eat anything substantial or hear any kind of explanation as to why they were being taken from one place to another. They demanded answers and were told that their orders had originated from 'the home government' – in other words, the British government back in London — who instructed that 'all the Dorsetshire trade unionists were to be treated with the utmost severity and receive especially harsh treatment from their masters.'

So the Tolpiddle men were singled out for 'special treatment' as an example to anyone else prepared to swear an illegal oath. Their punishment would be severe, harsh and cruel on orders from judges, magistrates and lawyers at home in England. Who were the faceless men who had made these decisions? On what grounds were they made? How did they arrive as such judgements?

After being incarcerated at the barracks for a few days more, they were sent to work with one of the work gangs engaged in building roads, causeways, bridges, courthouses and hospitals in the rapidly expanding city of Sydney. To their surprise they were joined by James Brine and James Loveless before suddenly being removed from the gangs and confined to barracks for the next month.

The four Tolpiddle men were eventually summoned to appear before the principal superintendent who took them by surprise by saying that 'the home government has granted you a conditional pardon at the expiration of three years from your arrival in the colony and an order has been received from the governor that you are to proceed to the penal settlement at Port Macquarie for twelve months until His Majesty's further pleasure should be made known.' The authorities wanted James Loveless to agree to his wife and children being brought out and promised to allow him to receive them on their arrival. Notwithstanding their threats, promises and entreaties he refused consent.

John Standfield 'did not like the idea of going to Port Macquarie' and on 10 March 1836, he sent a letter to the governor requesting that, instead of being sent to Macquarie, he be returned to his former master in Balwarra or go with his father wherever he was sent – but not back to shepherding in the remote bush. The second request was granted and on 16 March they left the barracks without their companions James Brine and James Loveless. They had no information about the fate of James Hammett or George Loveless.

The Standfields were taken to Mr. Timothy Nowlan's Farm, at Hunter's River, a remote 2,000 acre government-sponsored sheep breeding station near Maitland. They were put in charge of a large flock of sheep with orders to watch over them night and day. Young Standfield also had to walk six miles daily to collect rations for his father and himself from the farm and another six miles back. During the time they were there, Thomas Standfield had a severe illness after being caught out in a storm and was confined to bed for two months.

After nine months on the Nowlan sheep station John Standfield was casually informed by another farm worker that George Loveless had been sent to Van Dieman's Land. Now he could be sure that the remaining five Tolpiddle men were still serving sentences for crimes they did not commit in different parts of New South Wales and in Van Dieman's Land. But although they might be suffering in different ways, they were all still alive in the same part of the world.

James Brine's Story:

At the age of 21, James Brine was the youngest of the Tolpuddle Six to be transported – but was far from being the youngest to be taken from England to a place of punishment at the other side of the world. The youngest to be sentenced was a boy of 7 accused of stealing some clothing and in 1814 alone five children aged 11, seven aged 12, seventeen aged 13, thirty-two aged 14 and sixty-five aged 15 were transported to Australia for a minimum of seven years. Their crimes were minor by today's standards – stealing small amounts of money, picking pockets, burglary and petty theft. Their sentences were decided by magistrates and judges whose judgements depended on their whim on a particular day. On a good day they might receive a week in jail or even a good telling off; but on others they could be sentenced to a hanging or the relatively new punishment of seven years transportation to a penal colony in Australia. In 1812 of the 4,659 people who were transported 1,116 were aged less than 21.

After arriving in Sydney on 4 September 1834 Brine was assigned to Dr. James Mitchell, a Scots-born physician and surgeon at the Government Hospital. After a short time, at the request of Mitchell who had business interests in the Hunter River area, he was transferred to the farm of Robert Scott, a magistrate in Glendon in the Hunter River Valley for six months.

To reach his destination, Brine, like the rest of his comrades, made his own way by ferry and on foot. His overnight sea journey took him from Sydney to Morpeth, from where he had a 30 mile hike to the small settlement of Glendon. Brine's Master, Mr. Scott had arranged for his new farm hand to be supplied with a small roll up bed and a blanket to take on the journey plus a shilling to cover expenses. He was kitted out with new 'slops' – a pair of prison-issue trousers made from calico, a shirt of striped cotton and a jacket made from grey wool. In Brine's mind Mr. Scott sounded like an agreeable fellow and he looked forward to meeting him.

Shortly after arriving in New South Wales, James Brine was assigned to the farm owned by Robert Scott, a magistrate at Glendon in the Hunter River region. (*State Library of New South Wales*)

On arrival in Morpeth 'weary and fatigued, I laid down to take rest under a gum-tree.' Brine fell into a deep slumber and, while he dreamt of home, 'bushrangers' – a group of ne'er-do-wells who had abandoned social rights and privileges to take up robbery under arms using the bush as their base – came across his sleeping body. They 'robbed me of all I possessed and helped themselves to my shoes, new 'slops' and the small amount of food I brought to eat on my journey, leaving me with the old clothes I was sleeping in and first issued in Portsmouth before leaving England.'

On September 7 a barefooted Brine limped onto the Glendon estate 'exhausted from want of food, having had but one meal for three days'. Here he saw a fine stone house built for Mr. Scott by convict labour, containing six large rooms connected by a wide wooden verandah. The house was the centrepiece of the Glendon Estate and sat in the middle of the 80,000 acre farm, home to 300 horses, 9,000 head of horned cattle and thousands of sheep. There was also an extensive garden, stables, stores, workshops and a collection of small huts to house convicts.

Brine was met by the overseer, William Moody, also a convict, and taken to meet 'the master', Mr. Scott, who immediately demanded to know where his 'slops' and bedding were. Brine told him that bushrangers had robbed him but Scott swore that he was a liar and said he 'would give me a dammed good flogging in the morning'. This was not what Brine was expecting and was taken aback by Scott's angry attitude towards him. He was even more surprised by Scott's next remark: 'You are one of the Dorsetshire machine breakers, but you are caught at last.'

He gave Brine nothing to eat until the following day when he was employed to dig post holes in the hard stony ground. Scott came to visit Brine several times that day to ask how he was getting along. Brine said, 'I am doing as well as I can but not able to do much through weakness and that having walked so far without shoes, my feet are so cut and sore I cannot put them to the spade.' On hearing this Scott erupted: 'If you utter another word of complaint I will put you in the lock up; and if you ask me for an article for six months to come, or if you do not do your work like other men, or not attend to the overseer's orders, whatever they may be, I will send you up to Mr. Moody, where no mercy shall be shown you.' Brine found a piece of hoop iron (used for binding the staves of casks or tubs) on the ground and wrapped it around his foot and for the next six months went without shoes, clothes and bedding, laying on the bare ground at night.

Shortly after this angry exchange took place, Brine was sent to the pool to wash sheep and for the next seventeen days worked 'up to my breast in water. I thus caught a severe cold and having told my master that I was very ill, asked him if he would be so good as to provide cover for me at night, if it were only a piece of horsecloth.' 'No!' barked Scott. 'I will give you nothing until you are due for it. What would your masters in England have had to cover them if you had not been sent here? I understand it was your intention to have murdered, burnt and destroyed everything before you, and you are sent over here to be severely punished, and no mercy shall be shown you. If you ask me for anything before the six months is expired, I will flog you as often as I like.'

Scott then demanded that Brine explain to him the designs of the union 'and said if I would tell him it would be a good thing for me as he would try to get me a ticket of indulgence [allowing prisoners various privileges in return for good conduct]. I told him I knew nothing of what he was talking, and that the unions had no idea of murdering, burning or destroying.' Scott went red in the face and yelled: 'You know all about it and it will be better for you to tell me.' Brine repeated that he had nothing to communicate. Scott grabbed him by the collar and pulled his face close to Brine's. 'You dammed convict,' he spat. 'If you persist in this obstinacy and insolence, I will severely punish you! Don't you know that not even the hair on your head is not your own. Go to your hut, or I will kick you.'

Towards the end of 1835 a constable was sent 'to forward me to Sydney'. Brine must have been delighted to say farewell to the deeply unpleasant Scotsman and even pleased to enter a dark cell in Maitland for two days and nights with only twelve ounces of bread and half a pint of water for sustenance. On the third night he was chained to fifteen more prisoners who all had to lie together in the open yard until morning. They were then marched to the steamboat ferry and taken to

Newcastle 40 miles away. On arrival they were bundled into another prison where they stayed for two weeks without once being examined and not conscious of having committed the slightest offence. Brine was then chained to twenty others and boarded onto another steam boat bound for Norfolk Island 'where those only of the convicts who have committed some heinous offence are sent and where the most inhuman and cruel punishments are practised daily by the authorities upon the unfortunate and wrenched prisoners'.

The voyage steamed through a terrific gale and the wind drove the ferry back to Newcastle. Brine recalled: 'Being chained together on the deck, the waves kept continually dashing over us and we were wet and miserable. In this situation we were taken on shore and locked into cells for the next three days.'

The next stop was Sydney, where the prisoners arrived during the night and Brine was ordered into cells with condemned men 'but I strongly protested and demanded to know what charge was lodged against me, to cause me to be thus treated'. After some delay Brine was marched to the barracks and placed in a lock-up for 24-hours. The following day the prison muster-master – an officer in charge of roll-calls – came to visit. Brine begged him to tell him what offence he had been charged with and pleaded to be told why he had been put in chains with condemned men. He ordered Brine to be taken to a cell where he was issued with a blanket

> … which was a great comfort having been so long without one … And the next morning I saw, to my great satisfaction, two of my brethren in captivity, Thomas and John Loveless and in a few days after James Loveless, also with whom I proceeded to Mr. Brennen's farm at Prospect, where I remained until I left the colony.

James Loveless' Story:
James Loveless, the 26-year old younger brother of George, left the convict ship *Surrey* in Sydney on 4 September 1834 and was locked up in Hyde Park Barracks. Within two days at the prison he was told he had been assigned to a remote agricultural estate called Strathallan 500 miles from Sydney. He was relieved to have the cold shackles removed from his ankles and looked forward to a long walk free of the manacles that had restricted his movement for the past four months. He left the barracks carrying only flour and raw beef wrapped in a blanket.

The journey was rough and took him down endless stony tracks, across hills and plains, through gum forests, bush, valleys and gorges, alongside rivers and through tiny settlements. Very few roads led from Sydney and James Loveless was told that so long as he stayed on the main track he could not possibly get lost.

The younger Loveless never recorded the route he took from Sydney to Strathallan but it probably followed a track leading south towards Wollongong before turning west inland towards Goulburn and onwards in the direction of Gundagai and south west to Albury. At night he washed in rivers or streams and slept under gum trees to the sound of kookaburras marking out their territory, the barking and howling of wild dingoes and screeching of parakeets. He would have met few people along the way apart from native aborigines who must have left him alone as he made no mention of encounters with tribesmen. From Albury James Loveless would have walked the dusty track to Wangaratta before heading towards Shepparton and Elmore before turning north to the banks of the Murray River and his final destination at Strathallan. The journey took two weeks and he arrived exhausted, dehydrated, hungry and dirty.

Archibald McMillan, owner of the Strathallan Estate where James Loveless worked as a stockman. (*Elizabeth MacMillan*)

The Strathallan estate covered 3,250 acres and was well stocked with sheep, cattle and horses. Its owner, Mr. Archibald McMillan, JP, lived in a large stone house and several wooden huts had been built nearby for twelve assigned convicts working on the estate. James Loveless worked at Strathallan for 19 months and found McMillan an agreeable man.

In November 1835 a letter was sent to McMillan asking if Loveless had behaved himself since joining him and three months later McMillan was ordered to send him back to Sydney. Presumably McMillan provided Loveless with more provisions for his two week return hike than those he received for his outward journey.

When he arrived at the Sydney barracks, the Irish-born Principal Superintendent of Convicts, John Ryan Brenan wanted to know why he had returned. Loveless told him about the letter sent to McMillan asking for the prisoner's return. The Superintendent was at a loss and told Loveless he must remain in the barracks until called for. He remained there for the next three months 'not knowing what they were going to do with me, for I was informed the order was not to let me out of the barracks'.

He was eventually summoned to Superintendent Brenan's office and told the Governor wished to know if he would agree to have his wife and family brought out to join him. 'I said I could not agree under the present circumstances – not while I was a prisoner.' Brenan said he was certain that the Governor would grant him a free pardon as soon as his family arrived, but Loveless said he preferred to be in possession of a pardon first. Brenan gave Loveless two days to think it over and was later told that the prisoner could not consent 'as it was my intention to return to England whenever I obtained my liberty'.

Brenan was surprised by this remark being under the impression that the prisoner would wish to stay in Australia because 'you would do better here than at home'. Loveless said he thought otherwise as 'I have seen nothing but misery in the colony here'. Brenan said this would not be the case once he had become a free man so he had better make up his mind to remain in the colony. Again Loveless refused.

Brenan then thumped his fist onto the table and said that if Loveless would not consent to his family being brought out to Australia he would be sent to the Port Macquarie penal settlement – a place for 'troublesome prisoners' located on the Mid North Coast of New South Wales, 242 miles north of Sydney, 'until His Majesty's pleasure should be further known'.

Two days later he was summoned back to Brenan's office where he was made a surprising offer. Would Loveless prefer to go to the penal settlement at Port Macquarie – or to Brenan's own farm at Prospect, 22 miles from Sydney? 'Having heard of the dreadful ill-treatment experienced by prisoners at Port Macquarie, I preferred going to Prospect and proceeded there accordingly,' he recalled.

Loveless tells us nothing about his journey to Prospect or what life was like at the farm and cattle station four miles from Parramatta, described by a visitor 'as undulating grassland interspersed with magnificent trees and a great amount of kangaroos and emus.'

On 17 August 1836 *The Sydney Gazette* carried a government advertisement that jumped from page four like a bolt from the blue. James Loveless read:

Colonial Secretary's Office

Sydney, 13th June, 1836.

HIS Excellency the Governor directs

Colonial Secretary's office
Sydney, 13th June. 1836

HIS Excellency the Governor directs
it to be not fied, that the Right Honourab e
the Secretary of State for the Colonies has signified
His Majesty's gracious commands that Absolute and
condi i nal Pardons to granted to the undermen-
tioned individuals, viz—

Despatch, dated 31st Jan. 1836, No. 101.
ABSOLUTE PARDON.
Farrell James, Surry.
Despatch dated 12 November, 1835. No 72.
CONDITIONAL PARDON.
Brine James, Surry
Hammett James, Surry
Stanfeld John, Surry
Stanfield Thomas, Surry—
On condition of residing in New South Wales for
the term of Two years from the day of their arrival.
Loveless James, Surry
On condition of residing in New South Wales for
three years from the day of his arrival.
Despatch dated 17th November, 1834.
Dickinson John, Stren—
On condition of residing in New South Wales for
two years from the day of his arrival.
By His Excellency's Command,
ALEXANDER M'LEAY.

it to be notified, that the Right Honourable the Secretary of State for the Colonies has signified His Majesty's gracious commands that Absolute and conditional Pardons be granted to the unmentioned individuals, viz –

Despatch dated 12 November, 1835. No 72.

CONDITIONAL PARDON.

Brine James, *Surry*

Hammett James, *Surry;* Standfield John, *Surrey*

Standfield Thomas, *Surrey* —

On condition of residing in New South Wales for the term of Two years from the day of their arrival.

Loveless James, *Surrey*

On condition of residing in New South Wales for Three years from the day of his arrival.

Despatch dated 17th November, 1834.

By His Excellency's Command,

ALEXANDER McLEAY.

On 17 August, 1836 the *Sydney Gazette* announced that conditional pardons had been awarded to James Brine, James Hammett, Thomas Standfield and James Loveless. (*Trove – National Library of Australia*)

There was no mention of George Loveless and James began to wonder if his older brother was to be detained for a longer sentence in Van Diemen's Land. And why was he, James Loveless, being detained a full year longer than his other four comrades? And why had it taken eight months for a conditional pardon, dated November 1835 to appear in June 1836? Brenan provided the answer to the last question: 'The reason you had not obtained your pardon sooner was through a mistake of the Home Secretary, Lord John Russell who has taken over the duties of the Secretary of State for the Colonies.'

Brenan also revealed that the 'home government' considered James Loveless 'one of the ringleaders.' 'Ringleader of what?' asked Loveless 'Of your secret combination; and you may think yourself well off in not being hung, as I believe you were bordering on high treason. Your brother in Van Diemen's land is very likely in the same situation as yourself.'

Secret combination? Hung? And exactly who in the 'home government' was responsible for making these decisions? James Loveless, with the rest of his comrades, was an innocent man punished for a crime he did not commit and held against his will, far from his loved ones in a fly-blown country on the other side of the earth.

Brenan offered to take James Loveless on as a 'paid worker' at his small estate called Garryowen House, two miles from Sydney. James was to claim this handsome house, which stood in 30 acres of land, was two miles from Sydney (although James made a surprising claim that the distance was fifty miles). It was on the Parramatta River and commanded distant views of the Kurryjung Mountains. It had large rooms, stables for five horses, two coach houses and was surrounded by a 190ft wooden verandah. There was also 'a shingle shed' which is, presumably, where James Loveless resided.

Loveless was a good worker who could lend a hand to almost any task in the grounds and pastures surrounding the big house. He remained at Garryowen until December 1836 when he made his way to Sydney to obtain more information about his 'conditional pardon'. At every stage he was referred to Brenan for answers, which were not forthcoming. He asked if the Home Government intended to give himself and his five companions a passage home to England. 'No,' replied Brenan, 'only a pardon in the colony.'

Loveless returned to Garryowen after being assured that a free passage back to England might be forthcoming in the fullness of time, but it was not stipulated when the time might come. He was, however, assured that when the time arrived, he would secure a passage 'at the first opportunity'. 'But that gentleman [Brenan] neglected to fulfil his promise, wishing to keep me in his employ,' recalled young Loveless.

James Hammett's story:

Always an outsider and a loner, James Hammett chose not to record his time as a convict in Australia. What we know is that he was a silent and thoughtful man, not given to long conversations and discussions, yet quick to defend himself when challenged. He was not related in any way to the other Tolpiddle men nor had he been a member of the local Wesleyan Methodist congregation. He was, in many ways, his own man.

Hammett was born in 1818 and, aged 11, was sentenced to four calendar months of hard labour behind bars at Dorchester's House of Correction 'charged on oath on suspicion of having on or about the 28th day of February in the year 1829 stolen three pieces of iron, the property of Mr. William Brine of Tolpiddle.' He could have been transported for the crime but instead the 11-year-old lad spent every day for 16 weeks at the Dorchester House of Correction walking a tread wheel where prisoners toiled at the turning wheel for up to eight hours each day. Prisoners would step onto the 24 spokes of a large paddle wheel, and as the spokes turned, gears were used to pump water or crush grain. In gruelling shifts, prisoners would climb the equivalent of 7,200 feet daily – nearly twice the height of Ben Nevis.

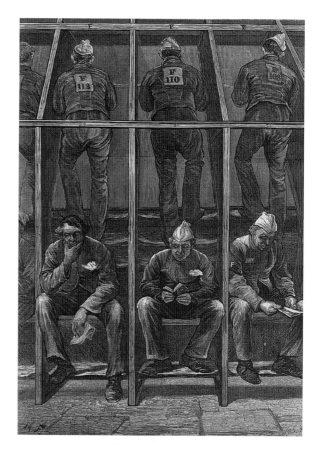

In Australia James Hammett recalled being sent to the treadmill in Dorchester jail as an 11-year-old boy and was expected to work on it for up to eight hours a day, climbing the equivalent of 7,200ft. (*Illustrated London News*)

The exertion, combined with poor diets, often led to injury and illness, but prisons throughout the country continued to install tread wheels.

Dorchester's tread wheel was installed in April 1822 and produced flour – all proceeds from the sale of which enabled the gaol to pay for the costs of the prisoners. Later, however, tread wheels produced no end products and were walked just for punishment. They were loathed by prisoners.

On Hammett's first visit to prison the initials 'J.H. 1829' were tattooed on the inside of his left wrist; a few years later he had another tattoo 'H.H.' etched on his inside lower right arm after he married Harriet.

Hard labour was introduced to teach prisoners the value of hard work, remove the temptation for idle men get into to mischief and deter others from committing crimes. In the 1830s around 500 prisoners were annually committed to hard labour in Dorchester's House of Correction, of which in 1834 25 prisoners age 17 and over were transported for periods of between seven years and life with a further 28 convicts under the age of 17 transported with varying sentences.

Prison and confinement was nothing new to Hammett when he entered the House of Correction for the second time in February 1834. But he was not a bad man, a thief, a murderer, a rabble-rouser or a work-shy. At the age of 22, he was a respectable married man with a baby son and working as a farm labourer on one of Mrs. Northover's properties. When he left the convict ship *Surrey* he was one of many men sold like a slave for £1 a head to dealers or agents who drew lots for cheap labour to work on farms, road gangs or as builders in England's fledgling nation at the other side of the world. He was quickly snapped up by agents seeking young, strong and healthy men with experience in agriculture and animal husbandry.

Towards the end of his life, Hammett spoke for the first time about transportation to Australia and recalled he was waiting in the Hyde Park Barracks prison yard to be taken to his cell when 'a man was brought in, a barrel was rolled into the middle, the man was stripped, tied across the barrel and given twenty-five lashes on the bare back, twenty-five on his backside and twenty-five on the calves of his legs.' He had no idea who the man was or why he was being punished so brutally but had witnessed his first taste of life as a convict in Australia.

Shortly after arriving Hammett was given the name and address of his new master living 'up country'. His name was Mr. Edward John Eyre, an Englishman who had purchased a 1,260 acre estate called Woodlands at Molongo Plains, near Queanbeyan in the south-eastern corner of New South Wales. He asked the agent who had 'bought' him, where Queanbeyan was located and was told: 'Not far, 400 miles.' Hammett asked who was travelling with him and was informed he would be hiking alone. He asked: 'How am I to find the right road?' and was assured: 'You'll find the road right enough. Go to Brickfield Hill and enquire for Liverpool. You're sure to find your way.'

Hammett's destination was, in fact, 180 miles away from Sydney – not 400 miles – and he was given rations for a 22-day journey and told to 'get drink as best you can and find your sleeping places where you might.' He was given one shilling by the agent to buy anything he might need on the journey. Hammett's feet were tender even before he began his journey having been cramped on the convict ship with only two hours daily exercise on a voyage lasting nearly four months. The soles of his boots, however, would have cushioned his feet and after a few days he was probably able to cover at least 20 miles each day.

After tramping 20 miles south-west of Sydney he found Liverpool easily enough and was given further directions. No record exists of his exact route but the quickest would have been to follow the track towards Wollongong, a town still being built and inhabited by new settlers. A further 50 mile hike would have taken him through rugged country, dense forest and in blazing sunshine to Bowral, another new town in the Southern Highlands of New South Wales. Queanbeyan, on the Southern Tablelands in south-eastern New South Wales, was on the banks of the Molonglo River. At the time of Hammett's arrival the settlement was about to be officially proclaimed a township with a population of nearly 50 people; it is close to where Australia's capital city, Canberra, stands today.

The Woodlands estate was home to 3,000 sheep owned by Edward Eyre, a rugged frontiersman who would later go on to become one of the most intrepid explorers of the unforgiving Australian outback. He had been assisted on the farm by two convicts and at the time of Hammett's arrival another four prisoners were assigned to the farm. Hammett's home at Woodlands was a lonely hut on the sheep-run some distance from the main house and other farm workers, which probably did not worry the solitary Hammett. Of the five Tolpiddle men sent to New South Wales, Hammett's allocation to the sheep station was the remotest and furthest from Sydney.

One day in May 1836 Hammett's work was interrupted by Mr Eyre who had ridden out to give his convict-shepherd some new orders. As he took these from his saddlebag an old London newspaper fell out which Eyre gave to Hammett to read at his leisure. 'By the providence of God,' Hammett later recalled, 'my eyes caught sight of my own name and I read that we had been pardoned and were to

Edward John Eyre, an Englishman and rugged frontiersman running an 'up country' estate at Molongo Plains, employed James Hammett as a shepherd. (*Whyalla News*)

be sent home again.' The following day he went in search of Eyre and pleaded to be sent home.

At this point Hammett's story becomes confusing. Eyre apparently received a message to release his convict-shepherd with instructions to return him to Hyde Park Barracks. On his way, however, Hammett either got lost or diverted and ended up in Windsor, a township 35 miles north-west of Sydney and 182 miles from the Woodland Estate. He may have fallen ill on the way or become lost after taking the wrong track or decided to take a different route back to Sydney. What is known is that in September 1837 he was arrested and detained following 'an assault charge' and marched back to prison for the third time in his life.

It is likely that the assault (upon whom is not recorded) earned Hammett an extra 18 months sentence undergoing physical punishment such as a return to some distant farm in the outback or chained to a work gang building roads or bridges. Hammett did not return into the spotlight until February 1839 when he wrote a letter – he called it a 'memorial' – to His Excellency Sir George Gipps, Governor of New South Wales:

> The Humble Memorial of James Hammett sheweth that your memorialist is one of the Dorchester Labourers tried in 1834 and arrived in this Colony by the Ship *Surrey* under sentence of transportation. That Memorialist received his pardon in 1836 with other labourers sent here under the same circumstances who obtained a free passage to England. That Your Memorialist would have obtained the same indulgence but he was unfortunately detained at Windsor charged with an assault when the other labourers left the Colony.
>
> That your Memorialist is now anxious to return to his native land and he trusts Your Excellency will take his case into your humane consideration and order your Memorialist a passage to England which he unfortunately lost on the former occasion and your Memorialist in duty bound will ever pay.
>
> (Signed) James Hammett

Hammett's request was rushed through as a matter of urgency. The Office of the Commissary General, in charge of placing all convicts on work details, appears to have lost all trace of where Hammett had been sent and was unable to inform him that a free passage home had been available for some time. The Commissary General's office was supposed to conduct periodic 'musters' at which convicts were expected to return to Sydney for inspection or inspectors sent out to interview them, but nobody seemed bothered about checking Hammett's whereabouts. No doubt officials had been in touch with Edward Eyre at his Woodlands Estate to ask if he might have any idea where Hammett might be, but by 1839 Eyre had sold his farm and moved on to new adventures in Adelaide and probably never received any official communications from the Commissary General.

Chapter 16

The London-Dorchester Committee

August 1834

They used to treat him as they liked
In the evil days of old,
They thought there was no power on earth
To beat the power of gold:
They used to threaten what they'd do
Whenever work was slack,
But now he laughs their threats to scorn
With the 'UNION' at his back!

The Grand National Consolidated Trades Union's mass demonstration from Copenhagen Fields had no immediate effect on politicians, apart from generating acres of column inches in newspapers the length and breadth of England. As the convict ships sailed on with their prisoners, families of the Tolpiddle men began writing letters of their own 'in the hope of awakening the sympathies and obtaining the aid of a generous British public on behalf of the orphan, the widowed and oppressed'.

The following letter was penned by George Loveless's wife Betsy to a 'Mr. Goode, Butt's Lane, Coventry' – presumably a contact passed on by the Grand National Consolidation Trade Union. Betsy signed the letter along with Sarah Loveless and Harriet Hammett while Dinniah Standfield and Catherine Brine marked their names with an 'X' mark.

Sir, it is with feelings of gratitude that I address you; but since the arrest of our husbands our distress have been great; our husbands were taken from us on February 25 and left us destitute of any thing for our support, for their wages were only seven shillings per week, and when we had received the few shillings they had due to them, we were obliged to pay it all to persons to who it was ow'd, and it was not sufficient.

Then we applied to Mr. Woolaston, the Magistrate, for relief but he said I was to apply to a union club, for he should not allow us any thing. I told him I knew of no union to apply to; he told me to go along. After that, Dianna, the wife of Thos. Standfield applied; and all of us went to the County Hall at Dorchester to get relief, but they told us to go along, for they meant us to suffer for the offences of our husbands.

And be it known to you, sir, we also applied to the Parish Relief and all the redress we could get was that we and our children must suffer because our husbands had committed such a heinous crime. But sir, I afterwards went to the Lord of the Manor, Mr. Frampton, who said there was nothing for me; I told him I could not remain to see the children perish for want, I would rather go into service and leave the children with them; they said if I did they would transport me for it; and, sir, had it not been for kind friends, we must have perished for want; out of a little they gave us a little, for none of the labourers here have but seven shillings per week to find house, fire, clothes and food and some of them have families to support with themselves …

But, sir, on Tuesday last a gentleman came from London to enquire into our circumstance, and relieved us; he gave us £2 3s each, all equal alike; had it not been for this I cannot tell what we should have done. But since that time the overseers knowing our distress, and not knowing we had a friend, gave us a few shillings, not six a piece.

But, sir, Tolpiddle have for many years been noticed for tyranny and oppression and cruelty, and now the union is broke up here, for the committee and rules, list and all is taken, and now others is suffering on its account.

Such, sir, is some of the treatment which we have here. Sir, I have not exaggerated that you may comment on it.

o0o

Frampton's spies, including Tolpiddle's vicar, the Revd. Dr. Thomas Warren were out and about everywhere – in the Crown Inn eavesdropping on the conversations of beer drinkers, at church trying to catch two or more men talking about trade unionism after the service and in Tolpiddle's small shops where wives gathered and chatted about life in general and their husbands in particular. These spies immediately relayed any information they picked up to Frampton and presumably were rewarded for their work. Frampton wrote to Lord Melbourne shortly after the Tolpiddle men were arrested that a spy – the Guard of a Mail Coach heading for London – had informed him that

A very well-dressed person, tho' not a gentleman, came from London last night and got off the Mail at Milbourne, a village about half way between Blandford and Dorchester; he said he should not remain there as he said he was going into the county. He evidently knew about the unions and the six men who have been transported and he made many enquiries about this neighbourhood. He said he should return to London in a few days and that he should send a letter to London tonight and expected a parcel from thence. The Guard, who lived with me as a butler for some years, informs me that if I had not been at Dorchester at the Sessions he should have come to me at Moreton to tell me such a man was in the county as he considered him a very suspicious person. I have thought it my duty to mention the above and I beg leave to add that you may depend on my using my best endeavours to have this person watched in this county.

Three days later, Frampton had more Tolpiddle intelligence to share with Lord Melbourne:

I have the honour to inform you that the man I mentioned to your Lordship in my last letter as having been set down by the Mail Coach at Milbourne, went immediately from thence to Tolpiddle and returned to the inn at Milbourne at night. He went again to Tolpiddle on Wednesday and returned to Milbourne as before. Yesterday he went to Bere and called on a man by the name of Bridle, a Methodist who keeps a Grocer and Drapers shop there [and had been ejected by the Crown from the trial of the Tolpiddle Six] but came back to Milbourne in time to go by Mail to London accompanied by George Loveless's wife and son. The Mail being full he remained at Milbourne. G. Loveless's wife and son went back to Tolpiddle and this man left Milbourne about half past four o'clock this morning by the Herald Coach for London. He is described to me as being about 5' 4" high, dressed in black coat and Trowsers (sic), dark waistcoat and black cravat. The features of the upper part of his face are short and compressed together and he has a sore on his under lip.

A few days later Frampton's spy identified this mystery man as

… a person by the name of Newman, a cabinet maker who makes cases for timepieces for the Guards and Mail Coaches and resides in Cromer Street, Gray's Inn Lane and it was known amongst his friends in London that he came into this neighbourhood for the purpose of conveying money to the wives and families of these convicts. It is understood that besides giving money to the Loveless and Standfield families he also left a sum of money in the hands of Bridle, the shopkeeper in Bere for the same purpose. Bridle says he is going to London in the course of this week to settle rates of pay to be allowed to these women and children. Previous to Newman coming from London, Dr. Warren, the Clergyman of Tolpiddle received a letter from a person signing himself Mr. Robert Morrison, 1, York Street, Middlesex

Hospital, London, requesting him to convey some money to the wives and families of the convicts. But when Dr. Warren heard no more of it, as he supposes he did not speak sufficiently favourably of their character in his answer, tho' he offered to distribute any charity.

o0o

Viscount Howick, Under Secretary of State, asked Frampton to confirm that wives of the Tolpiddle men had been refused any assistance from parish funds. He disdainfully replied on 4 May:

It is perfectly true that I and the Justices acting with me refused to order any parochial relief to the wives and families of these convicts, and we gave as our reason for doing so that we had ascertained from the gaoler that they had been supplied by their wives with more food than they could consume during the time that they were in the jail, which would have been continued after their conviction had the regulations of the prison allowed it. [George Loveless does not mention this and Frampton quotes no source so his claim is doubtful.] We also told them that on their husbands entering the union, the leaders of it engaged to maintain all families of those who joined the union, for so long a time as they were thrown out of work and deprived of their earnings, in consequence of their belonging [to] the union. And that therefore they ought to apply to those leaders and require of them to keep their promise. Our object in doing this was to prove to the labourers that the leaders of the union had deceived them, if they did not support their families, and if they did maintain them to lessen the funds of the union, at the same time as it relieved the parish.

We however explained to the overseer, though his instructions were not to relieve them, he was to watch over the parties and assist them as if from himself, if he found they were

On May 4, 1834, James Frampton wrote to Viscount Howick (Earl Grey), Under Secretary of State, who asked him to confirm that wives of the Tolpiddle men had been refused assistance from parish funds. (*Caldesi, Blanford & Co*)

really distressed; in fact he did relieve one of the families (that of George Loveless) in that way, which immediately caused the others to apply for relief, which he refused – but however he tells me that since that time he has occasionally relieved them all except Catherine Brine [the mother of James who ran the local church school for a modest stipend].

Very soon after the first application for relief, the person by the name of Newman came down from London and gave them money. We have reason to believe those families are now maintained by the union, through the medium of a man by the name of Job Bridle, a shopkeeper of Bere Regis and the Justices have had no application from them since. The Revd. Dr. Warren, the clergyman of Tolpiddle, has also received some money from a Mr. Morrison for their use since my letter of April 19, which he has distributed to them.

With regard to other statements in the letter, it is also perfectly true that we, as Justices, directed the overseer not to allow parochial relief to any persons whose names appeared in the book which was proved on the trial of the six men to contain a list of those who had taken the illegal oath and had joined the union and we did this because we considered that no person could be entitled to receive parochial relief who could afford to pay a shilling on entering and a penny a week afterwards to the support of the union, which would thus in fact be maintained by the money of the parish and as none of these persons have ever acknowledged their error or expressed any sorrow at having joined the unions, we have seen no occasion for altering our opinions.

I am requested by the overseers to assure your Lordship that no person of the vestry ever made use of any threat of transporting the women if they left their children and went into service.

I am anxious now to state that the Justices have particularly recommended to the farmers (who have expressed themselves most willing to follow our advice) that every encouragement should be given to those labourers who did not join the union by increasing their wages, and placing them in all the most profitable work, so that they may feel the advantage of their good conduct, by making a marked difference between them and the unions, and on no account at present to make any addition to the wages of the latter, lest it should have the slightest appearance of being done through fear.

o0o

Regular sums of money from individual trades unions and private individuals continued to find their way from London to the Tolpiddle families until in August 1834 an official organisation was created called The London-Dorchester Committee which operated from The Turk's Head Tavern, King's Street, High Holborn. It was made up of a committee of sixteen working men and union members whose object was to continue putting pressure on the government to bring the prisoners home and provide moral and financial support for their families. Its founder was Robert Hartwell, a working class printer and compositor, who shortly afterwards started the Chartist newspaper *The Charter*.

Henry Hetherington, another radical printer and publisher of newspapers including *Penny Papers for the People*, *The Radical* and *The Poor Man's Guardian* (which sold 230,000 weekly copies) also joined the London-Dorchester movement. He travelled around the country addressing large groups of workmen and making collections to send to Tolpiddle families. Following each meeting Hetherington penned reports for his radical newspapers reflecting the sweep of Chartist, trade unionist, social democrat and working class opinions during an era that witnessed the rise of Britain's socialist movements.

Following a visit to Manchester in October 1834, Hetherington personally collected £15 10s 'for the wives and children of our ill-used fellow countrymen, the Dorchester Labourers'. Hetherington told readers that 'the journey was necessarily attended with considerable expense, which, however, was amply repaid by the great pleasure I derived from being the bearer of a sum which, I am sure, will greatly mitigate the sufferings of these poor but interesting families.'

Hetherington reported that he found the wives and children of the Tolpiddle men to be all well. The three children of George and Betsy Loveless had suffered from the measles; the two oldest had recovered while the youngest (Thomas, age 5) 'is still in a state of progressive recovery'. He continued:

Poor Dinniah Standfield – she has five children besides the one transported, two absolutely dependent upon her exertions for support. The Loveless' are her brothers and when I reflect upon the circumstances that she had a husband, a son under 20 and two brothers, all unjustly and cruelly torn from her, merely because they had endeavoured to obtain fair remuneration for their labour, I could not help ejaculating a curse upon the unfeeling masters who had inflicted such misery and desolation upon these poor people, whose previous circumstances were sufficiently destitute and unhappy. She is now residing with her children, wholly dependent; a son, a fine young man about 17, who toils from morn till night for six shillings per week; and two daughters who make shirt buttons for 1s or 1s.2d per gross, for which they formerly obtained double that sum. By hard work they can make two gross a week. Poor Dinniah, in whose house the union held its meetings, is, it seems, to be severely punished. By order of the magistrates, all parochial aid is rigidly denied her. The parish authorities refuse her even the most trifling assistance, on the plea that the elder children (from the wages they receive) must support the younger; and that she, poor woman, must support herself.

Elizabeth Brine, whose son was likewise sentenced, appears not to be in want. She keeps a school, under the patronage of the clergymen, in which between 30 and 40 attend. The clergyman is partial to her, she having lived with him in the capacity of servant; and being unencumbered with a dependent family, I considered her as not standing in need of pecuniary assistance, and therefore did not include her in the distributions.

Money was distributed in the following manner:

£2 to each wife and 16s 8d to each child.
To Elizabeth (Betsy) – wife of George Loveless, three children – £4 10s 0d
To Sarah – wife of James Loveless, three children – £4 10s 0d
To Dinniah Standfield – wife of Thomas Standfield – two children wholly dependent) – £3 13. 4d
To Harriet Hammett – one child – £2 16s 8d
Total: £15. 10s 0d
I am, Gentlemen, your friend in the cause of Justice and Liberty,
H. Hetherington

William Loveless, another brother of George, wrote from Burton, near Bridport, on 20 November 1834 to thank Hetherington for his kindness to the family. He said that the last words of his brother George to him were, 'William, do your best that the tyrants do not starve my dear wife and children. I care not for myself so that my wife and children be taken care of.'

Chapter 17

The Two Laws

1835

A funny ditty I am going to pen,
About the King and his parliament men,
Like devils to him they all did splutter
About the fishes, the rolls and butter.

On 12 June 1835 the new Home Secretary Lord John Russell ordered Colonial Secretary, Lord Glenelg, to send letters to General Sir Richard Bourke, Governor of New South Wales and Sir George Arthur, Lieutenant-General Governor of Van Diemen's Land:

His Majesty's Secretary of State for the Home Department, having had under his consideration the case of (names inserted here) who was/were convicted at Dorchester, March 1834 of administering unlawful oaths and transported to Van Diemen's Land/New South Wales for seven years in the *William Metcalf/Surrey* has requested me to authorise you to grant a pardon to (individual names of the men inserted here) providing his/their conduct has been good since his/their transportation on condition they reside in Van Dieman's Land/New South Wales for the remainder of their sentences. You will accordingly grant a pardon to the prisoners on these terms and conditions.

Home Secretary Lord John Russell, who had stepped into the job following Lord Melbourne's promotion to Prime Minister, admitted to forgetting that an 1832 Act had been passed preventing any pardon for convicts who had spent less than four years on a seven year sentence. (*John Jabez Edwin Mayall*)

The letters would take four months to arrive, but no sooner had they been dispatched than Lord John Russell was informed by his law officers that an Act had been passed in 1832 which prevented any pardon to a transported convict until he had completed a minimum of four years on a seven years sentence. This meant that legally none of the convicted men could be granted conditional pardons for sentences in less than four years. The prisoners would also receive news about their pardons only to be told at a later date to forget the contents of their letters. That is, providing the prisoners could be found. So disorganised were prison records in both New South Wales and Van Dieman's Land – to say nothing of record keeping in the Colonial Office in London – that nobody could be precisely certain which prisoner was where or for how long.

oOo

The next important man to nail his penny to the Tolpiddle mast was Thomas Wakley, a doctor, publisher of *The Lancet*, parliamentary reformist and Member of Parliament for Finsbury. Wakley, the youngest of eleven children was born in Membury, Devon, in 1795. He left grammar school at the age of sixteen to be apprenticed as an apothecary in Taunton. He loved the work and decided to become a surgeon. After training at London's Guy's Hospital, Wakley qualified in 1817.

He established himself as a doctor in Argyll Street, one of the most expensive areas in London, and in February 1820 married the daughter of a wealthy iron merchant. In 1821 he met the radical journalist William Cobbett who published the weekly newspaper *Political Register*. Wakley told Cobbett about the need for reform in the medical profession and Cobbett suggested that Wakley publish a journal to be used to campaign for such reform.

In October 1823 he began publishing *The Lancet* in which he criticised the autocratic powers of the council that ran the Royal College of Surgeons. Wakley also campaigned for a united profession of apothecaries, physicians and surgeons and a new system of medical qualifications to improve the profession's standards.

In 1828 his involvement in campaigns for parliamentary reform brought him into contact with other political reformers and in 1832 he was asked to become the Radical parliamentary candidate for Finsbury. With 330,000 potential voters, this new constituency was one of Britain's largest. With the support of his two closest political friends, Joseph Hume and William Cobbett, Wakley campaigned for an extension of the vote, removal of property qualifications for parliamentary candidates and repeal of the Corn Laws. He was defeated in 1832 but won when he ran again in 1835.

Wakley spent the next seventeen years in the House of Commons. He was, at first, an infrequent speaker but, six months into his Westminster career, his maiden speech attacked the conviction of the six Tolpiddle men. He was determined to use this opportunity to display his talents as a speaker.

The fate of the Dorchester Labourers inspired his honest indignation and deep pity. Wakley was seen by increasing number of trades unions, political activists and ordinary working men as the best possible mouthpiece for a vigorous protest in the House of Commons against the harsh sentences. He was from the West Country and considered highly suitable to plead the cause of the Dorsetshire men and campaign for a major parliamentary debate focussing on the severity of the sentences and questionable legality of the prosecution.

Joseph Hume, MP for Middlesex told the House of Commons that it should 'redress the cruel and unjust act that has been perpetrated'. (*Public Domain*)

Scores of petitions had been submitted to parliament from different parts of the country. Major Aubrey Beauclerk, MP for Surrey Eastern presented a petition signed by 20,000 men from Leeds; Joseph Hume, MP for Middlesex presented another from Marylebone containing 3,000 signatures; Sir William Hutt, MP for Kingston-upon-Hull brought along a petition signed by 7,000 constituents. On 27 March, Wakley presented no less than sixteen petitions signed by 20,000 men. In total 221,517 signed petitions for release of the Tolpiddle men.

Wakley urged the labourers' cause in a brief speech, stating that the wives of the men, 'who, poor wretches, have been reduced to the direst straits of poverty by the transportation of their husbands, and roughly refused relief on applying to the parish authorities.' He revealed that he would move a resolution that their sentences must be commuted.

The date planned for the resolution was 25 June 1835 and Wakley was more than ready to make his maiden speech. Lord John Russell, however, requested Wakley to postpone the motion as he had already made a recommendation to the King to grant pardons to the men 'on condition that they remained in the colonies'. Lord Russell also said he was ready to recommend that James Hammett, John and Thomas Standfield and James Brine should receive a full pardon once they had been overseas for two years. George and James Loveless, however, were regarded as 'ringleaders' and would not be allowed to return home until they had fully served their seven years term. Wakley refused to stand down.

The 40-year-old novice parliamentarian rose in a crowded House to trigger his first serious debate. He spoke with moving eloquence, skill, dignity and courage. Hansard recorded:

He began by expressing his astonishment that the foreman of the Grand Jury should endeavour, even before the case was heard, to interpose between the sufferers and the seat of mercy. The Member for Dorsetshire, William Ponsonby, had also been foreman of the Grand Jury and was brother-in-law to the Home Secretary Lord Melbourne.... Now under what circumstances were these men prosecuted? I beg the attention of the House for if I should fail in my objective, I can only say that the people of England will, hereafter, look in vain for justice at the hands of this assembly.

On hearing this a number of Tories present in the House made it known loud and clear that their land-owning constituents were utterly averse to showing the Tolpuddle men any kind of mercy, especially those refusing to improve wages paid to their own labourers. But slowly and surely they quietened down and listened to what Wakley had to say. He spoke from his heart. There was no garish sentiment, no thump of unrestrained gesture and not a single ill-chosen word. He delivered a simple yet learned summary of the legal aspects of the labourers' case, a determined but temperate demand for justice and a sober appeal for mercy, all couched in the clearest possible phraseology, informed with good taste and tinged with passion.

I believe that everyone in the House knows well that the Trades Unions were instituted in London in 1824,' Wakley added. 'When was the union of Tolpiddle instituted? Ten years after Trade Unions had been established in London. Hundreds of men now belonged to them and Government permitted – at least had not interfered with – them. No party was prosecuted and thus, by acquiescence at least, Government gave their sanction to those unions.

The Dorsetshire Labourers having received notice (pray let gentlemen mark this) that their wages were to be reduced from 7s a week to 6s a week, they having wives and families, they wrote to their brothers in London and communicated to them their distressed condition.

Wakley then spoke about the character of the convicted men and asked the House:

Was it proved in court that any of the men had been guilty of threatening their fellow labourers in any degree or given offence to their neighbours? On the contrary; I have evidence that six better labourers and more honest men did not exist in the kingdom. Two of them – men who had never been anything in their lives but common labourers – had, by dint of study and application, become so qualified in mental capacity as to be enabled to give lectures in the neighbourhood to their fellow labourers and have been received into the Wesleyan Conference as preachers. I fear very much that this was their great offence.... George Loveless at the age of 28, with a salary of 7s a week, has succeeded in purchasing a small theological library and had studied with so much assiduity that there is no man in the neighbourhood who could compete with him in point of theological knowledge, but I can prove that in political discussions he had taken no part ... It has been admitted by all persons acquainted with the characters that six more honest, peaceable and industrious men were not to be found in the county of Dorset ... Who, then, can describe the cruelty of the sentence passed on these meritorious men?

Wakley then read from a recent letter Betsy Loveless had received from her husband describing life in Van Diemen's Land. It had taken four months to travel from Hobart to Tolpiddle:

From what I can observe of this country, it is not such a paradise as is generally supposed by the people of England. Bread is uncommonly dear; more than double the price of bread in England, and other provisions in proportion. Clothing is dearer than provisions; thousands of persons are actually starving in this country, as many cannot get employment and many are too idle to work. As yet I see nothing to attract my attention, to make me stop in the country one day after I obtain my liberty and have the means to return; in fact at present I despair of ever getting money to go to England, and yet nothing would yield me so much satisfaction – nay, nothing in this world will satisfy me until I return to you and the children.'

Wakley asked the House:

What mitigation of punishment would that be which is attended with such reservation as five years' [in fact it was seven] domiciliation in such a country under such afflicting circumstances? My prayer to this House is for the restoration of all the prisoners to their families. I beseech you to concede the favour, to gratify the humane wishes of the working people of England, who have implored the House for mercy to their fellow labourers. The people of England, I can assure the House, feel deeply on the subject. To the working classes especially it is a constant subject of agitation, and unless the men are restored that agitation will continually increase. The (union) society was legal with the single exception of the oath; and when the object was legal the oath alone cannot make the society illegal. I hope the House will interpose its authority ... I am convinced that no evil will arise from the restoration of these individuals to their native country.

It was at this point in his address to the House that the matter of the so-called 'secret oath' entered the debate. Wakley compared the unionists 'secret oath' with the 'perfect impunity with which members of Orange Lodges had committed as great, if not greater offence but had been allowed to escape.' He added:

> It certainly appears to me not a little extraordinary that persons of high station, of character, of great talents and large experience should be allowed to commit with impunity an offence that Orange Lodges had committed, while persons so ignorant and so unacquainted with the law they were transgressing, as those unfortunate labourers, should be visited with the heavy punishment inflicted on them.... It appears that a declaration was taken by the members of Orange Lodges, requiring secrecy in their proceedings, exactly similar to that taken by the Dorchester Labourers. Now, every Orangeman that assented to and took the declaration came under the operation of the secret oath act as fully and as completely as those unfortunate men. The country must demand that these men should not any longer be subjected to the punishment they were now undergoing, after those disclosures respecting Orange Lodges. If all those Orangemen thus accused were not prosecuted, the people of England would be satisfied that there was one law for the rich and another for the poor in this country.

Wakley's entire speech on behalf of the Dorchester Labourers took two and a half hours to deliver and he held the closest attention of the House throughout. Loud support was frequent and forthcoming from both sides of the chamber. When he sat down the general applause was so hearty and unrestrained that he could not but feel he had achieved a real oratorical triumph in Europe's most critical assembly.

The motion was seconded by Joseph Hume, who expressed the feelings of the House with highly complimentary references to Wakley's speech. Lord John Russell – Home Secretary and the government's

Parliamentary reformer Thomas Wakley became a Radical candidate for Finsbury in 1828. He spent the next seventeen years in the House of Commons, where his maiden speech was a spirited attack on the decision to convict the six Tolpiddle men. (*Journal of the Royal Society of Medicine*)

chief spokesperson in the House – supported the action of the Crown in refusing clemency, a view also taken by Opposition Leader Sir Robert Peel.

Daniel O'Connell, the Irish political leader, said that the House recognised Wakley's oratorical powers, but they would have no practical result when it came to casting their votes. He, therefore, urged Wakley to withdraw his motion and generate more petitions from outside Parliament and to bring the matter to the earnest attention of the government. In a brief reply, Wakley said it was his duty to press his motion 'for an address to the King, praying that His Majesty would be pleased to grant a pardon to, and direct the recall of the six labourers'. O'Connell's prophecy was, indeed, correct as only eighty-two members voted with Wakley and three hundred and eight were against.

His speech, nevertheless, had been an impassioned and impressive appeal for speedy justice. It was now up to the people of England to determine whether proper and correct justice had been administered to the Dorsetshire labourers. Conditional pardons had been offered to four of the men but the stalwarts of the agitation were determined that these should give way to full and free ones for all six.

The Dorchester conviction caused the oath to be dropped ostensibly from future trades union initiation ceremonies. In April 1834 the Builders' Union formally abolished the oath. The Grand National Consolidated Trade Union quickly adopted the same course and the Leeds and other unions followed suit. But it was too late to save the six Dorchester Labours now serving tough sentences under the heat of the Australian sun.

Chapter 18

As Opposed To Democracy As It Is To Sin

1834/35

I'm what they call a Methodist, one of the noisy few;
I shout when I am happy, and that I ought to, oh!
Some say I am too noisy, I know the reason why,
And if they felt the glory, they'd shout as loud as I.

Few people in 19th century England questioned the existence of God. Some, however, chose to let their faith play a bigger part in their lives than others; men like George and James Loveless, Thomas and John Standfield dedicated their lives to serving God as committed Christians in the Methodist tradition. Religion influenced all areas of their life including their work on the land, what they read and wrote and how they behaved. They also stood by a strong moral code that they believed would bring the whole world closer to God and were prepared to take the rough with the smooth in order to achieve this. They also believed in justice and equality.

When Thomas Wakley stood up in the House to speak in defence of the Tolpiddle men details about their arrest, trial, deportation, petitions and demonstrations had appeared prominently in newspapers for over a year. Many articles, particularly those appearing in radical publications, had stimulated working people to sign petitions calling for their return home. But what was the Methodist Church itself and its own newspapers doing to help free the men, particularly the lay preachers now serving sentences on the other side of the world? The answer was: *nothing*.

The Wesleyan Methodist leadership at that time was staunchly conservative in its outlook and in dealing with its congregations. It was led by the autocratic Manchester-born Jabez Bunting – known to many as 'the Pope of Methodism' – who was President of the Methodist Conference. It was around the time of the arrest of the Tolpiddle men that Bunting stated that Methodism 'is as opposed to democracy as it is to sin', which was far from true, particularly in northern regions where Methodists supported reformist and radical political activity. But Bunting's Methodist church had no interest in or concern about local problems in rural England at that time.

Bunting was prepared to stand against any form of radicalisation to the point of crushing opposition within his own organisation. He refused to intervene in the case of the Tolpiddle Six and after their arrest and transportation, Robert Owen's Grand National Consolidation Trade Union wrote to Bunting asking him to intercede on behalf of the men unfairly tried and sentenced. He received no reply.

The Methodist leader showed no sympathy with the political aspirations of working people. Bunting disliked anyone involved in political reform, such as the Luddites who protested against (and often broke) new machinery which they considered a threat to their jobs. He similarly opposed all participants in the Swing Riots against the arrival of threshing

Jabez Bunting – known to many as 'the Pope of Methodism' – was President of the Methodist Conference and stated he was 'as opposed to democracy as he is to sin.' (*National Portrait Gallery*)

machines and other labour saving devices which had made thousands of farm labourers redundant. There was no apparent support either from local leaders of the Weymouth Wesleyan Circuit, under which the chapel at Tolpiddle was a part, and no evidence of anyone within the circuit signing a petition for their release or making a collection on behalf of wives and children of the deportees. So much for John Wesley's plea for brotherhood and support in hard times; it appeared that nothing of that kind was forthcoming from the Methodist community in Dorset or elsewhere to the Tolpiddle men.

The bible was central to worship and study for all Methodists – particularly the Loveless and Standfield families. They would have read passages regularly, probably more than once a day and preaching in chapel was based on biblical passages. Preachers like George Loveless would have known large biblical passages by heart and he would study a great deal in order to understand how to interpret 'the Word' in a way that would help the lives of his congregation. They would also have used the bible to help their children learn to read.

The Methodist community should have taken a leaf out of their own prayer book to observe the words of the hymn written by Wesley's brother Charles, known as *The Covenant Prayer*. This commits believers to accept God's will which may involve hardship and suffering and would have helped the Tolpiddle men see the injustice and privations they experienced as prisoners for themselves and their families as part of God's purposes for the good of humankind:

> *I am no longer my own but yours.*
> *Put me to what you will,*
> *rank me with whom you will;*
> *put me to doing,*
> *put me to suffering;*
> *let me be employed for you,*
> *or laid aside for you,*
> *exalted for you,*
> *or brought low for you;*
> *let me be full,*
> *let me be empty,*
> *let me have all things,*
> *let me have nothing:*
> *I freely and wholeheartedly yield all things*
> *to your pleasure and disposal.*
> *And now, glorious and blessed God,*
> *Father, Son and Holy Spirit,*
> *you are mine and I am yours.*

Chapter 19

I Do Not Myself Much Care

1836

Ha, my dear friends pray 'ow de-do?
I 'opes I see you well,
Peer'aps ye don't know who I is -
Well, I'm a Westminster swell.
My chambers is in Shoreditch,
And I fancy I'm a toff -
From top to toe I really think,
I looks immensely posh!

Lord Russell was in a tight corner. He had sent letters to the Governors of Van Diemen's Land and New South Wales telling them that the Dorchester Labourers were pardoned, but now learned that this was not to be the case. He should have been aware the Act had been passed or informed about it by one of his advisors, but neither was the case. Mention of the pardons had already been made in Parliament on the same day as Thomas Wakley made his historic speech but it appears Russell had forgotten that the information was now in the public domain and it was the job of his bumbling Westminster mandarins to keep him informed.

On 29 June 1835 Russell wrote to Lord Glenelg saying 'he had only just become aware of the Act preventing convicts being released early' and ordered him to write to the colonial governors asking them for reports about the conduct of the six men. If the response stated they had all been well behaved, Russell hoped that 'His Majesty's gracious intention of extending mercy to them might be carried into effect under the Royal Sign Manual', which allowed the King to use his prerogative of pardon to overrule official statutes. But by 29 June Russell had still to approach the King about the issue. Even if he had, he knew King William IV to be a most obstinate man who would very likely reject the request.

Glenelg again wrote to both Governors enclosing copies of the letter from Lord Russell. He also wrote private notes to each Governor. To Governor Arthur in Hobart he wrote: 'I do not conceal from myself that I impose upon you a duty which may possibly be in some degree at variance with the terms of the statute to which I have referred.' To Sir Richard Bourke in Sydney he wrote: 'I trust, however, that it may be in your power to accomplish the immediate release of these prisoners from penal labour without involving yourself and the government in a responsibility which, it must be confessed, is not lightly to be undertaken.' In other words, 'keep this quiet, chaps, try not to make a fuss and go about this matter swiftly.'

Things were not helped by the thirsty bloodhound Thomas Wakley who continued to agitate Russell at the Home Department for total remission of the sentences. On 23 February 1836, Sir William Molesworth, Radical MP for East Cornwall, seconded a motion by Joseph Hume for the suppression of Orange Lodges, contending they were illegal by swearing illegal oaths. He insisted that the Dorchester Labourers had been condemned for a far more innocent act. The difference was that their chief, George Loveless,

Lord Glenelg was given the job of preventing Lord John Russell from appearing stupid before the Governors of Van Diemen's Land and New South Wales by writing carefully worded letters to both men. (*Wikimedia Commons*)

was not a Prince of the Blood like the Orange Order's Grand Master, the Duke of Cumberland, fifth son of King George III and Queen Charlotte.

A few days later, again in reply to the indomitable Wakley, Russell stated that four out of the six convicts would, as had already been stated, be able to return at the end of two years and that period would expire in October 1836. Since the recent discussions about the Orange Lodges he had thought it his duty to recommend to His Majesty that such part of the sentence upon two of the labourers that called on their continuance in the colonies for the whole period of their transportation should be commuted. At the same time, if other 'favourable circumstances were brought to my knowledge, I know of nothing to prevent me from recommending to His Majesty a further extension of royal mercy'.

To demonstrate that the case of the Tolpiddle men was still uppermost in his mind, Russell sent an urgent note to the Revd. Thomas Warren, Vicar of Tolpiddle asking him to call on the wives of George and James Loveless and ask if they might consider taking their families to Van Dieman's Land and New South Wales to join their husbands. He received a reply dated 3 August 1835 saying that George's wife, Betsey, was anxious to join her husband in Hobart but James' wife, Sarah, was not so enthusiastic but agreed to go 'if it is his desire'. The letter concluded: 'As

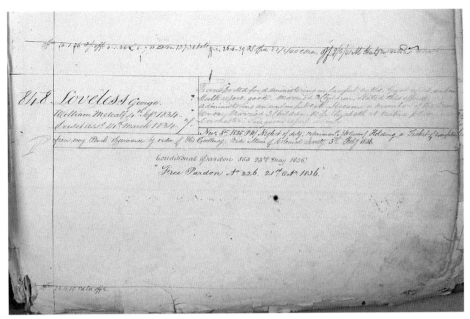

A document confirming that Prisoner 848 George Loveless became the 226th person to be granted a free pardon on October 1836. (*Tasmanian Archive and Heritage Office*)

soon as they receive an answer to their respective letters, if their husbands wish to receive them and their families, they will petition you for this indulgence.'

On Russell's instruction, Lord Glenelg dispatched further letters to the colonial governors asking them to enquire whether the Loveless brothers wanted their wives and children to join them. While waiting for a reply Russell had quietly secured conditional pardons from the King under the Royal Sign Manual, which allowed the Standfields, James Brine and James Hammett to return home at the end of two years and the Loveless brothers at the end of three years.

George Loveless's pardon was an elaborate affair, signed by King William IV at the top with a flourish and approved with the red royal seal. It was addressed to 'Our Trusted and Well-beloved Lieut. Col. George Arthur, Lieut. Governor of our Island of Van Diemen's Land. The Lieut. Governor of our said Island for the time being, and all those whom it may concern, by His Majesty's Command' and it continued:

Whereas George Loveless was at the Lent Assizes, 1834, holden for the County of Dorset, tried and convicted of administering unlawful oaths and sentenced to be transported for seven year for the same – we in consideration of some circumstances humbly presented unto us are graciously pleased to extend our grace and mercy unto him, and to grant him Our Free Pardon for such crime, provided his conduct has, during his residence in Our Island

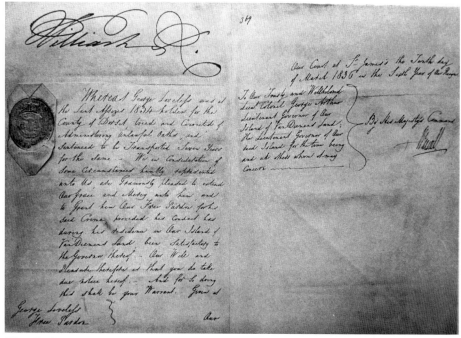

King William IV personally signed George Loveless's Royal Pardon – but it would still be a further 10 months before the agricultural labourer from Tolpiddle boarded a homeward-bound ship to England. (*Dorset History Centre*)

of Van Diemen's Land has been satisfactory to the Governor – our Will and Pleasure therefore is that you do have due notice thereof – And for so doing this shall be your warrant. Given at our Court at St. James the tenth day of March, 1836, in the sixth year of our Reign.

It would be just over 10 more months before George Loveless boarded a homeward-bound ship for England.

From Lord Melbourne to Lord John Russell, 13 October 1835:

I do not myself much care what is done respecting the Dorchester Labourers. But you know the feeling which exists against their being brought back to the country.

From the Tolpiddle wives to Lord John Russell, 18 March 1836:

May it please your Lordship,
    My Lord, we whose names are hereunto fixed with feelings of our warmest Gratitude and of our most humble acknowledgments return to you our Grateful thanks for your Kindness shown towards us by Procuring for our

Handwritten letter from Prime Minister Lord Melbourne to Lord John Russell – October 13, 1835: 'I do not myself much care what is done respecting the Dorchester Labourers. But you know the feeling which exists against their being brought back to the country.' (*National Archives*)

Letter from Tolpuddle wives to Lord John Russell offering 'grateful thanks for your kindness shown to us.' (*Dorset History Centre*) husbands, the son and relatives His Majesty's most Gracious Pardon viz. on the Dorchester unions. But those especially by procuring Pardon for the two Lovelesses to return with the others at the end of two years and Hearing of your unworried diligence for them and us. We will as in duty bound pray for your Lordship's health, Happiness and prosperity.

(Signed) Elizabeth Loveless, Sarah Loveless, C. Brine, Dinniah Standfield. H. Hammett.

From the Home Department, Whitehall, 21 March 1836 to Colonial Governors:

Sirs,

Lord John Russell having thought it right, upon further consideration of the case of George Loveless and other.... I am directed to transmit to you the enclosed warrants, which the King has been graciously pleased to grant for that purpose, and to request that in forwarding the same to Governors of the Australian Colonies, Lord Glenelg will also convey instructions that the convicts may be provided with a free passage to this country by the first favourable opportunity.

'I have the honour to be your most obedient and humble servant,

'J. M. Phillipps, Permanent Under Secretary, Home Department.

From Downing Street, 24 March 1836 to Lieutenant Governor Arthur and Governor Sir Richard Bourke:

Sirs,

With reference to my Dispatch of November 12 last, which I forwarded to you conditional pardons for certain prisoners who were convicted at Dorchester for administering unlawful oaths, I have now the honour to transmit to you a copy of a letter which I have received from the Home Department, enclosing a free pardon, which His Majesty has been pleased to grant to those persons, and to request that you will give them the benefit thereof.

I have further to request that in the event of all, or any of them, wishing to return to this country, you will provide them with free passages by the first favourable opportunity, the expenses of which will be chargeable on the funds applicable to convict services.

I am your most obedient and humble servant,

Glenelg.

From Betsy Loveless to Lord John Russell, 24 July 1836 after hearing that her husband is to be pardoned and she and her children are to be offered a free passage to Van Diemen's Land:

'My Lord – I am gratefully obliged to your Lordship for the offer you have given me. But I cannot think of going to my husband as I know he have received a pardon and from what I have learned I hope to see him in a few months. I'm also thankful for the privilege of receiving the letter from my husband.

   I am, my Lord, your humble and most obedient servant.

       E. Loveless'

Chapter 20

No Better Than Slavery

1836

I had a dream, a happy dream,
I thought that I was free;
That in my own bright land again
A home was there for me.
England's tide dash'd bravely on,
I saw wave roll o'er wave;
But in my full delight I woke
And I was still a slave.

While still at the Government Farm in Hobart, Loveless wrote to Governor Arthur 'hoping I might be allowed to be assigned to a master, but I received no answer.' Sometime in November 1835, the Governor contacted the farm's overseer, a man called Fitzpatrick, with enquiries into Loveless's character. Over the next two months more enquiries were forthcoming, the last one asking Fitzpatrick: 'Is there no fault whatever to be found with Loveless? Does he never reply when you bid him to do something? Does he never neglect any part of his work?' Little did Loveless know that he would be given his ticket to freedom 'providing his conduct has, during his residence in Van Dieman's Land, been satisfactory to the Governor'. Loveless was a hard worker on the farm and Governor Arthur was reluctant to let him return to England to be replaced by an inferior stockman. But if there might be just a small misdemeanour, it might be possible to detain him in Van Diemen's Land for a few more years.

Loveless treated his cows and sheep as if they were his own, tending them from sun-up to sun-down. He had even given the nine cows in his care individual names just as he had his plough horses back in Mrs. Northover's Tolpiddle farm. In December 1835 Loveless was busy milking his cows when a constable appeared who marched him and Fitzpatrick to the police office charged with 'neglecting his duty'. William Gunn was the sitting magistrate at the time. He asked the overseer why Prisoner 848 had been brought before the bench. 'For neglect of duty' replied Fitzpatrick. 'In what manner has he neglected his duty?' asked the magistrate. Fitzpatrick explained that Loveless was a shepherd and stock keeper on the government farm in charge of all tame and wild cattle. 'He is expected to see them all every day. Nine of the wild cattle were taken to the public pound yesterday and he did not miss them until this morning,' explained the overseer.

Mr. Gunn looked long and hard at Loveless and told him: 'I have not heard a clearer charge of neglect of duty for a long time; what have you to say Prisoner 848, in answer to this charge?' Loveless said it was true. 'I am in charge of all cattle and I am expected to see the wild cattle in the bush once every twenty-four hours. I rise in the morning at sunrise, or before, and take the sheep to the bush to feed. I then return to the farm and milk nine cows and suckle as many calves. I am requested to follow the sheep and not lose sight of them for fear of dogs which often get among and worry them. I am ordered to search for the wild cattle to see that none of them are missing. I had just been weaning the lambs, and the ewes being very restless, I was afraid to leave them. And this, sir, was the reason the cattle were taken to the pound and I did not miss them.'

Gunn asked Fitzpatrick if Loveless had been telling the truth. 'Yes sir,' came the reply. 'How long have you known this prisoner?' asked Mr. Gunn. 'Nine months,' answered Fitzpatrick. 'Did you ever know him to neglect his duty before?' continued Gunn. 'No sir, never,' was the reply. 'Then you do not think that he went away from his duty now, but that, as he says, he was with the sheep in consequence of having weaned the lambs,' queried Gunn. 'Yes sir, what he has told you is true, but then he has neglected his duty in losing the cattle,' explained Fitzpatrick. 'But do you not think the man has more duty than he can perform. I really think it is a great pity you should have brought the man here,' said Gunn before turning to Loveless and said: 'I shall return you to your duty, Prisoner 848.'

Loveless thanked the magistrate and left the courtroom fully expecting to receive fifty lashes when he returned to the farm. But there was no further punishment. Punishment, however, was shortly to be given to Fitzpatrick, for embezzling a quantity of hay from the government farm, the property of the Crown, and he was discharged from his job.

On 29 December 1835 Loveless was summoned back to the police office to answer a note received by Acting Chief Magistrate, Josiah Spode, wanting to know if his wife and children should be sent out to Van Dieman's Land to join him. Loveless said he had a question: 'Am I about to obtain my liberty?' Spode nearly fell off his chair: 'Liberty? What do you mean?' Loveless answered: 'Is there a prospect of my obtaining my free pardon?' The Magistrate answered: 'Not that I know, that depends on the ministry at home.' That was the answer Loveless was expecting and replied: 'Then sir, I can have nothing at all to say on the subject while I am a prisoner.' Spode grew red in the face as if he was choking and then spluttered: 'You audacious rascal, will you come to insult me thus, after I have been at pains of writing and sending for you and all for your own advantage?' Loveless said he had not intended to insult Mr. Spode. The Magistrate brought his fist down on the table with a bang before pointing at Loveless and said: 'You liar, you rascal, you did; and do you mean to continue, you obstinate fellow?' Loveless remained silent, knowing what Van Diemen's Land's cruel penal system would have exposed him to if he had replied. He would have been accused of insolence and punished accordingly. Spode snapped: 'Go back to your work, Prisoner 848, and go instantly or I will give you a dammed good flogging.'

On 7 January 1836, he was brought back before Spode who told him: 'Well Prisoner 848, I have sent for you once more.' Loveless replied: 'Yes sir, and here I am.' Spode leaned forward and gently told Loveless: 'I want to know if you have any objection that your wife and family should be sent over to you? And let me tell you before you answer me, it is intended for your advantage.' Standing upright and looking straight ahead, Loveless replied: 'Nothing could give me so much satisfaction as to join my wife and children had I my liberty, but I do not want them here while I am still a prisoner.' Spode began banging the table again: 'You want to be above the government and tell them what they must do, eh?' Wearily, Loveless replied: 'No sir, but I tell you, rather than be the instrument of bringing my wife and children into the distress and misery of this colony, such as I feel it, I will remain as I am as long as I live.' Spode angrily ordered Loveless to be returned to the farm.

On 24 January Governor Arthur himself came to the farm in person and asked Loveless to 'walk and talk' with him through the fields. As they strolled across a meadow, Arthur gently asked Loveless if he had any objection to the government sending Mrs. Loveless and the children to join him at the government's expense. Loveless said he had objections and Arthur asked him to name them. 'I should be sorry to send me my wife and children to come into misery,' he said. Arthur was surprised by this answer: 'Misery? What do you mean?' asked the autocratic and authoritarian Governor who lived a life of wealth and luxury among other like-minded people in Hobart well away from the poverty and strife facing other new citizens in the colony. Loveless did not hold back with his answer: 'Why sir, I have seen nothing but misery since I came into this country about seventeen months ago. The food and clothing allowed to government men only renders them miserable. It is no better than slavery.'

Governor Arthur stopped in his tracks: 'Oh no, there are no slaves under the British dominions, you are only prisoners.' Loveless responded with: 'You may call it by what name you please, sir; I call it slavery and that of the worst description.' They carried on walking once more. 'But are you willing that your wife should come over? Don't you think that you could do very well together here?' asked Arthur. 'I do not know that I could,' said the prisoner. 'How is it you don't know?' asked the Governor irritably. 'You are a good farming man and you are a good shepherd, are you not?' Loveless was unsure how to answer. 'As to that, other people are the best judges. I know nothing of what the colony can afford,' he said.

Arthur replied: 'Well, I think you could do well with your wife in this country; she would do very well here.' Loveless replied firmly: 'Sir, I should be a monster to send my wife to come over here and see no way of supporting her; what could I do with my wife while I am a prisoner?'

They turned and headed back to the cattle pens. 'I have no doubt but you will have your liberty as soon as your wife arrives. I would gladly give you indulgence myself, but that I dare not, in consequence of an act of parliament that no seven years' man is to obtain a ticket of leave 'till he has been four years on the colony. Government has sent out to know how you have conducted yourself since you have been here and I have sent home an excellent character of you to them. How would you support your wife and family in England?' 'By my labour, sir,' Loveless replied. 'And why cannot you support them by your labour here?' asked the governor. 'I consider, while they are in England they are surrounded by friends; if they were here it might be otherwise.' The Governor told him to think it over and let him know his decision in two or three days.

On 27 January Loveless wrote to Betsey requesting her to come to Van Diemen's Land and sent it, unsealed, to Governor Arthur for approval. Nine days later he received a note from the Governor's office ordering him to come to the police office 'without delay, repair thither as soon as possible'. On arrival, he was greeted by Acting Chief Magistrate Spode who handed him an envelope. Inside was the following note:

> I am directed by his Excellency, The Governor, in accordance with His Majesty's government, to give George Loveless (prisoner 848 from the *William Metcalf*) a ticket, exempting him from the government labour to employ himself to his own advantage until further orders.

It was signed by the Principal Superintendent's Office, Josiah Spode, on 5 February 1836. But he was prevented from taking 'the ticket' away with him until he was able to find somewhere to call home and recorded as where he would be located when needed.

Loveless was now no longer a convict but a free man once more.

Part VI

A Stranger in the Colony

1836/37

O pity the fate of a poor wretched stranger,
That's wander'd thus far from his home;
I sigh for protection from want, woe and danger
But know not which way for to roam.

Loveless later recalled:

I now had my liberty to prove what the colony could afford; and I soon found, to my sorrow, the force of the observation I made to the Governor a few days before. I was a stranger in the colony, without money, without clothes, without friends and without a home. In this situation I travelled the country seeking employment; and I have walked fifty miles without breaking my fast. I soon returned to Hobart Town. After a week or two I got a little employment; and as soon as possible advertised for a situation and found a master, in whose service I remained until I left the country.

His master was a gentleman called Major William de Gillern, a German-born landowner who had served in the British army and risen to the rank of Major. He had purchased a farm called Glen Ayr in the new settlement of Richmond, 16 miles from Hobart in the heart of the Coal River Valley. Richmond was an important military staging post and convict station linking Hobart with Port Arthur. The farm supplied the barracks and commissariat in Hobart with fresh vegetables and hay.

Major de Gillern and his English-born wife Harriet arrived in Van Diemen's Land thirteen years before and opened a distillery near New Town in Hobart. They later moved to Glen Ayr where they built barns, re-built their distillery and sold gin commercially, which was not difficult in such a hard drinking colony.

In addition to providing Loveless with a wage-paying job undertaking general farming duties at Glen Ayr, the Major also provided accommodation in a stone built cottage close to his own large family home nearby. The Major took a liking to George Loveless. He found him a man of intelligence and good character, a hard

Ruins of Glen Ayr, the once fine mansion near Richmond, 16 miles from Hobart where George Loveless was provided with a wage earning job with owner Major William de Gillern. (*Rebecca Mayo*)

worker, prepared to labour long working hours when needed. The two men enjoyed regular conversations and the Major passed on copies of his newspapers once he had finished with them so they could discuss what was happening in the small world of Van Diemen's Land and the larger world outside. Early in September 1836, the Major passed on a copy of the *Weekly Dispatch* dated 2 April containing a report about a speech given by Sir William Molesworth, a radical British politician, talking about Orange Lodges, the conduct of the Duke of Cumberland (Grand Master of the Orange Order), Lord Kenyon and the Bishop of Salisbury all of whom were said to be part of a plot to overthrow Princess Victoria who was to become Queen on the death of William IV and replace her with the Duke. Loveless wrote: 'It stated that shortly after this speech was delivered Lord J. Russell gave notice that orders were forwarded that the Dorchester Unionists were not only to be set at liberty, but also to be sent back to England, free of expense and with every necessary comfort.' Loveless jotted down this paragraph of the story in case he might need it as evidence to his freedom at some time in the future.

Another article keenly followed by de Gillern and Loveless involved Governor Arthur and his use of Van Diemen's Land as a prison. Considerable agitation had been taking place on the island against what was considered to be Governor Arthur's severity and maladministration. Other newspapers regarded Arthur as little more than a tyrant and demanded his recall to London. Since taking the role of Lieutenant Governor in 1823 Arthur's main objective had been to turn the island into an efficient gaol; this he did with an iron fist. He introduced chain gangs to deter prisoners from escaping and used them extensively for punishment. To increase the 'dread' of transportation back in England, Arthur told the Colonial Office that convicts 'should be kept rigidly at the spade and pick-axe and wheelbarrow ... from morning till night, although the immediate toil of the convicts be the only beneficial result of their labour'. The basis of Arthur's system had been to assign prisoners to work for settlers, and it was here that his imprint had been most obvious. Not only did servants face punishment for misconduct, but they might be withdrawn if their masters ill-treated them, gave them grog, failed to keep the Sabbath, or broke other regulations.

The outspoken English-born editor of the *Tasmanian* newspaper, Robert Murray, reported that 'order had been sent from the Home Government to work the Dorchester Unionists in irons on the roads' but – apart from one week – Governor Arthur had not carried out the order and sent George Loveless to work on the government farm. Murray also remarked that 'No doubt Governor Arthur has already sent George Loveless back home.'

Loveless wrote to Murray at the *Tasmanian* on 19 September 1836:

'Sir, Of late, frequent mention has been made in the *Tasmanian* of the men known as the Dorchester Unionists, and of the home government in reference to them. Last week you mentioned the subject again, and observed 'no doubt that Governor Arthur has already sent George Loveless back home.' I do not know whether Governor Arthur has received orders from home; I should like to know. If His Excellency has received intelligence to that effect, I hope he will have the goodness to communicate that knowledge to me before he leaves these shores. I hereby offer you my sincere thanks for the sympathy you manifest towards the fate of some half-dozen humble individuals who, in 1834, were transported to these colonies for unwillingly and ignorantly giving offence. Few can imagine – experience alone teach – what it is to be bereaved of, and torn from, those who are dear to us; and who are still dearer to me than could possibly be all the treasurers of the world – wife and children.

Signed: A Dorchester Unionist.

A week or so layer, Major de Gillern received a letter from the Governor's office asking that if Loveless was still working at Glen Ayr, he should be informed that the Governor wished to see him at Government House. Unfortunately, in communicating this message to Loveless, de Gillern failed to tell him that the Governor wanted to see him and some time elapsed before he became aware of it. He was eventually notified on 8 October by the Governor's Principal Superintendent of Convicts, Josiah Spode, that he could have a passage home on the passenger and cargo ship *Elphinstone*, the same ship carrying Governor Arthur back to England.

Loveless answered:

> 'Sir, I highly appreciate the kind offer of His Excellency the Governor in giving me a passage to England by the *Elphinstone*. I would most gladly embark, as I have a strong wish to go back; but consider that I have placed myself in a very awkward situation. His Excellency knows that I have been persuaded to send me my wife, and it is probably that she is now on her way here, it being nine months since the invitation left this colony. It would be a dreadful thing for her to find, when she arrives at Hobart Town, I had gone to London. I hope I may be allowed to remain until I hear from her, and if she is not coming, to claim a free passage to England.'

Spode replies a few days later:

> George Loveless, in answer to your note wishing to know if you could be allowed a passage to England in a few months, I have to inform you, that unless you go by the present opportunity, the government will not be able to give you a free passage.

After receiving Spode's note, de Gillern gave Loveless leave to go to Hobart to try and sort his passage out. He managed to get an appointment with Spode and recalled the following conversation:

> Loveless: I have called, sir, to know if I can be allowed to stop in the colony until I shall receive a communication from my wife.

> Spode: You have been told what can be done; you seem to pay no attention to the authorities; nothing more can be done for you.

> Loveless: I think, sir, that mine is a hard case; I was urged by the Governor to send for my wife and family and I know not but they are coming, and yet I must be forced to leave before sufficient time has been allowed me to ascertain whether they will come or not.

> Spode: Well, why did you not obey the Governor when he sent for you; it appears you altogether treat the authorities with disrespect.

> Loveless: I have no wish to disobey those in authority, but the reason I did not proceed to Hobart Town, in compliance with the first request, I was not

told that I was wanted. My master only told me the Governor wanted to know if I was living in his service; and lately I could not come in consequence of my master's illness, he having been for some time at Hobart Town under the doctor's care.

Spode: Well, but the Governor has an order to send you back by the first ship.

Loveless: I think, sir, you have had a free pardon for me in your office some considerable time longer before I knew about it, than I have delayed in coming since I have known it.

Spode (getting flustered): Yes, my good fellow, but the reason of that was, we did not know where to send to you.

Loveless (firmly): I beg your pardon, sir, that could not be the reason, as the place I called my home was registered in the police office by order of the Governor. You say, sir, the King's pardon for me is in your office, and yet I am to be sent home as a prisoner. I was sent out as a prisoner, contrary to my wishes, and with a free pardon I am to be sent back a prisoner, contrary to my wishes. I hope Mr. Montague (sic) will place himself in my situation a few minutes. I know he is a husband and farmer.'

Spode (after a long pause): Well Loveless, what do you want?

Loveless: I want a promise from the Governor that I shall be indulged with the privilege of stopping a few months until I shall receive a letter from my wife, and if she is not coming to Van Diemen's Land, to have something to show that I may claim a free passage to England.'

Spode: I will draw up a memorandum myself, and see what can be done for you, and you shall know the results in a few days.'

A message from Spode's office dated 24 October 1836 was delivered to Glen Ayr:

Memorandum, with reference to a former notification addressed to you from this office, relative to a free pardon having been ordered for you from England, I am now to inform you that His Excellency, the Lieutenant-Governor, is pleased to approve of that indulgence being issued to you immediately: and I am to further acquaint you, in consequence of your having expressed your disinclination to embark for England by the *Elphinstone*, from having written some months ago to your wife, to join you with your three children in this colony, and that you are therefore anxious to await the result of that communication, that, in the event of your expectation not being fulfilled, as it regards the arrival of your family, and which an interval of three or four months may determine; His Excellency has been pleased to direct that a free passage is to be then offered you by the government that you may return to England.

Desperate to share his news with Betsey, Loveless dashed off a short note to his wife:
Hobart Town – October 30 1836:

I have seen in the newspapers lately that my free pardon was ordered and free passage to England. I made application to the Governor, to know the truth of it, who assured me it was so and wished me to embark with him in the ship *Elphinstone.* I have absolutely refused the offer, in consequence of having invited you to come to me; for it would be a sad thing if you were in Hobart Town and I in London. If I don't hear from you before April or May 1837, doubtless I shall think of going to England. By the time this reaches you, I might be ploughing the mighty deep; and I cannot say any more at present, or it will be too late for the post.

Loveless now waited on tenterhooks for a letter from Betsy, which finally arrived, via the Home Office, three days before Christmas 1836 'assuring me she did not intend coming to Van Diemen's Land and wishing me to return as soon as possible'. He scribbled a quick letter to the Colonial Secretary of Van Diemen's Land, John Montagu:

This will inform you that George Loveless (Prisoner 848, per *William Metcalf*) has received a letter from his wife, through the Home Office, refusing the offer to join him in this colony, and as through your kind interference, a promise was made him by the government, of granting him a free passage to England, on receiving information that his wife was not coming, he therefore earnestly entreats and humbly demands of His Majesty's Government in this colony, to provide for him a free passage to England. Relying on your goodness, he offers you his warmest gratitude and acknowledgement and subscribes himself your humble and obliged servant.
George Loveless.

o0o

Unbeknown to Loveless, correspondence on behalf of the Tolpiddle wives was being exchanged between Robert Hartwell of the Central Dorchester Committee and Lord John Russell through his Secretary, Mr. J. M. Phillips:

London – January 18, 1837:

My Lord, The families of the Dorchester Labourers having received information, by a letter, that their relatives were all prisoners in August last, and feeling great anxiety on the subject, I am required respectfully to solicit from your Lordship an answer to the following questions: Whether the free pardon was dispatched in March 1836; whether an order accompanied it to send the men home at the expense of the government or whether the men will have to make their way home in the best manner they can? An early answer to these questions will tend to relieve the painful suspense under which their families are now suffering and greatly oblige.

My Lord, yours respectfully,
R. Hartwell

After two weeks Hartwell received a reply:

Sir, I am directed by Lord J. Russell to acquaint you in reply to your letter of the 18th instant, that if any of the family of the persons therein mentioned will call at this office, information on the subject to which you refer will be communicated to them; or if either of the parties, not being able to attend at the office, will address a letter to the Secretary of State, the requested intelligence will be immediately granted.

I am, sir, your most obedient servant,
J. M. Phillipps

This apology for an answer was sent to Betsey Loveless and the other Tolpiddle wives who immediately met together to write to Lord John Russell. Three weeks later they received a reply:

Whitehall February 18, 1837:

Elizabeth Loveless is acquainted, in reply to the letter to which her name is affixed, that a free pardon for the persons therein referred to was forwarded to Australia in March 1836, with instructions to the Governor to provide them with a free passage home at the first favourable opportunity.

I am your most obedient servant,
J. M. Phillipps

The *Eveline* brought George Loveless home from captivity in Van Diemen's Land departing in January 1837 and arriving in London in June. (*National Maritime Museum*)

Hartwell sent copies of the correspondence to newspapers sympathetic to the cause of Dorchester Labourers with the following covering letter:

> The Dorchester Committee deem it their duty to lay these letters before their fellow workmen and the public. They require but little comment. It appears that there is a probability the men may not yet arrive for some time, for it entirely depends upon the authorities in the colonies when they think a favourable opportunity may occur. Why did not the government order them to be sent home immediately on the arrival of their pardon? No, that was too straight-forward a course for the Whigs to pursue; their policy is always crooked.... The public may depend that some decisive steps will be immediately taken by the committee on the subject.

oOo

At the end of January 1837, Loveless requested another two days leave from Major Gillern to go to the police office in Hobart and enquire if any letters might be forthcoming. He was informed that a letter had been delivered to him, via Major Gillern at Glen Ayr, that very morning. It was from Josiah Spode and read:

I am to inform you that you can be allowed a free passage on the ship *Eveline*, Captain Jamison, in the forecastle [almost certainly in the crew's quarters] with steerage passenger's allowance, providing you are satisfied with the accommodations; as this vessel will sail in the course of the month, you had better proceed to Hobart Town immediately, and satisfy yourself respecting it, and inform me of your decision – Josiah Spode.

Loveless records:

I instantly went on board and agreed with Captain Alexander Jamieson who told me the ship would sail on Sunday January 29, 1837. I returned and told Mr. Spode that I had seen the Captain and was satisfied with the promised accommodation, and the same night returned to my master. Saturday, January 28, I proceeded to Hobart Town and went on board the ship and on Monday January 30 at nine o'clock at night, we drew anchor and embarked for London where I arrived on June 13, 1837.

On the long voyage home, Loveless had plenty of time to reflect on his time as a convict in Van Diemen's Land and how it might have affected his thinking and frame of mind. But he later wrote:

Transportation *has not* had the intended affect on me, but, after all, I am returned from my bondage with my views and principals strengthened. It is indelibly fixed on my mind that labour is ill-rewarded in consequence of a few tyrannising over the millions; and that through their oppression, thousands are now working in chains on the roads, abused by the overseers … and punished by the flagellator … is this the plan to reform men? I say no. If they were bad before, they are tenfold the children of hell now.

The groans and cries of the labourers ere long will bring down vengeance on the heads of those who have been and are still the authors of so much misery.

I believe that nothing will ever be done to relieve the distress of the working classes unless they take it into their own hands.....Nothing but union will or can accomplish the great and important object, namely the salvation of the world. Let the producers of wealth firmly and peaceably unite their energies – and what can withstand them?

o0o

After learning that his uncle, George Loveless, was in Van Diemen's Land and not in New South Wales, John Standfield wrote to him at Glen Ayr on 27 November

1836 and received an answer the following January. Loveless told his nephew that he was soon to sail for England and provided young Standfield with instructions on how to go about getting a free passage home for himself and the others, none of whom had any idea what had happened to James Hammett or where he was.

John Standfield immediately wrote to his uncle, James Loveless, telling him the good news about Uncle George and asking him to make an application for their passage home. He asked the farm superintendent, Mr. Brennan to post the letter for him – but Brennan conveniently forgot to carry out the task for several weeks. According to John Standfield this was because 'Brenan wanted to keep us in the colony'. James Loveless, however, persevered and a passage was finally obtained for himself, the Standfields and James Brine even though, as young Standfield later recalled, 'not the slightest communication was ever made to me or my companions by any government officer of our free pardon having been received.'

Chapter 21

The Homecoming

1837

The dearest spot on earth to me
Is home, sweet home;
The fairy land I've longed to see,
Is home, sweet home.
There how charmed the sense of hearing,
There where hears are so endearing,
All the world is not so cheering
As home, sweet home.

A small welcoming party from the Central Dorchester Committee awaited George Loveless on the landing stage at the London Docks. These were men Loveless had never met before but had tirelessly championed for his release and freedom for the other men. His return did not attract any newspaper publicity, probably because King William IV was close to death 'from an affection of the heart'. The King finally passed away in Windsor on June 20, leaving behind him the memory of a blundering and belligerent monarch who had achieved little in his lifetime. He was to be replaced by his 18-year-old niece Princess Victoria of Kent, who was virtually unknown to the British public. That was to change radically during the 63 years, seven months, and two days of her reign.

Loveless travelled by coach back to his home and family in Tolpiddle. There was no village welcoming party to greet him as nobody was exactly sure when he might return. It must have been an amazing sight when he walked through the door of his humble home to be greeted by Betsy and the children, George now 12, Robert, 10 and Thomas, 8. Loveless knew in his heart that one day he would be reunited with his family and was thankful he did not have to endure the full seven years of his original sentence.

After resting he rose early the next morning to have his customary walk around the village at daybreak – to the stables at West Farm to be reunited with his carthorses where he would have checked them over thoroughly, onto the village green to stand under the large sycamore tree, the scene of many a meeting with his union companions, and across to the small Methodist chapel he had helped to build and where he had preached many a sermon. It was good to be home.

He still, however had much work to do. Before travelling home after arriving at the Port of London, Loveless had a long conversation with members of the Central Dorchester Committee about activities which might take place when the other Tolpiddle men arrived back. He suggested that it might be best to do nothing at all for the time being, but the committee proposed to draw up plans in readiness for their return. Committee Secretary Robert Hartwell suggested that Loveless might consider writing a pamphlet outlining the story of how and why the Friendly Society of Agricultural Labourers was born, his arrest with five others, their confinement in prison, the scandalous perversion of the law at their 'sham' trial followed by the horrors of transportation and life in a penal colony on the other side of the world. This would give Loveless an opportunity to tell his side of the story, share his experiences and thoughts about the men responsible for taking three years of his life away and his ideas about how to improve working conditions and wages for ordinary working men. He would also find the writing experience cathartic and a chance to get matters off his chest. Hartwell proposed that a pamphlet should be printed, bound and sold for a small sum of money with all profits for Central Dorchester Committee funds.

Loveless was unsure if he could write such a pamphlet. His previous experience of writing had been confined to sermons and letters and he had doubts that he could produce a coherent story of his struggle that people might like to pay for and read. On the bumpy coach ride home, however, he determined to try and after a few days rest he boldly set out to put his story down on paper.

As the committee was still providing a weekly allowance to families of the six men there was no pressure on him to return to the plough for a measly crust. He purchased paper and writing materials and spent the rest of June and all of July 1837 writing and re-writing his story. He decided to call it *The Victims of Whiggery – A Statement of the Persecution Experienced by the Dorchester Labourers; with a Report of the Trial and also a Description of Van Diemen's Land and Reflections Upon the System of Transportation and dedicated (without permission) to Lord Melbourne, Grey, Russell, Brougham and Judge Williams. By George Loveless, one of the Dorchester Labourers.*

Each evening following a full day's writing, Loveless read out what he had scribbled to Betsy who, on occasions, would break down and cry as she learned for the first time about how her husband had been so wretchedly treated in England and Van Diemen's Land. Robert Hartwell volunteered to pen an introduction to the pamphlet, stating that the Central Dorchester Committee was

... of the opinion that it would be highly desirable for an authenticated statement of the persecution of the Dorchester Labourers to be laid before the public, which, while serving as a memento of Whig hypocrisy and tyranny, might also be beneficial in aiding that fund which is now raising to confer some recompense upon these ill-used men on their return, and from which their families are supported during their exile, suggested to George Loveless on his arrival in June last, the propriety of his writing such a statement.

Venomously Hartwell added:

The committee feel it necessary to remind the public generally, but especially the labouring classes, that it is a duty they owe to themselves and their order, never to forget who were the authors and abettors of this cruel violation of the laws of humanity – of this unparalleled outrage upon the rights of industry. It was the WHIG GOVERNMENT – the REFORM MINISTRY of William IV, under

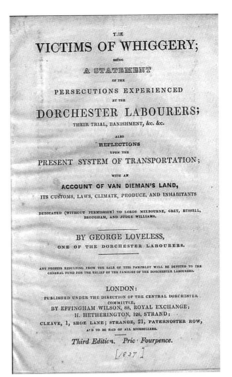

George Loveless wrote *The Victims of Whiggery* shortly after returning to England. It sold for 4d per copy and sold over 12,000 copies in four editions. (*Author's Collection*)

the auspices of Lords, Gray, Melbourne, Russell and Brougham – it was these men who carried into execution, with haste as unfrequent as it was indecent, the cruel sentence of a Whig Judge (Baron John Williams), created by themselves but a short time previous, and who was then making his first circuit. Truly this man has earned an ignoble fame! Yes fellow countrymen, it remained for these men, carried into office and supported by the mass of the population; who had their political life breathed into them by the power and energy of the working millions; who boast of the great affection they feel for the people, in contrast to the hatred of their colleagues in political profligacy – the Tories: it remained for these men, to turn round upon the industrious and confiding working men of England and in an obscure village, seize upon and transport six of their honest and industrious brethren....in defiance of the prayers, entireties, and remonstrances of the people, from all parts of the country.

More rant followed:

Monstrous hypocrites! To tear six of their unoffending countrymen from their native land, from the partners of their bosom, and from the arms of their young and helpless families.... to doom them to a species of punishment, which they themselves had boasted to have made worse than death; to keep them in the colonies after they had been granted a free pardon, reluctantly wrung from them; and after doing all this, still to talk of liberty – of their love for the people and call on the working classes for support! Whenever a mere Whig utters these sophistries in an assemblage of working men, they should raise such a cry of 'Dorchester' as would shame him into silence, or drive him into obscurity.

oOo

Two months after George Loveless had returned to English soil, the following short article appeared in some regional newspapers:

August 12, 1837 – Return of the Dorchester Labourers:

It appears that one of the Dorchester Labourers, George Loveless, has reached this country, and it is probable that the rest of the men will be home in two or three months, though they had not received their free pardon when he left Hobart Town.

oOo

The Victims of Whiggery went on sale for 4d a copy on 4 September 1837. By January 1838 it had sold over 12,000 copies in three separate editions with a fourth on the way. The Central Dorchester Committee said it hoped a copy would be 'in every home throughout the kingdom'. Advertisements promoting the pamphlet and where copies could be obtained appeared in leading regional newspapers telling readers that 'all profits resulting from the sale of this pamphlet will be devoted to the general fund for the relief of the families of the Dorchester Labourers.'

The pamphlet received a glowing review in the radical newspaper *The Champion and Weekly Herald* which reported:

This pamphlet is so cheap as to be within the reach of everybody, and we make no doubt that it will be, as it ought to be, extensively read.... The tale which Loveless tells is a horrid one. Yet it is so circumstantial and told in language so full of moderation that it bears the appearance of truth. If it be false, those who are most interested have the power of disproving it, and if the truth of it be not disputed, let those who read the details say what the

Whigs deserve in return for their treatment of George Loveless and his fellow labourers.

The relief fund had been providing funds to the Tolpiddle families for the last 27 months. Each family received weekly cash payments personally delivered to them either by a member of the Dorchester Central Committee or another trustworthy who travelled from London by coach carrying the funds. At no stage was any person bearing money ever prevented from visiting the families or stopped and questioned about the purpose of their visit to Tolpiddle. By July 1837 and after payments to the six families, £600 was still in hand with royalties from the *Victims of Whiggery* rolling in each week. The question was now posed: what was to be done with the Tolpiddle families once all the men had returned home?

Chapter 22

Sons of Freedom

1838

Sons of freedom, hear my story,
Mercy will become the brave:
Humanity is Britain's glory –
Pity and protect the slave.

The four Dorset labourers made their way to the Sydney quayside on 11 September 1837 where the 540 ton three-masted merchant ship *John Barry* was moored and waiting to board them. The ship had previously been anchored for several weeks at the North Head Quarantine Station in a remote part of the port after arriving with a ship load of passengers suffering from typhoid, thought to have been brought on board by Irish emigrants who boarded her in Queenstown (Cork). Of the 379 men, women and children the *John Barry* had been carrying nearly 40 had died of the disease on its 106-day crossing to the new world. In quarantine, the ship was scrubbed and disinfected from stem to stern in readiness to return via Port Chalmers in Dunedin, New Zealand where it would spend several weeks loading timber for export to England. Most of the timber was native kauri spars – long poles made from kauri trees used for masts and booms much in demand by the Royal Navy at His Majesty's Dockyards. Also travelling on the ship were quantities of whale oil, kauri gum and hemp.

Once on board John Standfield sought out Captain John Robson and negotiated a deal whereby the four exiles would work their passage home on board the *John Barry* in return for wages, giving them money to buy 'new clothing and other necessities on our arrival in England'. The ship left Sydney later that evening and the four Tolpiddle men must have been relieved to see New South Wales slowly disappearing into the distance. Three years and one month earlier they had arrived in the colony as prisoners in chains. Now they were leaving as free men returning home to their wives and children and, hopefully, to their old jobs on Tolpiddle farms.

On arrival in Dunedin the *John Barry* spent nine weeks loading timber and other cargo into its hold before heading home to Plymouth. The passenger manifest recorded the occupations of the four new crewmen as 'Pardoned, illegal combination.'

The four Tolpiddle men arriving home on the *John Barry* set foot back on English soil in Plymouth's Sutton Harbour where this plaque records the occasion. (*Labour: Coast and Country*)

After 'a rough and boisterous voyage' the *John Barry* nosed into Plymouth's Sutton Harbour on 17 March 1838 – exactly four years from the date of their trial. A small rowing boat was brought out to transport the men from the ship to the West Pier and dry land – English land, homeland, their land.

Once word got around Plymouth that the four Dorchester Labourers had disembarked in their town people flocked to West Pier to get a look at the famous men. They were invited to stay overnight at the Dolphin Inn on Barbican Quay by the landlord, Mr. Morgan 'who showed them every attention', according to the *North Devon Journal*. Scores of people followed them through Plymouth's winding lanes, firing questions at them and feeling a need to touch their clothing. That evening even more people turned up at the Dolphin hoping for a glimpse of at least one Dorchester Labourer and offering to buy them tankards full of foaming cider or ale.

A *North Devon Journal* correspondent cornered Captain Robson of the *John Barry* 'who spoke in the highest terms of their behaviour during the voyage'. The writer also managed to have a few words with James Loveless

> … who appears an intelligent, well behaved man; but he complains very much of the delay in communicating to him that a free pardon had been sent out for him. He says that he only received it in November 1836 while two (pardons) were released in the March previous. Various attempts were made to induce him to send home for his family, but he invariably refused and at last he was ordered home.

The following day the men moved into the Plymouth home of James Keast of the Friendly Society of Operative Bricklayers and stayed there for the rest of their time in the town. Several members of Keast's union suggested the Tolpiddle men should stay a few days more to attend a public meeting of working men who wished to officially welcome them home. Anxious as they were to return to Tolpiddle and their families, they agreed and the meeting took place at the Plymouth Mechanic's Institute in Princess Square where 'a large number of persons were present, principally the working classes', reported the *Plymouth, Devonport and Stonehouse Herald*. They all crammed into a small room to congratulate the men on their safe return to England. A penny collection was made for them at the door and the next day they left in a four-wheeled closed post-chaise to Exeter where they were to attend another public meeting before travelling on to Dorchester's Antelope Hotel where they stopped for refreshments and to change horses.

The Dorchester County Chronicle had heard that the Tolpiddle men were expected back in the same town in which they were convicted four years before, but were unsure as to exactly when they were arriving. A band had been hired and other preparations made for a triumphant return to Dorchester and when news arrived that a smart post-chaise had just pulled into the Antelope, the Chronicle hurried a correspondent over to interview them. He arrived just as the men were boarding their carriage and they had no time for interviews. But the writer did notice that they 'were dressed in handsome new suits of clothes and travelling caps, and the carriage was loaded with portmanteaux and other luggage'. The correspondent learned that 'they are going to stay for a few days with their families and then go to London, but for what purpose has not transpired.'

The post-chaise jogged along the same seven-mile long rough road they had marched in custody of the constable on the day of their arrest. Everything looked so different to the wild country in which they had spent their last years. Its every detail was familiar and for the returning men no country in the world could appear so pleasant as the trim Dorset fields and hedgerows they sped past on that spring morning. The coach sped along until they at last could see the tower of Tolpiddle's parish church. Everything looked much the same as when they had left; the run-down cottages, the village green, the giant sycamore tree, the Crown Inn, their beloved Wesleyan chapel and, finally, their own homes. John Standfield later recorded that 'we finally arrived home safely to the great joy of our relatives and friends.'

The *London Dispatch* reported:

Whilst we hail with heartfelt satisfaction the so-long-looked-for return of these ill used martyrs [apparently the first, but certainly not the last, time they were so described] to the cause of the millions, we must not forget that the working classes owe them a vast debt of gratitude. The Dorchester Committee have exerted themselves with untiring energy to raise funds to put these men on their return home into some reputable mode of business, but much still remains to be done. We call on the working millions to come forward manfully and contribute to the Dorchester fund. Let a public meeting be called to greet these returned sufferers and at it let subscriptions be raised. Many, of course, will be hindered from distance and other causes, from attending; but they can send their contributions to this office.

Daily life in Tolpiddle remained difficult for the Loveless and Standfield families. James Hammett's family were not regular churchgoers and the widowed mother

A four-wheeled post-chase transported the four returning Tolpiddle men from Exeter to Tolpiddle. (*Regency World at Candice Hern*)

of James Brine and her four children attended Tolpiddle's Anglican Church. As a result, they escaped persecution from people suspicious of 'dissenters' within their community. But their menfolk had also been branded criminals by a court of law and although their wives and children were innocent, they were still related to convicts in penal servitude on the other side of the world. Was there any greater crime than being the son or husband of a convict whose disgraced name had appeared in scores of newspapers across the land and in whose name thousands of everyday people – like themselves – had marched in protest through the streets of London demanding a revision of their sentence? Many still crossed the street whenever they saw the family of one of the men coming towards them. Some shops still refused to serve them, even though they now had money to buy basic groceries. Others refused to talk to them or look them directly in the eye.

Was Tolpiddle still a place where they wanted to live?

Chapter 23

England Rejoices

1836

All you who turn the sturdy soil,
Or ply the loom with daily toil,
And lowly on through life's turmoil for scanty fare,
Attend, and gather richest spoil
To soothe your care.

The single sheet poster sent out to different trade union branches supporting the London-Dorchester Committee read:

Fellow workmen – we are instructed by the London Central Dorchester Committee to acquaint you with the safe arrival in this country of George Loveless, one of the six ill-used Dorchester Labourers (with whose case we conceive you are fully acquainted) and of the recent arrival of other victims in the cause of Labour against tyranny of capital.

It being the wish of the committee and of the trades connected with it, upon the arrival of the whole of the men to receive them with a public procession of the trades of London, the committee are desirous of knowing, in the event of their so desiring, whether your trade would take any part in such a proceeding. The committee are of the opinion that a procession, numerous, organised and well conducted, in connection with the subscriptions raised for the support of the families, would not only prove that the working classes still remembered the outrage committed upon the rights of industry in the persons of their brethren, but that the moral effects resulting there from would materially advance the time when labour will be emancipated from the unjust power of the grasping and all-devouring capitalist. The committee respectfully solicit an early reply answer to this communication.

Another flyer, addressed to the 'Working men of Britain!' invited them to:

Come forward with one united effort – form a committee in every city, town and village, to receive subscriptions for the Dorchester tribute – let it be done quickly and promptly – simultaneously; and the result will be a sum sufficient to raise a memorial in favour of our brethren, that will show the enemies of labour they cannot invade its rights with absolute impunity and afford our children an example of what might be effected by union, integrity and perseverance.

The idea for an enormous 'public procession of the trades of London' through the streets of the capital was carefully explained to the Tolpiddle men by Robert Hartwell on one of his visits to Dorset. He told them that he envisaged a long and colourful procession of trade union members 'escorting' the Dorchester men through London's streets in a horse-drawn open carriage where they would be seen by everyone. They would be accompanied throughout by various brass bands playing bright and sprightly tunes for the entire length of the journey. He told them that the procession would start at the famous Horns Tavern, Kennington (of which none of the Tolpiddle men had ever heard) and follow a route towards Kennington Cross, Walcott Place, across Westminster Bridge, through Whitehall and on to Charing Cross. From there they would head toward Pall Mall, travel up Waterloo Place, through Regent and Oxford Streets and Tottenham Court Road into Bedford Square and Russell Square, into the Gray's Inn Road, onwards through Pentonville to the White Conduit House 'a celebrated Cockney place of amusement' where guests would be entertained at a lavish dinner after which ladies would be admitted to a ball, performances by singers and dancers and ending with a gigantic firework display.

There was a long silence after Hartwell had finished explaining his idea and the five Tolpiddle men will have found themselves gazing in silence at the floor. George Loveless would have most likely broken the silence by explaining that as Wesleyan Methodists they were not used to parading themselves in public and felt it was wrong to be at the centre of such a large demonstration which brought attention to each man. Hartwell would have explained that by showing themselves to the London public at large they would be saying thank you to one and all in a single swoop. And those turning out to see the men would be appreciative, grateful and thankful for their safe return.

Hartwell then gently broached another subject. He was aware that things were, and remained, difficult for Tolpiddle families whose husbands had been transported and suggested they might like to consider moving elsewhere – perhaps to their own farms outside Dorset and the kind of trouble that had followed them around for the past few years. This should be considered as compensation for the horrors of transportation they and their families had endured. The cost would be underwritten by ordinary working people buying a copy of George Loveless's pamphlet and making generous donations to their cause. It would also permanently remove the men from the power of their former persecutors in Dorset. Hartwell said that sooner or later they would again be exposed to the petty tyranny which their squire, local magistrates and landowners imposed on people they referred to as 'the lower classes'.

Hartwell's remarks took the Tolpiddle men and their families by surprise. Most of them had been born in or around Tolpiddle and had never thought about moving despite their treatment by neighbours and the local gentry. Hartwell explained that, with the funds already available to the London-Dorchester committee, the on-going income generated by sale of *The Victims of Whiggery* and profits from ticket sales from the proposed London dinner, sufficient resources might be found to lease farmland where the men could take their families and run their own businesses. Instead of being 'Dorchester Labourers' they would become 'Farmers' in their own right. These farms would be a living testimonial of the great esteem in which the six men were held by trade unionists and the general public. Had they heard Hartwell correctly? Did he say that the committee would pay for them to move to their own farms?

Hartwell asked the men to think over what he had said, discuss it among themselves and their families and get back to him with their thoughts. They soon made up their minds. They decided that the business of showing their thanks and gratitude in person to the working people of London was a good one. The brass bands, grand ball, singers, dancers and fireworks were, however, a little ostentatious and not the sort of thing ordinary Methodist folks like themselves indulged in. They had once been happy to dance a jig to a fellow playing a fiddle under the giant sycamore tree on the green at harvest time or join in a sing-song with a local band during a well-dressing weekend – but a grand ball? That was the kind of thing the gentry went to, not simple farming folk. They knew their place and it wasn't at a grand ball.

The idea of moving to farms they would manage themselves was something they found most agreeable. But being landlords, or leasehold tenants, of their own properties also frightened them. After all, they were farming men, not businessmen. Moving, of course, would also mean saying goodbye to their Wesleyan congregation and people they had known for years and who had supported them during troubled times. Life in Tolpiddle, however, was unlikely to improve and they decided to inform Hartwell that they agreed with his ideas, providing they were settled on farms close to one another.

Hartwell went about the task of finding suitable farmland for the Tolpiddle families with his usual zeal. Using contacts in the Grand Consolidated Trades Union, he began exploring possible sites that might accommodate them under one roof, but this proved impossible as all available farm accommodation proved too small for what amounted to over twenty men, women and children. He began looking for separate properties located close to each other. As nothing was available in the London area he began a wider search for a pair of affordable farms in Middlesex, Surrey, Berkshire and Essex. George Loveless was invited to view some of them with Hartwell or other members of the London-Dorchester committee. They were seeking properties that each came complete with plenty of arable land (at least 80 acres), rich meadows, woodland, good size farm yards, barns, stabling, cowsheds, outbuildings, orchards, farm tools and large farmhouses including gardens for child playgrounds. Preferably the farms would include cattle which could be provided by the committee.

o0o

First, however, the Tolpiddle men had to travel to London to take part in the public procession on Easter Monday, followed by the 'Public Dinner in Celebration of the Remission of the Sentences of the Dorchester Labourers and in Commemoration of the Moral Power displayed by the Working Classes of London in their Great Procession, April 1834'.

Large posters were produced promoting the events and pasted to walls on every street North and South of the river explaining where potential ticket buyers to the dinner could be found. The posters stated that the London Dorchester Committee 'feel great pleasure in their fellow workmen and all Enemies of Oppression' that the public dinner would be presided over by Thomas Wakley and listed the names of the London-Dorchester Organising Committee, including Robert Loveless, the younger brother of George, who now lived in Paddington Street, Marylebone and who had originally passed on details to his brother about how to start a trade union. The posters stated that tickets for the dinner and entertainments would cost 2s 6d each with double tickets – for a lady and gentleman – costing 4s 6d. The dinner would be served promptly at 2.30pm and 'in the course of the afternoon several appropriate Glees will be sung'. (These short songs were usually sung with at least three unaccompanied voices and could be convivial, fraternal, idyllic, tender, philosophical, and even occasionally comedic or dramatic.)

Public houses, coffee houses and working men's institutions acted as ticket agents and posters stated that:

> The whole arrangements of the day will be under the immediate superintendence of the London Dorchester Committee who pledge themselves that nothing shall be wanting on their part to ensure the comfort and convenience of those who may assemble to celebrate the day; and they feel confident that their exertions will be ably seconded by Mr. Peters, the landlord. The dinner will be served hot, of the best description, in the Large Room of the Tavern, and will consist of every sort of Roast, and Boiled Meats, Hams, Vegetables, Bread, Porter; Plum Puddings and Tarts.

In the evening 'in aid of the Fund for the support of the Wives and families of the Dorchester Labourers' there was to be 'A Concert and Ball under the direction

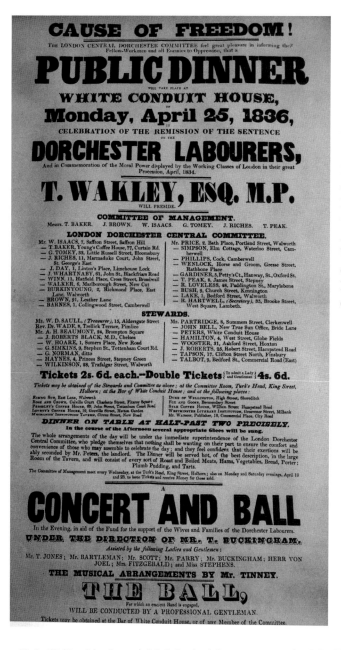

Five of the returned Tolpiddle men took part in a massive public procession through London's streets on Easter Monday, 25 April, 1836 followed by 'A Public Dinner in Celebration of the Remission of Sentences of the Dorchester Labourers and in Commemoration of the Moral Power displayed by the Working Classes of London in their Great Procession in 1834.' (*Author's Collection*)

of Mr. T. Buckingham with Musical Arrangement by Mr. Tinney.' Readers of the posters were told that 'The Ball, for which an eminent band is engaged, will be conducted by a Professional Gentleman.'

The men at the centre of all this attention must have dreaded waving to crowds of total strangers during the London street parade but looked forward with relish to roast meat, hams and plum puddings at dinner.

Crowds began arriving on Kennington Common for the start of the public procession at 7:00am and before 9:00am several thousand people attired in their best holiday clothing had also turned out. Large groups representing different trades arrived in procession, preceded by their colours and brass bands. Those intending to join the procession wore a square of crimson silk ribbon on their left breast. According to the *Morning Chronicle:*

> Amongst those most distinguished for the gaiety of their display were the farriers, the whitesmiths (also known as tinsmiths), bricklayers, blacksmiths, and glassblowers … [At 9:45am] a general huzza announced the arrival of the Dorchester Labourers. They rode in an open landau drawn by four fine grey horses and as they were carried through the lines were received with deafening cheers which lasted for a considerable time and which they acknowledged by taking off their hats and bowing to the assembled thousands of their brother labourers.

The paper described the labourers as 'good looking middle aged men, with one exception and he is a respectable looking old man'. This would have been Thomas Standfield who, at the age of 49 was oldest in the group, but hardly an 'old man'. The men were:

> … well dressed but not at all in an ostentatious manner … [At 10:15am] two rockets were discharged as a signal that all was ready for departure; after a short delay the procession began moving forward towards their destination. There was not a policeman to be seen on the common, and the presence of any was certainly not required, for good order, decorum and respectability of deportment characterised all present. Indeed the manner in which everything was conducted was highly creditable to all parties concerned and may be taken as one of the many proofs of the advancement of the people.
>
> … The procession was an enormously long one, and although the men walked four abreast and close, the leaders of it were at the distance of a mile before the Dorchester Labourers, who brought up the rear, had started. It was calculated that between 6,000 and 7,000 men were in the procession and four or five times that number made up the spectators standing along the route. When the head of the procession had reached Charing Cross, the landau of the labourers was still on Westminster Bridge. Along the whole line of the procession, the crowd anxious to witness it was immense and loudly cheered the labourers as they passed.

When the procession passed the Home Office in Whitehall, the band began playing 'See the Conquering Hero Comes', 'We'll Fight and We'll Conquer Again and Again' and 'Hoorah for the Bonnets of Blue.' The steps outside of the Home Office were noticeably empty of people as staff working there had been instructed not to stand outside and wave. The procession finally arrived at the White Conduit House …

… where a splendid tented pavilion had been erected for dinner. The pavilion was singularly beautiful and as the space which it covered was interspersed with trees, its magnificent awning was most conveniently supported by the branches. At one end it was terminated by the stage of a fanciful little theatre, which upon this occasion served as a platform for the tables at which the Chairman, the Tolpiddle men and other special guests were to be entertained and who were thus distinctly seen by the whole company. Nine lines of long trestle tables for general guests were placed down the whole length of the pavilion and smaller tables occupied vacant spaces at the sides. An overflow marquee for a further 200 diners had been erected alongside the main pavilion. The tables were so disposed that nothing could be possibly added to increase their convenience or effect. A number of chandeliers were suspended from the roof.

[At] half past two o'clock the procession arrived at the principal entrance and the Committee, having been admitted, the rush of the multitude towards

The procession ended at the White Conduit House, Islington, 'where a splendid tented pavilion had been erected for dinner'. (*British History Online*)

the gates was most tremendous. It was with the utmost difficulty that tickets could be collected from those demanding admission, so intense was their anxiety and arduous their struggle to advance forward. At length, however, the whole of those fortunate enough to possess tickets for dinner were admitted and in a few minutes afterwards not a single vacant place was observable anywhere inside the pavilion. When the whole company of probably more than 1,500 were seated, the general view was admirable.

Thomas Wakley presided over the occasion. On his right and left sat the five Tolpiddle men who, according to *The Times*,

> … were all unaffected looking men and had the appearance of respectable farmers instead of agricultural labourers. This may be accounted for by the fact that the two Lovelesses are men of good education for working men and had acquired an extensive district reputation as lay preachers… [Wakley spoke of the labourers' persecution and hardship and painted] a pathetic picture of the desolate state of their homes after their expatiation, which the honourable gentleman had visited for purposes connected with their case, and gave so touching a description of the hopeless, tearless state in which he had found a female there, who was at once the wife and mother of the Standfields and sister of the Lovelesses that many persons in the meeting, overpowered by their feelings, burst into tears.

There was a toast to the Tolpiddle men and John Standfield was elected to make a short speech in response, 'but was so overcome with appreciation and his heart full of gratitude that he was unable to speak'.

Wakley then announced that James Hammett 'might be expected home in the course of a fortnight. The delay was occasioned by his being far into the interior of New South Wales when the pardons arrived.' Quite where Wakley was obtaining his information about Hammett is uncertain and it would be another 16 months before Hammett sheepishly walked down the gangplank of a ship and reached Britain unannounced.

Then it was time to eat and plates of steaming food were served to diners in the pavilion by a team of 70 waiters. People in the overflow marquee

> … became apprehensive as they saw dish after dish of puddings borne away from one of the receptacles and a few of them ran after the waiters and endeavoured, amid thundering roars of laughter, to make them return the puddings. This the latter refused to do, alleging that there would still remain 200 more puddings. The waiters continued to pull one way and the 'greedy guts' as they were called, another, until at last a body of police had to come up

and clear a way for the steaming dishes – not, however, before a considerable quantity had been thrown about, to the no small chagrin of all parties, and the loss of several who were left altogether puddingless.

Wakley mounted the platform followed by the Tolpiddle men to propose a toast and instructed the crowd:

Look at these men beside me, do any of them look like dishonest men? (Cheers from the crowd and cries of 'no, no'.) Although these men now stand before you in the simple grandeur of upright integrity, there are still creatures – base monsters under human appearance, who had manacled these men (groans) and had wound the chains and irons of felons around their honest limbs (dreadful groaning and cries of 'shame, shame!'). If the people of England had their political rights, would it have been possible that human nature should be so disgraced? (Cheers and 'no, no!). Then let them take a little breath and give three hearty cheers for these men! (Enthusiastic cheering). Wakley's toast was dedicated to 'The People' 'and there are five of them beside me,' (huge cheers). [He allowed the crowd to settle before continuing] Let us resolve that the labourers should be labourers no longer. (Cheers) Let us make farmers of them all. Trifling contributions throughout the country will make them quite independent; there is a good sum of money in hand already and soon they will have all the rest.

It was now time for each Tolpiddle man to say a few words to the huge crowd. Wakley introduced them individually and each gave sincere thanks to the audience. George Loveless – to whom Wakley referred as 'the archbishop of Tolpiddle' much to his embarrassment – said he had suffered in the cause of truth, which he would 'always stand by or lose his life'. There was more cheering and stamping of feet.

It had been an incredible day for the Tolpiddle men. Never before had they seen so many people; men and women who had left their homes and places of work to catch a glimpse of simple everyday farming folk, fill them full of delicious and nutritious food so unlike the meagre slops dished out to prisoners and then make speeches in their honour. It is not recorded if the men stayed to watch the Grand Ball, listen to the singing, watch the classical dancing or gaze up into the night sky to watch the fireworks. Soon it would be time for them all to return home with happy memories of an amazing day of the kind they would never see again – not for the time being, anyway.

Chapter 24

The Church Shown Up

1838

Some go to church to take a walk,
Some go there to laugh and talk,
Some go there to meet a friend,
Some go there their time to spend,
Some go there to meet a lover,
Some go there a fault to cover,
Some go there for observation,
Some go there for speculation,
Some go there to dose and nod,
But few go there to worship God.

Back at Tolpiddle again, the men attempted to get their lives back on course. It was not easy. For someone whose name was in the newspapers every day, cheered on by thousands of friendly people while being driven through London's streets and guests of honour at a feast for over a thousand people, returning to work on a Dorset farm was going to be difficult.

George Loveless was comfortable. Writing *The Victims of Whiggery* had been such a cathartic and wonderful opportunity to get the story of his sentence and treatment out of his system that he eagerly took up Robert Hartwell's suggestion to write another pamphlet. He now turned his attention to the personal stories of his friends and how they had confronted and endured transportation to New South Wales. As James Hammett had not yet returned to England, Loveless was unable to include his story; he knew, however, that Hammett, the quiet loner, would almost certainly have refused to be part of the pamphlet if he had been present. Loveless's brother James, John and Thomas Standfield and James Brine all agreed to write their personal stories. John Standfield wrote his contribution in association with his father, Thomas, and related both of their stories together in a single article.

Hartwell also suggested that, because George Loveless's story in the previous pamphlet had been so well received by the public, the ploughman ought to write a companion piece about his own impressions of Van Diemen's Land and treatment of convicts there. Loveless could hardly wait to begin work. He had discovered that he was a natural writer and that words came easily to him. He would have made an excellent social commentator for one of the radical newspapers or even attempted to climb the Methodist ladder and become a full time preacher, but he did neither. Soon he hoped to become his own master on a farm which would partly be his and he knew that eventually this would consume all of his time. In his heart, however, he knew there were other things he wanted to describe and he would set his words down when the time was right.

A Narrative of the Sufferings of Jas. Loveless, Jas. Brine and Thomas and John Standfield, four of the Dorchester Labourers; displaying the Horrors of Transportation, written by themselves with a brief Description of New South Wales by George Loveless was the title of the pamphlet which went on sale later in 1838 published by the

A NARRATIVE

OF THE SUFFERINGS OF

JAS. LOVELESS, JAS. BRINE,

AND

THOMAS & JOHN STANDFIELD,

FOUR OF THE DORCHESTER LABOURERS;

DISPLAYING THE HORRORS OF TRANSPORTATION,

WRITTEN BY THEMSELVES.

WITH A BRIEF

DESCRIPTION OF NEW SOUTH WALES,

BY GEORGE LOVELESS.

ANY PROFIT ON THIS WORK WILL GO TO THE DORCHESTER TRIBUTE.

LONDON:
PUBLISHED FOR THE DORCHESTER COMMITTEE, BY
CLEAVE, 1, SHOE LANE; HETHERINGTON, 126, STRAND;
WATSON, 15, CITY ROAD.
1838.
Price Twopence.

A Narrative of Sufferings by four of the Tolpiddle men went on sale in 1838 chronicling the experiences of James Loveless, James Brine, Thomas and John Standfield in New South Wales. (*Author's Collection*)

London Dorchester Committee, price twopence. Many readers of the *Victims of Whiggery* invested a further two pennies in Loveless's new pamphlet. Clergymen across the land based sermons on its content, newspapers wrote articles using excerpts from the pamphlet to 'tell the real truth' of what it was like to be dragged from homes and families, chained and transported to the other side of the world. The pamphlet was discussed in parliament and became a main topic for debate in university discussion and debating groups.

o0o

Shuttling backwards and forwards between Tolpiddle and London was becoming commonplace for George Loveless who visited the capital regularly for meetings with the London-Dorchester Committee and to appear at various Chartist gatherings keen to see a Tolpiddle man in person.

On 12 May 1838 Loveless travelled to London with James Brine to attend a meeting of the committee at the Crown and Anchor in The Strand. Its purpose was to 'consider the means of establishing the Dorchester Labourers in independence…. and do justice to men who have been deeply wronged by an accursed system of misrule, under which the populace of this nation has groaned from time immemorial.'

Loveless and Brine were 'received with the most tremendous cheering' and those in attendance heard that £900 had been raised through penny donations and profits from *The Victims of Whiggery* and *A Narrative of Sufferings*. The meeting also learned that on their return from exile, the Tolpiddle families had been awarded £350 to share between them, but had agreed to return the money 'because the object of the committee was to fix on some plan for giving them the means of obtaining a decent and respectable livelihood'. Following return of the money, the Tolpiddle men and the committee agreed that 'the best way would be to settle them on land – to give each labourer five acres, by the cultivation of which, with industry and care, they might maintain themselves and their families.'

William Saul, a London businessman who was the committee's treasurer told the meeting that the cost of purchasing 30 acres of land at £30 per acre would work out at £900. The expense of stocking each portion of land would be a further £300 – a total of £1,200. To meet this estimate £670 was currently available 'and the remainder of the appeal must be made to the liberality of the working classes'. Saul said that 150,000 people each contributing one penny 'will raise more than the required sum'.

oOo

Loveless had no plans for a third pamphlet until word reached him that 'several gentlemen of the clerical order' were critical of *The Victims of Whiggery* and its author. The main critic was the Rev. Henry Walter, Vicar of the Anglican church of St. Mary and St. James in the Dorset village of Hazelbury Bryant (now known as Hazelbury Bryan) 12 miles from Tolpiddle.

Less than one month after returning home, Loveless had begun preaching again and one of the places he was allocated to lead a service at was Hazelbury Bryant's Primitive Methodist chapel. A full congregation turned out to hear him; many had read *The Victims of Whiggery* and all would have read extensively about their preacher of the day in newspapers.

Also in the congregation that Sunday was the village's Anglican vicar, the 38-year old Walter who, for some reason, chose to attend the Methodist Chapel service instead of attending to his own flock at the parish church. The more Loveless preached to his congregation, the more agitated the Rev. Walter became while sitting in his box pew. In his sermon, Loveless made reference to his arrest, trial and transportation and spoke about the suffering he had endured in Van Diemen's Land. He spoke about how 'a member of the upper class' had reported his actions in founding a trade union for agricultural labourers to senior members of the government and how that same upper class person had forbidden his farming tenants to increase labourers' wages to the ten shillings once promised. He said that his Methodist faith had given him strength throughout his ordeal and now he had returned that same faith had become stronger. Loveless suggested the world would be a much fairer place if a decent day's work was rewarded with a decent day's pay for everyone and that the only way to ensure this was for more people to join a trade union – if they had not already done so.

Unaware that the village vicar was sitting in his crowded congregation, Loveless told them that, since his return from exile, he had noticed the great rift between the established church and his own had grown even wider. He stated that the Anglican clergy was always at the forefront of oppositions to popular measures for the good of the people.

The Rev. Walter was an intelligent and educated man whose family was connected to the Austen family; his father was step-brother to George Austin, father of Jane. He had attended St. John's College, Cambridge and graduated with a BA in Mathematics. He was appointed professor of natural philosophy at the East India Company College in Hertfordshire and elected a Fellow of the Royal Society in 1819; in 1821 he was inducted as rector of Hazelbury Bryant and, while there, wrote various papers on religion, the bible and Christian principles.

Loveless was surprised to learn that Walter had been part of his congregation 'and greatly displeased by what he heard from the dissenter leading the service that day'. Walter complained that Loveless's language in the *Victims of Whiggery* 'could make labouring men dissatisfied and discontented' and that Loveless had stated that 'state religions and state churches are a curse to mankind'. Walter referred to Loveless as 'a criminal, a strife maker and a wicked man guilty of writing palpable falsehoods'.

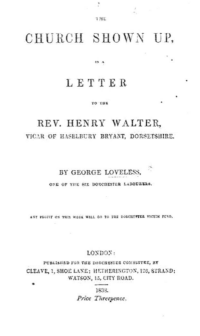

THE

CHURCH SHOWN UP,

IS A

LETTER

TO THE

REV. HENRY WALTER,

VICAR OF HASELBURY BRYANT, DORSETSHIRE.

BY GEORGE LOVELESS,

ONE OF THE SIX DORCHESTER LABOURERS.

ANY PROFIT ON THIS WORK WILL GO TO THE DORCHESTER VICTIM FUND.

LONDON:

PUBLISHED FOR THE DORCHESTER COMMITTEE, BY
CLEAVE, 1, SHOE LANE; HETHERINGTON, 126, STRAND;
WATSON, 15, CITY ROAD.

1838.

Price Threepence.

The Church Shown Up was the last of three booklets written by George Loveless. It took the form of a letter to the Rev. Henry Walter, Vicar of Haselbury Bryant who was critical of one of Loveless' sermons given in his parish. (*Author's Collection*)

Loveless decided to respond to Walter's accusations in the form of another pamphlet, his third since returning to England. He called it *The Church Shown Up in a Letter to the Rev. Henry Walter, Vicar of Haselbury Bryant, Dorsetshire by George Loveless, one of the six Dorchester Labourers*. Again it was published by the London Dorchester Committee and 'any profit on this work will go to the Dorchester victims' fund'. It sold for 3d a copy.

Loveless began the pamphlet by quoting from John Milton's 1644 text *Areopagitica*: 'Give me the liberty to think, to speak and to argue freely according to conscience, above all other liberties' and – directly referring to Walter in the pamphlet – stated that:

> In addressing myself to you I adopt the above as my motto, believing that liberty of conscience is every man's birthright; and as the Almighty Creator of man hath blest me in common with others with thinking and reasoning powers, I consider that I should be abusing those noble powers, were I to be silent at the present time and not to speak out boldly and freely in vindication of truth and justice; that I should be withholding an important obligation I owe to my fellow men; and that in so doing I should reproach my Maker and sin against my own soul. [Referring to Walter's negative remarks he continued that] had you confined your observations to the circle of your own friends, or even to your own parish, I should not have thought it worth my trouble to have noticed it; but as you chose to address others besides your own religious body to represent or rather to misrepresent my character and conduct to them, I thought it my duty to reply to those calumnies.

After hearing Loveless preach in the Hazlebury Bryant Methodist chapel, Walter had penned an angry letter to Edmund Grindrod, President of the Wesleyan Conference, complaining about the lay man's style of preaching, things mentioned in his sermon and messages he wanted members of the congregation to take home with them. Loveless queried Walter's motive in writing about 'one of whom the President most likely knows nothing and perhaps cares as little. Of the President of the Methodist Conference, as a private man, I know nothing, but judging of him from the situation he fills, I think I have nothing to dread from that quarter.'

Loveless pointed out that the Church of England was not the only religion in England. He observed that Walter disapproved of the Catholic Church and believed that the Anglican faith was England's only true religion; he contrasted this to his latest pamphlet demonstrating how completely he believed in and drew his strength from Methodism.

The Church Shown Up did not include the same elements of storytelling displayed in the previous two pamphlets but it sold well and produced further funds for the committee's bank balance.

Part VII

The Chartists

November 1838

Hurrah for old England and liberty sweet,
The land that we live in and plenty to eat,
We shall ever remember this wonderful day,
See the Chartists are coming, get out of the way.

By 1838 Chartist agitation was in full swing. Founded by The London Working Men's Association in 1836, Chartists wanted 'to seek by every legal means to place all classes of society in possession of their equal, political, and social rights.' The six points of what became known as The People's Charter were: votes for all men over the age of 21, voting by secret ballot, electoral districts of equal size, abolition of property qualifications to become an MP, salaries for MPs and annual elections for Parliament.

Chartist agitation was in full swing by 1838 and large meetings of the kind pictured here took place across the country. In November of that year a Chartist meeting was held at Charlton Down, near Blandford and John Standfield was guest of honour. (*From a contemporary print*)

The Charter was presented as a modern day Magna Carta and gained rapid support across the country. The Glasgow meeting to launch it in May 1838 was attended by an estimated 150,000 people. A petition was assembled at Chartist meetings across Britain and brought to London in 1839 to be presented to Parliament by Thomas Attwood, the Radical Birmingham MP. Despite 1,280,958 signatures Parliament voted not to consider it.

In November a Chartist meeting took place at Charlton Down, near Blandford, 12 miles from Tolpiddle. Placards were pasted to walls around the area announcing the meeting stating that Robert Hartwell from the London-Dorchester Committee would be the main speaker. According to the *Dorset County Chronicle*, 'George Loveless, one of the returned convicts, will also be present to call upon his fellow labourers to join the Working Men's Association.'

George Loveless was not present, but John Standfield attended and stood on the rail of a wagon to wave to the crowd who gave him three cheers. He did not make a speech. Over one thousand working men showed up but 3,000 had been expected. Many Chartists claimed they had been intimidated by local farmers and landowners who turned up on horseback to threaten labourers taking time off from work with losing a day's pay and risk losing their jobs. According to the *Chronicle*, 'the speechifying was of the usual ranting incendiary description', and included one speech in which it was said that labourers stood in fear of farmers and their only hope for the future lay in uniting to obtain political justice which would, in due course, bring them practical justice. The speaker, however, sensibly stressed this had to be done by bringing moral pressure to bear and not by the use of physical action. He also said that current wages in Dorset were still around seven shillings a week 'in comparison with the Queen Mother, who had recently complained that £20,000 was insufficient for a single lady to live on'.

Another radical newspaper, *The Operative*, reported that William Roberts, a solicitor from Bath who had recently defended 32 Chartists in court, told the crowd that the

> ... time had come when some great moral blow would be struck to emancipate the working classes of England from the chains of that oppression under which they laboured. The situation from which they sought to be relieved was this: that the millions who made the bread could not eat it, that the millions who fabricated the cloth could not wear it; they complained that this was contrary to the law of God, as developed in the Holy Scriptures; and to this they would no longer submit. The time had come when labour producing 7s a week should be paid more. He said that the greatest portion of the country's taxation was borne by the labouring classes – everything they ate or wore was taxed; and if anything was not taxed it was the silks and frippery and furbelows of the aristocracy.

Hartwell then informed the crowd that he had selected 'a most fit and proper person to represent the men of Dorset in the forthcoming General Convention of the Industrious Classes of Great Britain – Mr. George Loveless, late of Tolpiddle.' A cheer went up and hats were thrown into the air. The committee, on which Loveless represented Dorsetshire, had been set up to promote the adoption by Parliament of the People's Charter.

o0o

James Frampton did not attend the meeting but sent along one of his spies to report back. He also read the *Chronicle's* report with interest and forwarded a copy to Lord John Russell with a letter

… written by myself on behalf of several magistrates in the region of Dorchester, Blandford and Wareham who have received information from various people that certain labourers are at this time threatening great agitation. I am requested by these gentlemen to write to your Lordship and acquaint you with all the intelligence we have been able to obtain. I have also received the following information that the union is going on with great force in Bere Regis, Milton and neighbouring villages and that many labourers have joined it, that the numbers are increasing and are actively introducing penny subscriptions to members. The labourers intend to hold a special meeting of the union in the neighbourhood of these villages to discuss an increase in wages. They are meeting in groups of four and five at a time. I believe they are to get legal advice. Each man joining pays one shilling and agreed to pay one penny a week.

A handwritten letter dated August 9, 1838 from James Frampton to Lord John Russell 'written by myself on behalf of several magistrates...who have received information from various people that certain labourers are at this time threatening agitation.' (*Dorset History Centre*)

Frampton claimed that 'that the situation is again grave and fraught with dangers'. A note in the margin of his letter pencilled in by a Home Office official stated: 'All that can be done at the moment is for the magistrates to be watchful.'

Soon after receiving Frampton's latest tell-tale intelligence letter to his Home Office chums, the Tolpiddle men and their families would finally be out of his hair for once and for all.

Chapter 25

Unwelcome in Essex

August/September 1838

Farewell to old Dorset,
The land of my birth:
The scenes of my childhood,
My dear native earth.

George Loveless failed to attend the Charlton Down meeting because he and his family were busy re-locating from Tolpiddle to New House Farm in the parish of Greenstead Green near Chipping Ongar and Epping, 21 miles from London and 150 miles from Tolpiddle.

Despite the hostility the Loveless family had endured in Tolpiddle over the years, it must have been a great wrench to finally leave the village where George and his brother James were born, where he and Betsey had married, she had given birth to their children and where he worked on farmland he knew and loved. But they were probably not sorry to leave their decaying cottage which they would be exchanging for a spacious brick and timber-frame farm house in rural Essex which they would share with James Loveless, his wife and three children and young James Brine. A total of eleven people, including six young children, would live in the spacious house so unlike their tumbledown Tolpiddle cottage.

New House Farm covered an 80 acre site which included arable enclosed pasture land, a fine house originally built in the 17th century, an orchard, a wood, a large farm yard, a barn, stables and a number of outbuildings. The farm stood at the centre of a quiet community consisting of twenty-nine other homes housing 150 people and was pleasantly situated on high ground affording good views of undulating countryside reminiscent in some respects of Dorset. The property was available for lease over a seven year period for £600 and the London-Dorchester Committee agreed to allocate a further £40 for furnishings. George Loveless conducted visits to the property in the company of a farmer friend of Thomas Wakley. They inspected its buildings and walked over the arable land which appeared not to have been ploughed for some years. Loveless could see that a great deal of hard labour lay ahead, but he and his brother were no strangers to strenuous work in either England or Australia. On returning to Tolpiddle, Loveless shared his findings with his brother James who agreed there and then to accept the farm as their new home and business 'with every prospect of being enabled, by labour and perseverance, to obtain comfortable subsistence'.

A second property called Fenners Farm, four miles from Greenstead in Tilegate Green, High Laver, was leased for Thomas Standfield, his wife and their six children, including John Standfield. The farm covered 43 acres of arable land, plus a farm house, barn and outbuildings. Because James Hammett had still not returned from New South Wales and his wife wished to remain in Tolpiddle for the time being, the committee awarded her a sum of money sufficient to keep her in comfort until her husband's arrival.

The Tolpiddle families left their run-down cottages for the last time in August 1838 and immediately set about making repairs to their new homes. By early September the men had ploughed all but seven acres of land on the two farms, sown five acres of wheat, 15 acres of oats, one acre of barley, one acre of potatoes, eight acres of beans, two acres of peas and two acres of pasture. George Loveless reported to the Dorchester Central Committee: 'There will not be full crops because the land is so foul having lain uncultivated for three years, but it all looks pretty well at present and when the harvest is made, will enable us to get on pretty well for the next year, both in the way of living and finishing repairs.'

There was, however, still one problem left to solve. When the families moved onto their farms, the fund formed to handle donations still needed a further £500, but had only produced £162, leaving a shortfall of £338. But the committee was not concerned. A report in the *Trades Chronicle* on 1 September, 1839 stated: 'The committee trusts that those trades who have not contributed to the fund will now do so and remove all chances of failure, which, should it take place, would reflect an indelible disgrace on the working classes. About £100 or £150 would affect the desired object, a sum which the committee feel confident the working men of London will speedily contribute, upon their being put in possession of the facts.'

Within a week a further £7 2s 6d had been raised from the Tin-Plate Workers' Society, twine spinners, the landlady of the Red Lion pub, King's Street, Golden Square and the Camberwell Lodge of Carpenters. But the committee was still short of £331 and committee members wracked their brains to find ways of raising it.

Chapter 26

The Bonds Between Us

1839/40

Ye true sons of freedom I pray you attend
Unto these few lines which I have here penned:
These four years and better I have been in exile,
Once more I have returned to my own native soil.

James Hammett sailed back to England in the triple-mast, double decked 356-ton barque *Eweretta* owned by the Truman & Cook Shipping Company which departed from Sydney on 8 March 1839 in the company of 'invalid passengers returning home from Australia'. By August he was back in England three and a half years after his pardon and free passage home had originally been granted. He had spent five years and four months in New South Wales and, of the six Tolpiddle men, James Hammett was the longest serving convict.

Harriet Hammett and her son George, now aged 8, had remained in Tolpiddle and when word reached her that her husband was, at last, on his way home she contacted George Loveless to ask if she could now come to Essex with her husband and son to join the rest of the Tolpiddle families on their farms. No record exists about the kind of welcome Hammett received when he disembarked from the *Eweretta* after it had docked in the port of London or who was waiting to greet him on the quay. What is known is that instead of going back to Tolpiddle he headed in the direction of New House Farm. Once there Hammett's skills as a builder, plasterer and decorator would be useful as the Tolpiddle men continued to make improvements to their houses and farm buildings. The Hammetts lodged with the Lovelesses, James Brine and Brine's 20-year old brother, Joseph, who had also come to live at New House Farm.

In June 1839 the bonds between the Tolpiddle families were further strengthened when Thomas Standfield's daughter Elizabeth married James Brine at Greenstead's wooden church of St. Andrews, said to be the world's oldest wooden church built in AD 845. No convenient Methodist church licensed for marriages was nearby, so the happy couple were pronounced man and wife in a conventional – yet very attractive – Anglican Church. James Brine, however, had been christened into the Anglican faith which, presumably, persuaded St. Andrew's vicar, the Rev. Philip

James Brine married Thomas Standfield's daughter Elizabeth at Greenstead's wooden church of St. Andrews in June 1839. The Rev. Philip Ray was asked to perform the ceremony, but was unhappy about admitting former convicts into his church, despite three of them being Methodist lay preachers. The vicar lived in fear of Chartists invading his peaceful parish. (*ESAH160 – the Essex Society for Archaeology and History*)

Ray to perform the ceremony. Ray, however, was unhappy about admitting a clutch of former convicts into his church, despite the fact that three of them were Methodist lay preachers. He was so incensed that he went on to preach sermons in which he objected to having convicts in his parish. He also fired off an angry letter to the magistrates in Chelmsford and to Henry Maynard, 3rd Viscount Maynard and Lord-Lieutenant of Essex complaining that dangerous Chartists 'had invaded the area'. And so, the former Tolpiddle men now faced the third criticism of their actions from members of the Anglican clergy. First was Tolpiddle's Rev. Thomas Warren who had promised to help farm labourers fight for better wages before going back on his word; second was Hazelbury Bryant's Rev. Henry Walter who spread poisonous messages about George Loveless from his pulpit and now the Rev. Philip Ray who lived in fear of Chartists invading his peaceful parish.

The zeal of the Tolpuddle men for their Methodist and Chartist convictions continued in their new surroundings. Before long they had formed their own Chartist association and Sunday meetings were held at New House Farm where entire families turned out to hear George Loveless speak instead of listening to the Rev. Ray's sermons. When the house could no longer hold so many people they switched their meeting place to an adjoining large barn. Delegates began attending from other Essex and Hertfordshire villages including Waltham Abbey, Epping,

Harlow, Hatfield and Broad Oak. They all wanted to hear George Loveless talk about his Chartist ideals. These were part political and part Wesleyan chapel meetings and enormously popular among farming folk. Sometimes up to 40 London-based Chartists also found their way to New House Farm and before long the barn was packed with people who had chosen Chartism over Church.

As in Tolpiddle, these activities brought the men to the notice of Essex hierarchy who responded in the same way the Dorset establishment had done although with less firmness as there was, thankfully, no James Frampton among them. And just as the families began to enjoy peace and tranquillity away from the pressures and persecutions of living in Tolpiddle, harmful articles began appearing in national and Essex regional newspapers.

oOo

The Charter, 6 October 1839, from George Tomey, Secretary, London-Dorchester Committee:

To the Trades of London and all Friends of Humanity: Fellow countrymen – Five years since, you thought it prudent to call us into juxtaposition with one of the most heartless factions, the Whigs, that ever disgraced what should be a free and happy country. They transported your brethren, intending therefore to break up your unions and trade societies, and render you all hopeless and helpless. We cheerfully obeyed your call, began the work and, backed by you, wrung from the faction a pardon. The men returned to their homes, and once more enjoyed the caresses of their wives and the endearments of their children. In this our undertaking we have sacrificed our time with pleasure, knowing our cause was just and were in hope of finishing the work, with credit to ourselves, and an everlasting honour to those who should support us through with it. We now call on you for the last time, to rally round us on Tuesday next, October 8 at the Royal Victoria Theatre. The pieces will be, without fail, the historical drama of *King Harold: the Battle of Hastings*; the popular interlude of *Family Feuds*; the new popular drama of *The Lass of Gowrie*, and numerous other entertainments. The house is beautifully cleansed, painted, decorated and improved suitable to any company. The performers cannot be equalled by any house in London.

'I remain, fellow countrymen, your devoted servant on behalf of the Dorchester Labourers' Committee,

G. Tomey, Sec.

The notice was signed by 'G. Tomey' as secretary to the London Central Dorchester Committee because Robert Hartwell had been asked to resign 'under grave suspicion

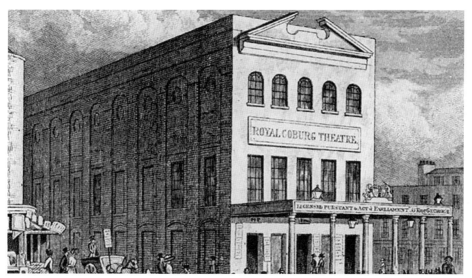

London's Royal Victoria Theatre, soon to be known as the Royal Coburg Theatre and today as The Old Vic, opened its doors to hundred of playgoers anxious to get a glimpse of the Tolpuddle men in October 1839. (*The Old Vic*)

of dishonesty'. After steering the committee since its inception in 1834, Hartwell had given countless hours of his time, energy and oratory skills travelling around the country organising fundraising events for the Tolpiddle men. But in 1839 a sum of money was missing from the committee's funds and on investigation was discovered to have been 'mislaid' by Hartwell. At this time Hartwell was experiencing personal financial difficulties with the newspapers he published, edited or was responsible for printing. He had also put himself up as a potential Chartist candidate when various constituency seats in the north of England became available, but found it difficult to raise sufficient funds to cover his election expenses. It would appear that he had not intended to steal money but 'borrow' small sums to tide him over until such time as he was able to repay. Instead of talking to the committee about what he had done in his role as committee secretary, he had helped himself to money which was not his. When the committee discovered that sums allocated to pay for leases on the two Essex farms had fallen short of the expected amount in its bank account, an investigation was launched and Hartwell named as the culprit. Despite protestations that he would pay the money back in full, the committee lost its trust in him and called for his resignation. With enormous regret and shame he had no option but to comply. He was replaced by George Tomey, a London-based tinsmith who would handle the committee's final activities, including the evening's entertainment at the Royal Victoria Theatre, an event designed to top up the shortfall in funds for lease of the two Essex farms.

By 1839 London's Royal Victoria Theatre – known today as The Old Vic – had become one of the capital city's most popular playhouses. While it attracted every type of audience, not everyone appreciated the high drama which was often on show. A few years before the actor-manager Edmund Kean had played *Richard III, Othello, Macbeth* and *King Lear* during a six-night engagement. At his closing night curtain speech Keen told his rowdy audience: 'In my life I have never acted to such a set of ignorant, unmitigated brutes as I have before me.' The crowd booed and pelted him with cabbages and tomatoes.

On the night of 8 October hundreds of ticketholders poured into the theatre and *The Charter* newspaper reported that 'the house was literally crowded to suffocation'. They had, of course, turned out to see the six Dorchester Labourers in the flesh but when the evening finally came around only four of them were able to attend. George Loveless sent an apologetic letter which was read out to the crowd. It stated that he (Loveless) and James Brine 'were prevented from appearing having been employed in arranging matters at our farms in Essex'. So it was left to the Standfields, James Loveless and newly returned James Hammett to show themselves to an adoring public.

After a short drama, comedy and an opera, the curtain opened to reveal 'the great attraction of the night' – four rather embarrassed looking men blinking in the direction of the audience with George Tomey in their midst. *The Charter* wrote:

They were greeted with one of the most enthusiastic bursts of approbation ever heard within these walls ... The majority of the audience rose, whilst the pittites [the occupants of a raised area of the front stalls who could present flowers to cast favourites] hurled gilded wreaths of evergreen (one for each labourer) upon the stage. As soon as the tumult had subsided, Mr. Tomey advanced and said, 'Ladies and gentlemen, I appear on behalf of the committee, to present to you four of the six Dorchester labourers.' Tomey then pointed to the man on his right who the paper described as 'a thin, pale looking individual who has evidently not yet recovered from the base and brutal treatment to which the Whigs subjected him.' This was James Loveless, who stepped forward in order to say a few words, but his agitation was so great that he was quite overcome and his voice all but left him. The warmth of his reception aroused him a little, however, and after a moment's pause he proceeded to thank the public for the support afforded to him and his wife and family, both during and since his unjust transportation. The situation of this generous-souled man was heart stirring and excited the sympathy of all. Would to God his base persecutors had been present it would have 'Reformed them altogether', they must have been moved at witnessing such a scene. Poor Loveless, eventually overcome, retired back to his companions, and gave vent to his feelings in a flood of tears.

Standfield (the younger) then came forward, and having a little more nerve than his friend, proceeded to thank his audience for the support he had received ever since he fell under the claws of his oppressors at which there was a perfect hurricane of applause. He was determined, he said, to bear all the attacks of tyranny with as great fortitude as he had done during his transportation (applause). He thanked the Dorchester committee for their unnecessary exertions and the public for their generosity and expressed his conviction that, whenever any great object was to be attained, they needed nothing but union – a determined union to achieve it (tremendous applause).

During Standfield's address, it was curious to observe uneasiness by various persons behind the scenes. What could be the matter? Those at either wing were beckoning Standfield off; this drew the attention of Mr. Loveless to him, who tapped his brave companion on the shoulder, as much as to say 'don't say any more.' This done, Mr. Tomey next whispered Standfield in the ear, who appeared not to know what they were all about and retreated back a few steps only just in time to save himself from being crushed with the heavy curtain, which descended with great velocity to the astonishment and indignation of all present; not that they wanted so many thanks, but when four persecuted men had come all the way from Essex to address the public, and that public had come from all quarters to hear then, surely the management might have evinced a little tolerance. The theatre had been taken for the night by the committee, and they alone should have regulated the proceedings.

Why had the backstage staff rung down the curtain so abruptly? It would appear that the Royal Victoria Theatre's management was worried that the government was out to terrify all public places needing a licence to operate and that anyone associated with Chartism or sedition – such as members of the London-Dorchester Committee – were to be regarded as sympathisers with these beliefs. This is strange because the theatre management were well aware of what was taking place that night and to whom their playhouse was hired.

The function, however, was a success and raised the final funds needed to complete purchase of the Essex farms. The event also brought the work of the London-Dorchester Committee to an end. For five years the committee had worked tirelessly to achieve all its objectives, including sustaining the wives and families of the Tolpiddle men morally and financially during long years of separation. It had maintained enduring pressure and fought for full pardons for the men. It had organised welcoming committees and dinners which had made the men realise they had not suffered in vain or been forgotten. It had raised the means of compensating them for their suffering. Committee members had been motivated by their feeling of the injustices done and now their work was complete.

o0o

The worthies of Essex were less enthusiastic to have the Tolpiddle families in their midst than the audience at the Royal Victoria Theatre. Soon after moving to the county 'alarming' news about what was happening at New House Farm reached newspaper editors who opened investigations about how new settlers to 'the hitherto quiet and well-conducted population of these parishes' had begun to 'agitate in a manner and with a degree of success which shows but too plainly that their mission of mischief has not been entrusted to unpractised or unskilful hands'.

On 20 December 1839 *The Morning Post* carried a letter from 'A Conservative Magistrate for the County of Essex' stating that Chartism was alive and well in the neighbourhood of Ongar and that shortly after their arrival Chartist newspapers were seen in active circulation. It was reported that a Chartist Association had been formed in the parish of Grinstead

> ... and by the combined or alternate influence of persuasion and terror, nearly the whole of the agricultural labourers in that and adjoining parishes were induced to join it...Frequent meetings were held – the time selected for this purpose being generally on Sunday morning, during the hours of divine service...The effect of these proceedings was to diffuse a general sense of insecurity throughout that part of the country, and so far to disturb the habitual relations between the farmers and labourers. [The letter branded] the dreaded Dorchester Labourers [as] poor, ignorant creatures who literally do not even know how to plough the land they occupy ... and should they attempt to disturb the peace of the county, they will be put down, not by military force, not by rural police, but by the good sense and strong arm of the true agricultural yeomen and labourers of Essex, who would follow their landlords to the last drop of their blood in defence of the good old cause – the cause of their religion, their laws and their own firesides.

At the same time the *Morning Post* wrote about 'the extraordinary purchase of the Essex farms' and spoke about the 'counter-colonisation from Botany Bay to the rural parishes of Essex' and how 'the hitherto quiet and well-conducted population of these parishes had been stirred into agitation by the Dorchester Labourers'.

On 6 March 1840 *The Essex Standard* weighed in with their own insult to the Tolpiddle men, and George Loveless in particular:

> The Story of the Dorchester Labourers is known to everyone; their transportation, their pardon and the location of some of them on snug farms in Essex, are still fresh in everyone's memory. We see that one of those worthies – George Loveless – instead of quietly fulfilling the duties of his station, and availing himself of the experience of his sufferings and misconduct, is still dabbling in the dirty water of Radicalism and is publishing pamphlets to keep up the old game.

Aware that that persecution experienced in Dorset had followed them to Essex, Harriet Hammett pleaded with her husband James to take her and their son back to Tolpiddle. It cannot have been easy for the Hammetts to live in such proximity to the Lovelesses and Standfields and new family members, James Brine and his younger brother. Unlike the rest of the group, the Hammetts were neither religious people or used to discussions about the bible and politics each evening around the fire. They must have felt out of place and Harriett Hammett desperately missed her Dorset family and friends. Early in 1841 they reluctantly left Essex and returned home where Hammett soon found employment with a wealthy builder who was a member of another dissident religious sect – the Congregationalists. If back in Tolpiddle he had found himself a marked man, a trade unionist and an ex-convict he was soon able to slip from the limelight he had never courted and remained in the village for the remainder of his life, until his time as a Dorchester Labourer unexpectedly came back to life 40 years later.

oOo

While in Essex the Tolpiddle families began to expand. George and Betsey Loveless had two more daughters, Louisa born in 1839 and Sina in 1840. James and Elizabeth Brine had a daughter, Mary Jane, born in 1839 plus two further daughters, Susannah born on Christmas Day 1841 and Charity in January 1844. During this period, John Standfield, the only unmarried member of the group went to the altar with Elizabeth Thurgood at Christ Church, Southwark on July 4, 1840. Their first child, Julian Wesley was born in November 1841, a second son Theophilus Washington in 1843 and daughter Charity Madeline in 1841.

The 1840s, later known as 'the Hungry Forties', was a time of great depression when Britain experienced an economic slump, causing misery among the poor. In 1839 there had been a serious drop in trade, leading to steep increases in unemployment, accompanied by three years of poor harvests. The population was increasing rapidly and the Corn Laws were keeping the price of bread artificially high. The economic and agricultural recession bit into Essex and East Anglia where there were repeats of the 'Swing' riots with widespread rick burning and general arson. The difficulties of trying to earn a living in such a harsh economic climate were greatly exacerbated by the need to support five families off a small parcel of land.

George Loveless continued to read everything he could lay his hands on; anything to broaden his knowledge, intelligence and understanding. During these difficult years for farming he began considering the next best move for his extended family. He considered moving elsewhere in Britain, perhaps Scotland or Wales. The country, however, was mired in recession so relocation within it seemed pointless. Australia was out of the question. New Zealand was a possibility and four of his fellow Tolpiddle men had spent some time in the country's South Island on their way home from exile and spoke highly of its agricultural richness and agreeable climate. He had also read about Canada, an underdeveloped country and home to 'sober industrious people' where 'from the high price of labour they are obtaining a comfortable existence'. A rosy picture also described 'vast tracks of undeveloped land at the disposal of emigrants, where the climate is the same as in England, perhaps a little warmer, and where on 100 acre blocks, crops look well'.

Further reading informed Loveless that there were Canadian farms which paid workers 30 shillings a week complete with board and where 50 acres of land was available with nothing to pay for three years. Canada's popularity stemmed from a highly liberal system whereby almost everyone who applied for land obtained it. The overwhelming

Come to Stay, printed in 1880 in the *Canadian Illustrated News*, was designed to stimulate emigration to the new 'Dominion'. The publication was widely circulated around parts of Britain where people were known to be interested in starting their lives in a new country. (*Library and Archives of Canada*)

impression gained throughout the early stage of emigration was that, with hard work and industry, there was no reason why an emigrant family might not prosper in the New World. The possibilities of emigration were therefore strongly promoted as a possible solution to relieve overcrowded parishes in Essex and East Anglia, including the families of former farm labourers who were now themselves hard working and industrious farmers.

The Lovelesses and Brines decided to leave England for Canada in 1844, giving up the New House Farm lease before it expired. The Standfields were not so sure about uprooting and making an ocean crossing to a new life in an unknown country. In the 1840s Thomas Standfield was in his mid–fifties and he decided to renew the lease on Fenners Farm with a possible view to join the Lovelesses once they had received positive reports back about their prospects in the land of opportunity known as Canada.

Chapter 27

A New Jerusalem

1844–1904

In Dorsetshire I've a farmer been
For thirty years or more;
But now the times are grown so keen,
We leave our native shore.
Unto Canada we sail away
And leave our native shore,
From dearest friends we're torn away,
We never may see them more.

From 1815-1850 Canada was the primary destination for English, Scottish and Irish emigrants seeking life in a new country, over 650,000 people re-locating there from all parts of Britain. Before 1900 most emigrants arrived in Quebec City, Montreal or Halifax, Nova Scotia on services departing from Poole, London, Greenock or Liverpool. The voyage took 11-12 days and the adult fare was £5 15s. Children travelled for half price and babes in arms were free.

Conditions on emigrant ships in the mid-1840s were dreadful. Owners sold excess ship space to agents whose only interest was to fill it with as many passengers as possible. Emigrants were crowded into unsanitary and crowded quarters which, although nothing new to the Tolpiddle men, were alarming for their wives and children.

Many early emigrant carriers were, in the words of the *Quebec Gazette* on 2 June 1834, 'the worst of all the merchant ships of Great Britain and Ireland; with few exceptions they are very old, very ill-manned, very ill found; and considering the dangers of an early spring voyage to this port from ice and tempestuous weather, it is astonishing that more serious accidents have not occurred.' There was an improvement in sailing vessels in the 1840s, which is remembered today as 'the golden age of sail'. The first Cunard liner, the *Britannia*, created a flurry of excitement when she arrived at Boston in 1840, but the Cunarders and those like them were only for the wealthy. The Lovelesses and Brine families would have crossed the Atlantic in a much rougher vessel on which mortality was high. In 1847 one passenger in 40 died on vessels sailing from Limerick. On vessels from Liverpool to Canada, 1 in 14 did not make the crossing. One factor appears constant: vessels from larger city ports had higher mortality. A Canadian quarantine surgeon attributed this to typhus which had been contracted ashore in slums where emigrants had lodged. They were also weakened on crowded ships lacking adequate sanitation.

Storms caused confusion above decks and frightened steerage passengers. The air was foul; hatches were battened down and with each roll of the ship passengers in crowded berths were bumped and bruised as they were hurled from side to side against rough partitions where there was real danger of children being crushed to death. Water leaked through the decks in such quantity that beds were soaked and the floor ankle-deep in cold sea water. Candle lanterns could not be lighted and a sudden heave of the ship often dislodged whole families from their berths and hurled them headlong among their companions who lay on the opposite side. A cabin passenger described the situation on a vessel where 180 people were confined in a dark space as 'not much larger than a drawing room'. The passenger recalled: 'I popped my head down for a minute or two, but the smell was too powerful for my olfactory nerves – children crying, women screaming; butter, biscuit treacle, herrings and potatoes, all rolling from side to side, made up a scene of misery and confusion such as I never saw before.'

George Loveless would have been aware what conditions were like on board a freezing Atlantic crossing taking his family to their New Jerusalem. He will also have known where they were heading once they arrived in Canada in the spring of 1844. They aimed to reach an area known as the London Township, in south-east Ontario close to two of Canada's Great Lakes – Lake Ontario in the east and Lake Erie to the south. He seems to have been corresponding from New House Farm with Edmund Stoney, the Irish-born Methodist Minister of London Township. Stoney must have invited the Tolpiddle families to come to Canada where plenty of land was available for experienced farmers and where they would be welcomed into the local Methodist community. The Tolpiddle men will also have seen posters nailed to trees in every English agricultural community by representatives of The Canada Company informing farmers that one million acres of land was waiting for them to come out and farm. Whatever the case, the Lovelesses and Brine families were crossing the Atlantic to join a community of hard-working Methodist farmers and family people wanting to improve their lives away from personal hardship in England.

The route taken by the Tolpiddle families to their promised land is uncertain but, in the 1930s, the great-grandson of John Standfield claimed that they sailed via New York from where they travelled onwards by steam locomotive to Buffalo and ship to Port Stanley before trekking by ox-team to London, Ontario. Another route could have been by ship from England to Quebec, Montreal, Toronto or Hamilton from where they would have headed west by ox-drawn wagons over

ON BOARD AN EMIGRANT SHIP—"LAND, HO!"

Conditions on board early emigrant ships to Canada were unbelievably bad for families crowded into chaotic and unsanitary quarters for their long voyage across the Atlantic. (*Illustrated London News*)

NEW EMIGRANT-SHIP, HESPERIDES, FOR THE SOUTH AUSTRALIAN LINE.

ON BOARD AN EMIGRANT SHIP.

EMIGRANTS BY THE SHIP CANCES DEPARTING FOR CANADA.

Conditions on board early emigrant ships to Canada were unbelievably bad for families crowded into chaotic and unsanitary quarters for their long voyage across the Atlantic. (*Illustrated London News*)

rough tracks through forests and swamplands to their destination, a journey that might have taken over a week.

Their Canadian voyage was distressing for the Loveless' four-year-old daughter, Sina, died on the high seas. She had been born a healthy child at the Essex farm in 1840 and the nature and timing of her illness is unknown. Emigrant ships frequently lost passengers during the voyage and carried the necessary materials needed for sea burials. The tiny child would have been wrapped in sailcloth or a hammock with weights attached to the four corners and dropped over the side. The ship would have stopped for a few moments while a short funeral service was read over the body – probably by George Loveless himself but possibly a doctor or ship's chaplain if one was on board. As soon as the service was over the ship would continue its journey.

Edmund Stoney had been expecting their arrival and arranged temporary accommodation and provisions until they were ready to venture into their new world and discover its possibilities. The colonial government had divided London Township into a grid system similar to street patterns that still exist in Canadian and US towns. Plots had been split into lots – or 'concessions' – for settlers wanting to purchase land outright. In 1847 George Loveless purchased 100 acres at Bryanston, twelve miles from London Town. In true pioneering fashion the Loveless family built a house in their New Jerusalem from logs, the most popular building material at that time. Four years later the family moved to a second 100 acre farm, including a wooden farm house, six miles north of London. Here Loveless held regular bible classes for people in the neighbourhood and again began preaching at divine services at Methodist locations around the district. By now he could afford to travel to services by horse and buggy instead of walking. In 1856 he and Betsey purchased a smaller 48-acre plot on which they built a comfortable timber frame house at Siloam, five miles from London Township. At Siloam Loveless also helped build the community's wooden Methodist church and he and his family became part of the backbone of the North London community there.

A Siloam resident known as 'Dickie', who as a boy knew George Loveless, later wrote in the *Canadian Farmer's Sun*, a progressive weekly periodical published in Ontario, that when the whole of his (Dickie's) family had diphtheria, and his half-sister had died, the local minister was too scared of infection to come near them. When he even shied from conducting the funeral his father appealed to George Loveless who was unafraid to come to the aid of the distressed family.

A man who remembered Loveless after his death in 1874 described his appearance as that of 'a saint and a poet'. Of his love of the beauty of nature, there can be no doubt. His flower garden was said to be the delight and envy of all who saw it. He was particularly fond of growing begonias. His grandson, Tom Loveless, recalled his grandfather's displeasure if anyone picked a flower. He would say 'you mustn't purloin one, but I will give you a hundred.'

Surprisingly, James Loveless decided not to remain a farmer after arriving in Canada. By 1856 he had moved with his family to London Township where he became the sexton of the recently-built North Street Methodist Church. His duties included supervising the maintenance and upkeep of the building. James and Elizabeth Brine first settled in Huron County but later moved to London Township to be closer to their old friends before moving again to Blanshard Township where Brine built a log homestead on a 100 acre plot which included an orchard. Parts of the farm, known as 'the old Brine homestead', still stand. In total the Brines produced eleven children. In

James Loveless became sexton of the North Street Methodist Church in London Township. (*Fadedgenes – A Chronicle of the people of the Methodist Church in Canada*)

Dorset Brine had been only an occasional visitor to the Methodist Chapel but in Canada he became a full and active convert.

Thomas and John Standfield and their families had obviously received good reports about Canada from Loveless and crossed the Atlantic in 1846. John purchased a plot of land in Bryanston where he built a house called 'Dorset Hall' in memory of his homeland which was shared by his father, mother and his own family of four children. John built a second house on a neighbouring plot a few years later and moved into it with his growing family, which now numbered seven children. Thomas Standfield remained at 'Dorset Hall' where his family took an active part in local Methodist life and he and his son used their fine singing voices to good effect in the church choir. John later moved to Bryanston where he opened two shops before moving again to London Township where he bought a hotel which he ran with great success. He became Mayor of East London while still finding time to sing with his choir which became famous throughout Western Ontario.

The swearing of an illegal oath in 1834 had brought trouble to the lives of six Dorset labourers and their families. Ten years later the former Tolpiddle men, now living comfortably in Canada, swore a second secret oath between themselves. They agreed that in their new lives they would never mention anything about their convictions and sufferings to anyone – including their own children and grandchildren. To outsiders they had worked on farms in Dorset before moving to Essex from where they eventually decided to relocate to Canada to take advantage of its many opportunities. The men were taking a risk by keeping silent about their previous lives. With Britons pouring into Canada, many of them attending Methodist churches, there was a real possibility of exposure. Someone might inquire if the Lovelesses, Standfields or Mr Brine might be related to those Dorset men whose names had regularly appeared in British newspapers a few years back after being transported for swearing an illegal oath and who were brought back to parade through London's streets before moving to Essex on farms paid for by public subscription.

It could have happened at any time but, if it did, it was unrecorded until 1907. After they had all died their story re-entered the public domain through an article in *The Methodist Recorder* written by the Rev. John T. Waddy, a Dorchester Circuit Minister. His research was based on a long forgotten 70-year-old copy

A photograph of George Loveless taken in later life and thought to be the only one in existence. (*Taken from Six Heroes in Chains by Harry Brooks* (*1929*))

of *The Victims of Whiggery* and correspondence with Mr. H. J. Brine who was living in Chicago and the grandson of Petty Constable James Brine – the man who had arrested the six men in February 1834. In 1904 Waddy was responsible for Methodist affairs in Tolpuddle and surrounding villages where the former

Thomas Standfield was the first of the Dorchester Labourers to be laid to rest at Siloam Cemetery, London, Ontario. He passed away in February 1864 at the age of 75 and is buried next to his wife Dinniah who died the following May. (*Dorset History Centre*)

labourers were still remembered. He took an interest in their story, carried out research and documented the first story about their lives in England, Australia and Canada to appear for over 60 years. His headline, 'The Tolpuddle Martyrs', is the phrase still used to this day.

oOo

Thomas Standfield was first of the Dorchester Labourers to die. The oldest member of the Tolpiddle Six, Standfield passed away on 9 February, 1864 age 75 and is buried with his wife Dinniah, who died the following May, at Siloam Cemetery, Fanshawe Park Road East, London, Ontario.

James Loveless passed over on 16 February, 1873 age 65 and was buried in the Wesleyan Methodist Cemetery in Rectory Street, London Town which was shortly after sold for industrial use. Over 400 bodies had to be removed to Mount Pleasant cemetery in Riverside Drive, London Town, but for some unknown reason there is no headstone for George Loveless' younger brother; the former Tolpiddle man lies in an unmarked grave simply identified as 264-B. Perhaps it is time for a headstone or commemorative marker to be placed on the site which marks the last resting place of this brave man.

The grave of George and Elizabeth (Betsey Loveless) in Mount Pleasant Cemetery, London, Middlesex contains the phrase: 'These are they which came out of great tribulation and have washed their robes and made them white in the blood of the lamb.' (*Photograph by Yvonne Aburrow – Gods and Radicals*)

John and Elizabeth Standfield are buried in Canada near their friends George and Betsey Loveless in Mount Pleasant Cemetery, 303 Riverside Drive, London, Middlesex. George passed away on 6 May 1874 age 77. As the average male lifespan in the nineteenth century was 40, Standfield, Brine and the Loveless brothers lived long lives. Would they have died any sooner if they had remained in England? The former farm labourers would have worked longer days on Dorset farms, continued to eat a poor diet and live in abject poverty, so there is every chance they would have died younger. After moving to Canada, the men and their families had escaped persecution, lived in better accommodation, had access to better food, could work at their own pace and were their own masters. The move not only lengthened their lives but also the lifespan of their wives. Elizabeth Standfield passed away in 1888 age 61. Betsey Loveless died in 1868, age 68. The average lifespan for a female in England at that time was 42.

On the grave of George and Betsey Loveless is an appropriate inscription taken from Revelation 7:14: 'These are they which came out of great tribulation and have washed their robes and made them white in the blood of the Lamb.' The inscription on John and Elizabeth Standfield's grave, chosen by their eight children on the death of their mother, reads: 'Dearest mother thou hast left us, Here thy loss we deeply feel. But in Heaven we hope to meet thee, Where God will all our sorrows heal.'

James Brine, the youngest of the Tolpiddle men, died in 1902 age 90 and is buried in Perth County's St. Mary's Cemetery with his wife Elizabeth who died in 1906 age 88. Their joint grave is now marked with the words 'A Member of the Tolpuddle Martyrs' which was added in the 1970s by one of the Brine's many great-great grandchildren.

Chapter 28

A Hammett Celebration

1875

No stone may mark the exiles' graves
In distant lands beyond the sea,
Who wore the clanking chains of slaves
Because they struggled to be free.

By the time he arrived back in England in August 1839, James Hammett had been away for five years and four months – three years and five months since his free pardon and passage home had been granted – a long sentence for a wrongly accused man. After spending less than two years with his wife and young child at New House Farm, the Hammetts returned to what has now become Tolpuddle in 1841 and he would remain in the village for the rest of his life. An 1841 census records that Hammett was first employed as 'an agricultural labourer' in Tolpuddle but he did not remain long in his old profession. Soon after he was employed by a wealthy builder and returned to the anonymity he had enjoyed before 1834.

Harriet Hammett produced four more children, two girls and two boys, but in 1860 when her husband was nearly fifty, she died age 49. Two years later Hammett remarried and the couple produced a baby girl who died in infancy and another son, William. After ten years of marriage both his second wife and his 18-year-old son, James, died. Later Hammett married for a third time and continued to live a quiet and industrious life in Tolpuddle. Some Dorset union members still recalled the Dorchester Labourers and considered the March 1875 41st anniversary of the

James Hammett, taken at his home in Tolpuddle in March 1875 at around the same time as he was honoured on the 41st anniversary of his arrest. (*Taken from* Six Heroes in Chains *by Harry Brooks* (*1929*))

Tolpuddle Six's banishment to the other side of the world an occasion worth remembering.

The event was held in a large field at Brianspiddle, one mile and a half from Tolpuddle, as nowhere large enough could be found in Hammett's own village. Or was it because Henry Frampton, son of James Frampton who had died in 1855, was now Lord of the Manor, and, remembering the events of 1834, ordered that no land in his manor was to be used for a union celebration?

James Hammett was there in person wearing his best suit along with his brother John. The *Dorset County Express* reported:

> There was a remarkable unionist celebration on Wednesday last when there was a great gathering of agricultural labourers, their wives and families, to do honour to Mr. James Hammett of Tolpuddle, one of the six men who on that day 41 years ago were sentenced to seven years transportation for being concerned in the formation of a labourers' union in the village where they had lived and laboured.
>
> Naturally, the unionists today in Dorset honour this early martyr in the cause, and it was determined to celebrate the 41st anniversary of their condemnation by the presentation of an address and some little testimonial.
>
> The local unionists mustered in the afternoon, wearing the blue ribbon of the union and they marched in procession through the village to the music of the band, and then held tea-drinking in the large tent erected for the meeting. About six o' clock the labouring class mustered in force, and amongst them was the hero of the occasion – Mr. James Hammett, but there was no self-consciousness of heroism in him. There he was, a simple-minded plain old man, who had done his duty according to his light in the past and now rather shrank from the prominence in which he was placed.
>
> Mr. George Howell, secretary to the parliamentary committee of the Trades Union Congress, told the meeting: 'This meeting fully approves of the efforts made by James Hammett and others in trying to form a union in Dorset in 1834, and is very proud this day to make known to the country at large that the righteous effort then crushed out by the arm of the law is today an established fact in the county of Dorset.' In the course of his speech he said the trial was a blow struck at unionism throughout the country, but he urged that unions had conferred great benefit on the working classes and were still required.

Howell said that 'of the men who condemned Hammett and the rest he would say nothing. They are now all dead, gone and forgotten and it is not worthwhile to say anything harsh about them. But I am afraid that they have plenty of grandchildren behind them.' Who *could* he have been referring to?

Hammett agreed to say a few words to the large crowd and when his name was announced he was greeted with a thunderous applause. He said: 'Gentlemen, I return my thanks for this kind testimonial presented to me. It appears to me a great deal better than what I got 41 years ago – a sentence of seven years transportation put on me. I was not the man who deserved it. I belonged to the union, but I was not there in the lodge at the time the men swore I was. It was my brother John, and here he is and can tell you.' Hammett beckoned his brother to come forward but John Hammett waved him away and said: 'That's alright.' James Hammett continued: 'I was transported to a foreign land and sold like a slave, but thank God I've got over it and come safe back again.'

Hammett was presented with an illustrated address inscribed on vellum in old English characters. It stated:

Address to Mr. James Hammett – We the members and friends of the National Agricultural Labourers Union are desirous of testifying to the esteem and regard in which you are held by us as one of the early Martyrs to the cause of unionism. The blood of the martyrs is the seed of the church, and we all feel that the cause of the union, the cause of true humanity, was hastened and gained strength by the outrageous penalties inflicted on you and your

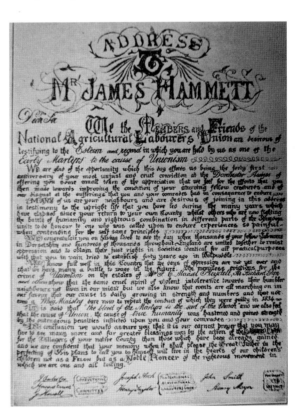

An illuminated address presented to James Hammett on the 41st anniversary of his wrongful conviction and signed by members of the National Agricultural Labourers Union 'testifying to the esteem and regard in which you are held by us as one of the early Martyrs to the cause of unionism'. (*Taken from* Six Heroes in Chains *by Harry Brooks* (*1929*))

comrades. We know full well in this country that the days of oppression are not yet over and that we have many battles to wage in the future.

He was also presented with a purse of gold coins and a gold watch on which was inscribed: 'Presented to Mr. James Hammett of Tolpuddle, March 17th 1875 by the members and friends of the labourers' union in Dorset as a mark of great respect for his patience and courage while undergoing a sentence of seven years' transportation for belonging to a labourers' union in Dorset in 1834.' Hammett held up the watch for all to see and then asked: 'Isn't that better than having seven years put on you, and that for a wrong cause? We only tried to do good to one another, the same as you're doing now.'

James Hammett died in Dorchester Workhouse in 1891, by which time he was blind and had told his family that he refused to be a burden on them. He was laid to rest in the churchyard of his native village at Tolpuddle's church of St John the Evangelist. Even in death Henry Frampton, son of the late James Frampton, was afraid that the late James Hammett might be an influence for the up-lift of down-trodden agricultural labourers, and that some might use the burial as an opportunity to deliver a trade union speech at the graveside. Frampton the younger and a dozen men from his estate positioned themselves prominently around the churchyard ready to jump on anybody daring to do such a thing.

Few today remember the Framptons. Many thousands remember the six men collectively remembered now as The Tolpuddle Martyrs.

James Hammett is the only member of the Tolpuddle Six to be buried in England. He rests in Tolpuddle's churchyard of St. John the Evangelist and receives flowers and wreaths each year at the annual Tolpuddle Festival which attracts thousands of visitors from across the world. (*Photograph: Alan Gallop*)

A Postscript

Tolpiddle or Tolpuddle?

From: Lord Melbourne Looks Down by 'Tomfool'
Yes surely I remember, Frampton,
That you and I between us clamped on
The irons which
The Titled Rich
Never degraded?
How can these ploughmen, herds and carters,
Whom we call criminals, be martyrs,
And now outbid
Our claims, who did
Nothing like they did?

By the time Queen Victoria came to the throne in 1838, the village of Tolpiddle had been renamed Tolpuddle. A move to change the name had been afoot for over fifty years, mostly thanks to prudish members of the landed gentry who insisted the name be changed to 'Puddle' due to 'Piddle' being an alternative word for 'piss'. The name of the small river that runs through the village, however, remains unchanged. It was and remains the River Piddle. Today's village of Puddletown was still called Piddletown well into the 1950s. 'Piddle' or 'Puddle,' by the 1890s 'piddle' was out and 'puddle' well and truly in, although the names of neighbouring villages also on the banks of the river, including Piddletrenthide and Piddlehinton have

A short postscript from the author.

remained untouched for centuries, probably because they did not have their fair share of gentry powerful enough to bring about a change of name. Hence the name 'Tolpiddle' has been used throughout this book.

For many people today, the only time they hear anything about Tolpuddle is in July each year when a huge two-day long free music festival is held in the Dorset village. Thousands of people attend. In addition to music there is plenty of political debate, stand-up comedy, poetry and lots of children's entertainment. Singer-songwriter and left-wing activist Billy Bragg is a regular participant along with the actor Maxine Peak and for many years the politician Tony Benn, an MP for 47 years and Labour Cabinet minister in the 1960s and 1970s, gave challenging talks to thousands of visitors attending before his death in 2014 at the age of 88. Current Labour Leader, Jeremy Corbyn is now a regular attendee.

Otherwise, visitors to Dorset often find themselves driving through Tolpuddle on their way to somewhere else and see a sign pointing to a free museum dedicated to the lives of the six trade union men from Tolpuddle. The small museum is packed with interesting information presented on a series of banners positioned around the room. A small shop sells books, souvenirs and memorabilia about the Martyrs. Seven miles away in Dorchester, visitors can see the old crown court in High West Street where the Martyrs were tried in 1834 and which is today a building of national and international significance in the history of Britain's trade union movement. Thomas Hardy later served as a magistrate at the court, an experience which inspired some of his writing. Time has stood still at the court house, particularly inside the courtroom and the gloomy cells below, which today remain unchanged from the time of King William IV.

A major project is underway to transform the old court into a visitor attraction offering high quality exhibitions, events and educational resources. Led by West Dorset District Council, the project has secured initial funding from the Heritage Lottery Fund. For further information visit: *www.dorsetforyou.gov.uk/shirehallproject*.

The Methodist chapel at which four of the Martyrs and their families worshipped still stands. It ceased being a chapel over 150 years ago and has subsequently been used as a barn and storage space for farming equipment. It has stood empty and unused since 2005 and has deteriorated alarmingly. A small band of determined and professionally-minded people from in and around Tolpuddle are, however, now working hard to restore, preserve and maintain this grade II listed building for the benefit of the people of Tolpuddle and anyone interested in the Martyr's story. It should be ready for use once again by 2019. Further information and updates about the Tolpuddle Old Chapel Trust can be found at: *www.tolpuddleoldchapeltrust.org*.

The story of the Tolpuddle Martyrs and the injustice served on them at their trial is a lesson to us all over 180 years after the men were sentenced to work at penal colonies on the other side of the world. Let us not forget that in the second decade of the 21st century, biased and corrupt justice is still meted out to innocent people living in countries including North Korea, Somalia, Afghanistan, South Sudan, Angola, Iraq, Libya, Haiti, Guinea-Bissau, Venezuela, Eritrea, Syria, Turkmenistan, Yemen and Uzbekistan. In that regard, the six farm labourers from Tolpuddle were lucky; people were prepared to stand up and shout loudly for them and eventually bring them home from their bondage. Those living in other countries mentioned here are not so fortunate to have such people fighting for their freedom.

Nothing changes.

> *They need no storied urn or bust*
> *Who once in yonder dungeon lay;*
> *The tyrant's fame is turned to dust,*
> *The felon's fame we sing this day.*

Bibliography

Greetings from Tolpiddle. (*Author's collection*)

The following publications have all been a valuable resource in the writing of this book:

A NARRATIVE OF THE SUFFERINGS OF JAS. LOVELESS, JAS. BRINE AND THOMAS AND JOHN STANDFIELD DISPLAYING THE HORRORS OF TRANSPORTATION AND WRITTEN BY THEMSELVES. Published for the Dorchester Committee by Cleave, Hetherington and Watson, 1838

ACCOUNTS AND PAPERS – Volume 10 – Session 19 February – 10 September 1835 – Vol. XLCI – Copies of the Indictment and Record of Conviction in the Prosecution against George Loveless and Others at the Dorchester Spring Assizes, 1834.

ACCOUNTS AND PAPERS – Volume 7 – Session 3 February – 12 August 1842 – Vol. XXX11 – United Gaol and House of Correction at Dorchester.

ACCOUNTS AND PAPERS – Volume 8 – Session January 31 – July 17, 1837 – Copy of all correspondence between the Colonial Office and the Governor of Australia touching on the Free Pardon and the Order for the Return of the Dorchester Labourers.

Ashton, John – MODERN STREET BALLADS – Chatto & Windus, 1888.

Ball, Roger – TOLPUDDLE AND SWING – THE FLEA AND THE ELEPHANT – Bristol Radical History Group, 2010

Brigden, Roy – PLOUGHS AND PLOUGHING – Shire Publications, 1984

Brooks, Harry – SIX HEROES IN CHAINS – J. Looker Ltd, The Wessex Press, Poole

CENTENARY COMMEMORATION OF THE TOLPUDDLE MARTYRS – Trades Union Congress General Council, 1934

Cobbett, William – RURAL RIDES – J. M. Dent & Sons, 1912

Cox, J. Stevens – THE PEASANTRY OF DORSETSHIRE 1846 (Reprinted from the Illustrated London News, September 1846) – Toucan Press, 1963

Cunningham, F. A. and Payne, J. – REPORTS OF CASES AT NISI PRIUS IN THE QUEEN'S BENCH, COMMON PLEAS AND EXCHEQUER TOGETHER WITH CASES TRIED IN THE CENTRAL CRIMINAL COURT AND ON THE CIRCUIT FROM MICHAELMAS TERM 1823 TO EASTER 1841.

Davies, David – THE CASE OF LABOURERS IN HUSBANDARY STATED AND CONSIDERED – Cambridge University Press, 2010

Groves, Reg – SHARPEN THE SICKLE – THE HISTORY OF THE FARM WORKERS' UNION – Marlin Press, 1981

Hall, Maggie – SMOCKS – Shire Publications, 1979

Hammond, J. L. and Barbara Hammond – THE VILLAGE LABOURER Vols 1 & 2 – Guild Books, 1911

HANSARD'S PARLIAMENTARY DEBATES – Vol. XXX – Tenth Day of September 1835 – A remission of the sentence on the Dorchester Labourers by Mr. Wakley – August 12, 1835

Hardy, Thomas – THE DORSET FARM LABOURER, PAST AND PRESENT – Dorset Agricultural Workers' Union, 1884

Harvey, Nigel – FIELDS, HEDGES AND DITCHES – Shire Publications, 1976

Hobsbawm, Eric and Rudè George – CAPTAIN SWING – Lawrence & Wishart, 1969

Howitt, William – THE RURAL LIFE OF ENGLAND – Volume 1 – Longman, Orme, Brown, Green and Longmans, 1838

Hughes, Robert – THE FATAL SHORE – Collins Harvill, 1987

Lewenhak, Sheila (Editor) – THE EARLY TRADE UNIONS INCLUDING THE FOUNDING OF THE NATIONAL TRADES UNIONS AND THE PROSECUTION OF THE TOLPUDDLE MARTYRS – Jackdaw No. 35 – Jackdaw Publications, Jonathan Cape, 1966

Lezard, Tim – THE SACRIFICE OF THE TOLPUDDLE MARTYRS – New Statesman, July 16, 2009

Lloyd, Thomas – GOD IS OUR GUIDE – THE TOLPUDDLE MARTYRS AND THEIR METHODIST ROOTS – Methodist Church Communications Office, 2007

Loveless George – THE CHURCH SHOWN UP – Central Dorchester Committee, 1838 and reprinted by the TUC Tolpuddle Martyrs Memorial Trust for the Tolpuddle Martyrs Museum, Tolpuddle, 2005

Loveless, George – THE VICTIMS OF WHIGGERY – Central Dorchester Committee, 1837 and reprinted by the TUC Tolpuddle Martyrs Memorial Trust for the Tolpuddle Martyrs Museum, Tolpuddle, 2005

Marlowe, Joyce – THE TOLPUDDLE MARTYRS – André Deutsch, 1971

Mitchell, George – THE SKELETON AT THE PLOUGH or THE POOR FARM LABOURER OF THE WEST – edited by Stephen Price – George Potter and T. Roberts – 1869

Norman, Andrew – THE STORY OF GEORGE LOVELESS AND THE TOLPUDDLE MARTYRS – Halsgrove, 2008

Oliver, W. H. – TOLPUDDLE MARTYRS AND TRADE UNION OATHS – Australian Society for the Study of Labour History, Labour History No. 10 – May 1966.

(Other broadside ballads used in this book can be found at BROADSIDE BALLADS ONLINE (http://ballads.bodleian.ox.ac.uk), which presents a digital collection of English printed ballad-sheets from between the 16th and 20th centuries, linked to other resources for the study of the English ballad tradition. This resource is maintained by the Bodleian Libraries and features the Bodleian's digital collections of ballads, with links to the English Broadside Ballad Archive's digital presentations. A visit to this site is highly recommended.)

Padden, Graham – TOLPUDDLE – AN HISTORICAL ACCOUNT THROUGH THE EYES OF GEORGE LOVELESS – Trades Union Congress, 1984

Palmer, Roy – THE PAINFUL PLOUGH – A PORTRAIT OF THE AGRICULTURAL LABOURER IN THE 19th CENTURY FROM FOLK SONGS AND BALLADS AND CONTEMPORARY ACCOUNTS – Cambridge University Press, 1972

Pree, Barry – EARLY DAYS DOWN UNDER (Vol. 2, part 13 of THE BRITISH EMPIRE, a 96 weekly part-work) – Orbis Publishing, 1979

Robertson, Geoffrey, QC – INTRODUCTION TO THE TOLPUDDLE MARTYRS – http/geoffreyrobertson.com – 2005

Robinson, David – THE TOLPUDDLE MARTYRS' CHAPEL – Architectural History, Vol. 44, 2001

Roebuck, JP – PAMPHLETS FOR THE PEOPLE – No. 4 – John Longley, 1835

Shepperson, Wilbur S. – BRITISH EMIGRATION TO NORTH AMERICA: PROJECTS AND OPINIONS IN THE EARLY VICTORIAN PERIOD – University of Minnesota Press, 1957

Squire Sprigge, S. – THE LIFE AND TIMES OF THOMAS WAKLEY – Longmans, Green & Co, 1897

Stephens, Henry – THE BOOK OF THE FARM – Volume II – William Blackwood & Sons, 1844

Stevenson, William – GENERAL VIEW OF THE AGRICULTURE OF THE COUNTY OF DORSET – The Great British Board of Agriculture, 1812

Tench, Watkin- A NARATIVE OF THE EXPEDITION TO BOTANY BAY – 1788 – Project Gutenburg

THE ANNALS OF CRIME and NEW NEWGATE CALENDAR – Number 37 – May 17, 1834

THE PUNISHMENT OF DEATH – A SELECTION OF ARTICLES FROM THE MORNING HERALD – Hatchard & Son, 1837

THE STORY OF THE TOLPUDDLE MARTYRS and TUC GUIDE TO THE OLD CROWN COURT IN DORCHESTER – Trades Union Congress, 1984

Tolpuddle Old Chapel Trust – EXTRACT FROM A CONSERVATION STATEMENT FOR THE FORMER CHAPEL, TOLPUDDLE – Jo Cox and John Thorp. Keystone Historic Buildings Consultants, Exeter. 2015

Various authors – THE BOOK OF THE MARTYRS OF TOLPUDDLE 1834-1934 – The Trades Union Congress General Council, 1934

Vince, John – OLD FARM TOOLS – Shire Publications, 1974

Webb, Sydney and Beatrice – THE HISTORY OF TRADE UNIONISM – Longmans, Green & Co, 1911

Wirdnam, Audrey – PIDELA – AN ACCOUNT OF THE VILLAGE OF TOLPUDDLE FROM EARLY YEARS – Beechcote Press, 1989

Ziegler, Philip – MELBOURNE, A BIOGRAPHY OF WILLIAM LAMB, 2nd VISCOUNT MELBOURNE – Collins, 1976

Index